B.45 .

CAVALRY SURGEON

CAVALRY SURGEON

THE RECOLLECTIONS OF
DEPUTY SURGEON-GENERAL

John Henry Sylvester, F.G.S.

BOMBAY ARMY

EDITED BY

A. McKenzie Annand

WITH A FOREWORD BY

The Marquess of Anglesey, F.S.A.

MACMILLAN

SBN boards: 333 00971 1

First published 1971 by
MACMILLAN AND CO LTD
London and Basingstoke
Associated companies in New York Toronto
Dublin Melbourne Johannesburg & Madras

Printed in Great Britain by
ROBERT MACLEHOSE AND CO LTD
The University Press, Glasgow

To
BERYL A. SYLVESTER HODDER
Granddaughter of the
CAVALRY SURGEON

Contents

List of Plates

The author and publishers are grateful to the following for permission to reproduce the illustrations: Miss B. A. Sylvester Hodder, 1; *Illustrated London News*, 11; National Army Museum, 8, 9, 14, 15; Lieutenant-Colonel J. B. R. Nicholson (Editor of *Tradition* magazine), 2; Royal United Service Institution, 3; Secretary of State for Foreign and Commonwealth Affairs, 4, 5, 6, 7, 12, 13; Wantage Urban District Council, 10.

List of Maps

Foreword by the Marquess of Anglesey, F.S.A.

THERE are scores of published first-hand accounts of the Indian Mutiny. Many of them were written by officers and men of the British regiments which helped to put it down. Among these, one of the more interesting is Assistant-Surgeon John Henry Sylvester's *Recollections of the Campaign in Malwa and Central India*, which was published in Bombay in 1860. By itself it would not, perhaps, warrant re-publication. Though it gives some details of the later phases of the struggle not to be found elsewhere, it is written in a style at once pompous and impersonal. This charge cannot be levelled, as the reader of *Cavalry Surgeon* will soon discover, at Sylvester's hitherto unpublished narrative, which forms the greater part of Mr Annand's skilfully edited book. Even less pompous and impersonal is the daily journal which Sylvester kept over many years. Extracts and information from this source have been used in the footnotes to good effect.

In many ways Sylvester, who was twenty-seven when the 'Great Indian Mutiny' (or 'the Sepoy War' as it was sometimes called) broke out, was a typical upper-middle-class Victorian male: similar to many another who spent the best part of his life in British India, helping to run that vast sub-continent. He was above average in his chosen field of medicine, which he never much relished, and a more than tolerable wielder of pen and paintbrush.

Robust of physique, hardworking and conscientious, he nevertheless possessed his fair share of human failings. His

ambitions outran his capabilities. His desire for recognition
in the form of honours and promotion was natural and
healthy, but his envy of others who achieved distinctions
was generally unjustified and sometimes bitter. He was by
nature restless and adventurous. Even after years of danger
and hardship as a medical officer in the field, he never quite
overcame his burning desire to be, instead, an actual
fighting cavalry officer.

His views on the Hindus, Mahomedans and half-castes
with whom he came into contact were the same as those of
the vast majority of Anglo-Indians of his day. His outlook
was neither intellectual nor liberal, and he had little
sympathy with their aspirations or needs. The less pleasing
aspects of his character were redeemed by an agreeable
sense of humour, of which there are numerous examples in
this book. One of the most typical is his remark about the
ruler of Kotah, 'who amongst his subjects had earned a
celebrity for prowess in arms, but to believe this it was
necessary not to see him'. Further, his powers of observation
were highly developed. He often succeeds in conveying,
with a delicately turned phrase, the immediacy and
atmosphere, as well as the pictorial features, of the scenes
and events with which he is confronted.

The India to which he went at the age of twenty-four
was very different from that which he left twenty years
later. In those two decades the march of Western civilisation
had advanced by momentous strides. Communications
were transformed out of all recognition. The long passage
round the Cape, and the Mediterranean–Red Sea route
(including the overland journey from Alexandria to Suez),
which Sylvester describes, were made obsolete by the
construction of the Suez Canal. India was beginning to be
covered with a network of railways, only a few miles of
which existed in 1854. In the year of the Mutiny an officer
of Bombay native cavalry could report that his men 'had
never seen a train, and were very much astonished at the

ag-gari (fire carriage)'.[1] The journey from Calcutta to
Peshawar which took three months in the 1850s, took only
as many days in the 1870s. The coming of the telegraph
was revolutionising the transmission of messages. When
Sylvester arrived in India a few internal telegraph lines
existed, but direct communication between Calcutta and
London had not yet been established.

The Honourable East India Company was still the
nominal ruler of British India. The reality of its role as an
autonomous trading concern had long since worn thin. For
more than half a century the policies of its directors in
London had been regulated by a Board of Control headed
by a Cabinet Minister. The Governor-General, though
technically the appointee of the Directors in Leadenhall
Street, was nearly always a politician nominated by the
Cabinet in Downing Street. His direct rule extended over
800,000 square miles, peopled by some 131,000,000 natives.
He also exercised varying degrees of control over numerous
native States, whose puppet leaders were as often as not
placed and supported on their thrones by his will.

Three separate armies were maintained, one in each of
the Presidencies of Bengal, Bombay and Madras. In 1857
these consisted of 232,000 native troops, formed into
regiments whose officers were British. Under them were
the native commissioned ranks. The most senior native
officer ranked below the most junior European cornet or
ensign. He could never aspire, except in the irregular
cavalry, to command even a troop or platoon. Attached to
each army were regiments of the 'Queen's Army' from
Britain. These were, in effect, hired out to the Company.
The 14th Light Dragoons, with which Sylvester served,
was such a regiment. Its tour of duty had already lasted
nearly sixteen years when the Mutiny broke out.

The largest of the three armies was that of Bengal, the

---

[1] Unpublished 'letters from "C.C." (Charles Combe, 3rd Bombay
Light Cavalry) to his family, 1856–1859.' This passage is quoted by
kind permission of the owner, E. Combe, Esq.

only one seriously affected by the Mutiny. At the time of the outbreak it numbered 151,000 men, of whom nearly 23,000 were Europeans. Very few of these latter were actually in Bengal proper. Some 13,000 of them were stationed in or near the Punjab. A former Governor-General had fixed a ratio of white troops to native troops, for the whole of India, of one to four. Below this it was considered dangerous to allow the armies to fall. Yet in 1857 it had become less than one to six. This decline was largely the result of withdrawals of 'Queen's regiments' for the Crimean War (which only ended in 1856), and for the short-lived Persian War, of which Sylvester arrived too late to see very much.

Nowhere does Sylvester attempt to analyse the causes of the Mutiny, which so altered his and millions of others' lives. He can hardly be blamed, for no simple answer exists. In this age of extreme nationalism, when self-government is the aim of all nations, it is hard to grasp that the Mutiny had nothing whatever to do with nationalism. 'It was in no sense', wrote Winston Churchill, 'a national movement, or . . . a patriotic struggle for freedom or a war of independence. The idea and ideal of the inhabitants of the sub-continent forming a single people and state was not to emerge for many years'[1] after 1857.

John Jacob, one of the finest leaders of irregular cavalry in the history of India, and a persistent agitator for reform of abuses in the Bengal Army, declared that:

the natives of India are quite incapable of self government. . . . They expect their sovereign to govern them absolutely and according to his own superior knowledge and ability, and not according to their instructions.[2]

He and other thinking Europeans in India believed that the slackening of the rulers' confidence in their moral right to

[1] Churchill, Winston S. *A History of the English-speaking Peoples*, IV, 'The Great Democracies', 1958, 70.

[2] Lambrick, H. T. *John Jacob of Jacobabad*, 1960, 350.

govern absolutely – the gradually increasing belief that the governed should have some say in how they were governed – was a root cause of the discontent which flared up in Bengal. In particular it was thought that the *sepoys* (infantrymen) and *sowárs* (cavalrymen) of the Bengal Army were unduly pampered, and their religious scruples paid too much attention to.

On the other hand there are other respectable authorities who say that threats to the men's religious scruples and caste taboos were, in fact, the chief causes. The General Service Enlistment Act of September 1856 is often quoted as an example. This required every recruit to undertake to serve wherever he might be needed. Until then his service had been limited to within India's frontiers. He saw this as an attack upon his caste feelings about travelling overseas. By crossing the *Kála pani* (black water) the Brahman was reduced to the same caste as a lascar. It is said, too, that the increasingly evangelistic outlook of many British officials led to fears (unjustified, in fact) that plans were afoot to convert the men to Christianity by force.

There were other, more potent, causes. Among these was the fact that a decreasing number of officers could speak the language of their men, either actually or metaphorically. Many commanding officers, who had once been as fathers to their men, had increasingly over the years lost touch with them. The advent in India of officers' wives in large numbers had certainly ministered to this, producing as it did an enlarged social and domestic life of an exclusively European nature. Further, disciplinary powers within the regiment had been whittled down to almost nothing. Since 1853, for instance, no commanding officer had been allowed to award a punishment more severe than five days' drill. Both in the Bengal Army and in other spheres of life, centralisation and Calcutta-inspired uniformity, characterised by an alarming increase in the use of red tape, had slowly but surely eroded the personal touch between ruler and ruled.

Nearly one-third of the Bengal soldiers came from Oudh, the central province of Bengal. These men, constituting a close-knit interest within the army, were in large part Brahmans. Others were Rajputs. Both were high-caste, full of bigotry and extremely resentful of any changes in the existing order. Three-fifths of the sepoys were high-born Hindus of one kind or another. Most of the sowars, on the other hand, were Muslims.

In the last thirteen years there had been four comparatively minor mutinies in the Bengal Army, all of which had been put down with vigour. A factor which contributed to this increasing unrest was the loss of prestige resulting from the Afghan War. In 1842, a considerable British Army, which included many Bengal units, had been annihilated as it attempted to withdraw from Afghanistan. For the first time, confidence in the invincibility of the 'Raj' had been shaken.

All these doubts and fears were exploited, and finally fanned into rebellion, by a growing number of dissatisfied native rulers. Many of them had recently been dispossessed of their domains, and pensioned off. Some, like the royal family of Nagpur, whose jewels had been publicly auctioned, had suffered humiliations. The Earl of Dalhousie, before he was succeeded as Governor-General by Lord Canning early in 1856, had added to Britain's possessions 250,000 square miles in eight years. The system of 'lapse', whereby a state became forfeit to the Company if there was no clear successor on the death of its ruler, certainly avoided the anarchy which so often occurred on these occasions, but it rendered dangerously idle numerous discontented men.

On top of all this, there came, like a spark to a powder-keg, the famous affair of the greased cartridges. The new Enfield rifle had cartridges which were believed to be smeared with the fat of cows and pigs, 'thus nicely', as one authority has phrased it, 'outraging the feelings of both Hindus, to whom the cow was sacred, and Muslims, to whom the pig was unclean'.[1] Though the order that the men were to bite off the ends of the cartridges (which so offended the Muslims) was quickly rescinded, and though upon the earliest complaints the men had been allowed to provide their own grease, the idea that their religious prejudices were being intentionally tampered with was not lessened. The withdrawal of the orders seemed to the soldiers to be a sign of weakness and of alarm at the discovery of a plot. 'The ingenuity of those who seized on the cartridge grievance', writes the historian of the first outbreak at Meerut in May 1857, 'and the tragedy of those whom it drove to frenzy, was the suggestion that the hand which nourished the sepoy proffered not only salt, but grease'.[2]

The terrible massacres of those early summer weeks, in which so many of the men killed their officers, as well as every white man, woman and child in sight, were condemned by a large part of Indians of all classes. This was because it was considered shockingly *immoral* to be faithless to one's salt. The fact of this widespread native condemnation ensured that what was essentially a military revolt could not develop into a nation-wide rising. It made it possible, too, to crush the revolt within a tolerable period. Without the devoted services of myriads of native camp followers, no European troops in India could make a day's march, let alone take part in campaigns. Delhi was recovered from the mutineers without a single white reinforcement from overseas. For every European in the British camp, there were twenty natives.

It was the Indian cook who brought the white soldier his dinner under the heaviest fire, it was the Indian bhisti who brought him his drink in the thickest of the fight, it was the Indian dooly-bearer who carried the wounded out of the danger zone and the Indian servant who looked after his general comfort.[3]

[1] Spear, P. *The Oxford History of India*, 1958, 667.
[2] Palmer, J. A. B. *The Mutiny Outbreak at Meerut in 1857*, 1966, 137.
[3] Sen. S. N. *Eighteen Fifty-Seven*, 1958, 413.

7,900 of the 11,200 effective troops fighting the mutineers before Delhi were native Indians.

In the Central Indian campaigns, in which Sylvester took part, the ratio of native to British troops was even higher. These campaigns were fought, of course, by troops from the Bombay Army, which was virtually untouched by the revolt. Why did the men of Bombay remain uninfected? It is clear that they had at least as much temptation to be untrue to their salt as their brethren of Bengal. Among them were many Brahmans and Rajputs from the very Bengali areas which were worst contaminated. Further, the three largest states recently annexed were Maratha, and the biggest single element of the Bombay Army was Maratha. Then again, much discontent had been engendered in landholders of the southern Maratha districts by a Commission set up to inquire into their tenure of land. Thousands of plots had been confiscated, many of them because the owner's documents had been destroyed by white ants.

Another reason why the Bombay army did not succumb to the temptation was that for many years there had existed jealousy, almost mutual contempt, between the men of the two armies. But the chief reason was a fundamental difference in morale and discipline. In Bengal there had grown up an increasing tendency to select the native officers from the ranks, on the sole ground of seniority, so that they were generally too old and inefficient to exercise control. In the Bombay regiments, right from the early days, the question of caste had always been very secondary. Promotion was decided upon merit. Even men of the lowest caste were constantly made officers. Above all, the excessive control from headquarters which had made commanding officers in Bengal (as one of them said) into mere sergeant-majors, had not been introduced in Bombay. A former Governor-General had called the Bengal Army the most expensive and inefficient in the world. The same could never have been said of the Bombay Army.

One of the most cogent summaries of the Mutiny and its causes comes from the pen of Dr S. N. Sen, the official Indian historian:

The patriots of Oudh [he wrote in his definitive *Eighteen Fifty-Seven*] fought for their king and country but they were not champions of freedom, for they had no conception of individual liberty. On the contrary they would, if they could, revive the old order and perpetuate everything it stood for. The English Government had imperceptibly effected a social revolution. . . . The Mutiny leaders would have set the clock back, they would have done away with the new reforms, with the new order, and gone back to the good old days when a commoner could not expect equal justice with the noble, when the tenants were at the mercy of the talukdars, and when theft was punished with mutilation. In short, they wanted a counter-revolution.

Nor was it a war between the white and the black. All the whites in India were indeed ranged on one side . . . but not the black. . . . It was, therefore, a war between the black insurgents and the white rulers supported by other blacks. It was the case of one slave rivetting the fetters of another under the supervision of their common master.

No moral issues were involved in the war of 1857. . . . The struggle may be characterised . . . as 'a war of fanatic religionists against Christians' but during the Mutiny the moral principle underlying their respective religions had little influence on the combatants.[1]

The stamping out of the revolt took as long as it did because of the obvious difficulty of coming to terms with men who had committed the most heinous of military sins. Though the famous 'Clemency Resolution' of Canning offered a vaguely worded guarantee that only those who had actually committed or assisted in atrocities would be executed, this was not generally believed. Nor, in practice, was it always observed. Implacable feelings of revenge too often actuated the white troops, both officers and men.

The Governor of Bombay at the time of the Bengal Mutiny was Lord Elphinstone, a man of excellent judgement and uncommon courage. He saw at once that he must send every man he could spare to the north-east to prevent the insurrection spreading southwards, and to help in quelling

---

[1] Sen, 412–13.

it. At the same time, by speedy and determined action, he made the most of the slender reserves which he kept back in Bombay to thwart the incipient signs of unrest which appeared in his own Presidency. The Dekkan Field Force, which he sent off in June under General Woodburn (soon to be succeeded by Brigadier Stuart), was necessarily weak. Beside the three troops of the 14th Light Dragoons to which Sylvester was attached, there were only one native infantry battalion and one European artillery battery. In December this 'flying column' had developed into the celebrated Central India Field Force, under command of General Sir Hugh Rose, later to become Commander-in-Chief in India, and Field-Marshal Lord Strathnairn.

As the weary years went by, and first the Rani of Jhansi, and then Tantia Topi, the two most skilful of the Mutiny leaders in the field, were slowly but inexorably hunted down, the force at Rose's disposal grew greater. Though increasingly mobile, it never became very large: at the most it never exceeded 6,000 men. Much of the campaigning was carried on during the hot season under the searing sun of the central Indian plain. The conditions were as appalling as any under which European troops have ever fought. Sylvester, in his descriptions of them, brings to the reader an intensely vivid feeling of being present – of actually experiencing the overwhelming heat, the overpowering fatigue, the tortures of thirst and the interminable fight against prostration and disease.

The historian of the British Army considered the march of a thousand miles to Kalpi and thence to Gwalior 'the most remarkable achievement in the history of the Indian Mutiny'. Sir Hugh Rose he thought 'beyond dispute the ablest commander' to emerge from it. Sylvester, when he first came across Sir Hugh, wrote in his diary, 'our new commander looks very effeminate, weak, and I should think unable to rough it much.' This is just about the most inaccurate description of the man it is possible to conceive. Sylvester was not alone in this first impression, and he

certainly modified it as time went on. He declares quite
rightly: 'How scarce an article is a good general!' He, and
all who served with him, were fortunate indeed to be
commanded by such an outstanding one.

Sir Hugh was a well known sportsman of varied military
and diplomatic experience. He had been British representa-
tive at French headquarters in the Crimea, discharging a
difficult task with skill. Behind a façade of delicate charm,
hid a man of steel. He had never been in India before, and
his methods did not commend themselves to officers of the
old India school. Nevertheless, intense activity of body, will
power of no common order, and the quickest of brains,
made him ideally suited for the command of a series of
flying columns, pursuing an enemy as tough and slippery as
any ever encountered before or since. Sir John Fortescue
wrote:

> No hostile army, though inspired by the bravest of the rebel leaders,
> the Rani of Jhansi, could stop Hugh Rose; no fortress, never so re-
> nowned or formidable, could long delay him. Lead, steel, and above
> all, disease might thin his ranks but could not discourage the remnant,
> nor intimidate their leader. He marched on irresistible, not to be
> turned from his purpose even by the orders of the Governor-General;
> and he prevailed.[1]

Sylvester was not the only man under his command to
resent the lack of rewards and recognition accorded to the
indomitable men of Rose's force. Neither special clasp nor
legitimately earned prize money ever came their way. It
was a shocking injustice which was never remedied.

Readers of this book will be deeply grateful to Mr Annand
for giving them an opportunity to experience vicariously
the turbulent years of Assistant-Surgeon Sylvester's life in
India a century ago, some of the background to which I
have attempted to depict in this foreword. Hardly less
absorbing and informative than the chapters on the Mutiny,
are those which describe Sylvester's furlough in Cashmere

[1] Fortescue, Hon. J. W. *A History of the British Army*, XIII, 1930,
394, 395.

and the little known Umbeylah campaign of 1863. This last was one of the seventy or so 'small wars' which were fought by the British throughout the Empire during what has come to be known, ironically, as 'The Long Peace'. Sylvester's account of his experiences in it will be of considerable value to military historians of the period, and like the rest of *Cavalry Surgeon*, will charm that mythical figure, the general reader.

Editor's Introduction

In the Lady Chapel of the parish church of Burford, Oxfordshire, stand tombs of many of the Sylvesters, an ancient family prominent in the town from the Middle Ages on. One name, however, is missing – that of John Henry Sylvester, probably the most talented and distinguished of them all.

John Henry Sylvester, son of John Jordan Ansell Sylvester and his wife Mary, of Fulbrook, near Burford, was born on 22 February 1830 and baptised at Shipton-under-Wychwood on 16 June of the same year. He entered King's College, London, as a medical student, when he gave early proof of those qualities which were to mark him as an extremely capable surgeon, soldier, and artist.

It is from the year 1848, when he entered King's College, that Sylvester takes up the tale which forms the context of this book, covering his early years in Bombay; sickness-ridden days in Persia during the campaign of 1857; stirring days of the Indian Mutiny; cantonment life in Peshawur and Mooltan, and the Umbeylah Campaign of 1863. To this narrative has been added an account of his life, up to 1867, drawn from the pages of the second and final volume of his diary.

He had already written much about the Indian Mutiny whilst it was still running its bloody course, in the form of articles which appeared in the *Bombay Standard* and were published in book form in 1860 as *Recollections of the Campaign in Malwa and Central India under Major General Sir Hugh Rose, G.C.B.* The narrative contained in this volume is not, however, a mere copy of what he had previously written: new incidents are included, and others omitted, and whilst the *Recollections in Malwa and Central India* were written in the third person, the present narrative is his own personal recollections and forms a chronicle of the important part he played in the drama.

It is not known exactly when the narrative was written, but it is almost certain that it was at some time after Sylvester's retirement in 1875; at the earliest on his return to England in 1873. Few liberties have been taken with it although it has been found necessary to correct an occasional error in spelling (but not in such cases as 'ancle', which form was then in use) and to insert a few unintentionally omitted words. The greatest liberty taken has been in punctuating and in breaking up the text into chapters and paragraphs, for easier reading.

The reader of Sylvester's recollections will perceive that though a talented medical man, his real inclination, at least in his younger days, was for the active life of a soldier. Perhaps regrettably, he took little pleasure in recording events connected with his medical duties, whilst revelling in the description of military actions. This side of his character is fully revealed in the manuscript, but it is understandably enough his diary, which is more revealing. There is to be found evidence of a shrewd brain seeking and finding ways of making money, always honestly, but making it nevertheless. Seldom did he get the worst of any transaction.

He was prone to despondency, as the following extract from his diary for 14 December 1860 shows: 'I have no inclination to read or write save letters. I hope all this will be a lesson to me to catch at shadows no more, it is useless striving for distinction or greatness, the Fates refuse both to me. . . . I think if I spent a trifle more on my personal comfort in stations, I should be more content and not always be so bent on change.'

After his return to Bombay in 1867, fortune smiled on Sylvester, for he at once obtained prominent appointments at the Grant Medical College and the Jamsetjee Jeejeeboy

Hospital, not to mention a very lucrative private local practice.

In 1869 he married a Miss Forman, by whom he had one daughter, but four years later he decided to retire and 1873 saw his departure for England on two years' retirement furlough. On Saturday, 8 March, the *Times of India* reported the impending departure of Sylvester (now a Surgeon-Major, to which rank he had been promoted on 4 December 1865). Before leaving, he was presented with a large illuminated address from the 'graduates and licentiates of medicine practising in Bombay', set out in that flowery language for which the Indian is unsurpassed. This address is now in the possession of his granddaughter, Miss Beryl Adeline Sylvester Hodder, together with five diplomas, four from King's College and one, dated March 1853, from the Society of the Art and Mystery of Apothecaries of the City of London.

Following his return to England by leisurely stages, and his retirement on 10 September 1875, Sylvester devoted much of his time to painting, with considerable success. The best known of his paintings are a portrait of the celebrated Lord Roberts, which he presented to the East India United Services Club, and that of Dr Carr Glyn, later Bishop of Peterborough. The self-portrait, reproduced in this book, in which he has depicted himself in his old uniform of Probyn's Horse, gives some indication of Sylvester's ability as an artist.

At the end of his life Sylvester lived at 16 Melbury Road, Kensington, and it was here that he died, as a Deputy Surgeon-General (in which rank he first appears in the Indian Army List of July 1880), at the age of 73, on 29 November 1903. His remains now lie in St Andrew's Avenue, in Brookwood Cemetery, Woking.

Acknowledgements

FIRSTLY, I have to express my thanks to Miss Beryl A. Sylvester Hodder, of Worthing, for her kindness in granting me permission to edit the recollections of her grandfather, Deputy Surgeon-General John Henry Sylvester, and further, for allowing me to quote from the pages of his private diary. To others I am also indebted, in lesser or in greater degree: to Mr A. J. Farrington and Mr A. H. Huntley, both of India Office Records, for the great assistance they have rendered me in identifying many of the officers mentioned by Deputy Surgeon-General Sylvester: to Miss E. M. Dimes, Miss K. Blair and Dr R. J. Bingle of the India Office Library: to the Director and members of the staff of the National Army Museum, who have given me similar help, as well as permission to reproduce several photographs, at one time in the possession of Miss Hodder, but now in the Museum: to Mrs H. I. Roosmalecocq, of Colchester, and to her sister, Mrs E. M. Shand, of Bournemouth, for information concerning their father, Captain Henry Thurburn.

Amongst those who have rendered me assistance in collecting what, it is hoped, is an interesting array of illustrations, I must also include Lieutenant-Colonel J. B. R. Nicholson (Editor of *Tradition* magazine) for the photograph of Colonel Gall; Virtue & Co., Ltd.; the Council of the Royal United Service Institution, and the London Electrotype Agency, proprietors of the *Illustrated London News*, and the Secretary of State for Foreign and Commonwealth Affairs.

I must in addition acknowledge help received from Mr Alexander Maitland (now working on a biography of

Lieutenant John Hanning Speke, the explorer); Mr H. G. Fletcher, Librarian of Cheltenham Public Libraries; Mr E. M. Kemp, Archivist of Thos. Cook & Son, Ltd; the Editors of the *Medical Directory* and *Crockford's Clerical Directory*; Mr R. W. Skelton of the Victoria and Albert Museum; Miss M. E. Beavan of the Geological Society of London; the London Necropolis Co. Ltd; Mr R. G. Harris, of Southsea, and Colonel H. J. Darlington, O.B.E., Regimental Secretary of the King's Own Royal Border Regimental Association.

Finally, I must remember all the help I have received from my wife who has spent so many long hours in checking and re-checking; wearisome and boring work, but without which this book could never have appeared.

A. McK. A.

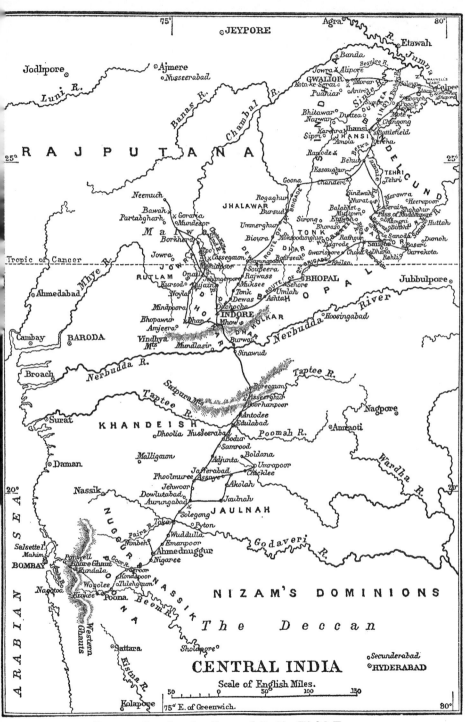

Route taken by the Central India Field Force

Northern India at the time of the Mutiny. Flags show the stations of British regiments in Bengal Presidency in May 1857

I

The Peaceful Years

In the year 1848, I entered as a matriculated student in the medical department of King's College, London, with the resolve to make the best use of the advantages obtainable from the excellent staff of teachers it then boasted; Todd, Fergusson, Farre, Partridge and Miller were among the number.[1]

Though reconciled to the study of medicine, I often encouraged an old longing for a more adventurous life, a desire dating back to my first acquaintance with Robinson Crusoe and the Swiss Family Robinson, and thus the idea of becoming an Army Surgeon took its shape. It appeared to offer a sort of compromise and was a bright hope for the future which cheered the monotony of a four years' course of study and residence in King's College.

I carried away some honours and served in most of the offices belonging to the Hospital in Lincoln's Inn Fields, and eventually qualified myself to practice in medicine and surgery; the time then arrived when I was compelled to choose for the future. The Navy was sufficiently easy to enter, but the pay and miserable advantages of those days rendered it entirely prohibitory: I never knew more than a single student of King's join that service. The prospects of promotion, rewards and pay in the British Army were but a degree better; it therefore required but little sagacity to prefer that best of all public services, the Honorable East India Company. Unfortunately however for me, its medical service was so coveted in the pre-competition days that I

---

[1] Professors Robert Bentley Todd, William Fergusson, Arthur Farre, Richard Partridge and William Allen Miller.

almost despaired of obtaining a nomination, but a fortunate
event gave me all that I desired.

It happened that at this period the Studentship in
Human and Comparative Anatomy, awarded every third
year by the Council of [the] Royal College of Surgeons of
England, was about to be competed for, and urged by Dr
Lionel Beale,[1] I became one of twenty-one competitors. A
fortnight's labour at the Animal Kingdom and I by no
means hopefully entered the list which dwindled very
considerably after the first day's examination. The ordeal
comprised the dissection of the nervous system of a Shorn-
back, and a detailed description on paper. As the number of
candidates fell off during the examination, I continued
more hopefully, and in the end was the victor.

At this time complaints were rife against the Directors of
the Honorable East India Company; whispers of abuse of
patronage were frequent, and perhaps this in a measure
was one of the causes which induced them to offer me
appointments. Be this however as it may, three offers of
nomination at once followed my success at the Royal College
of Surgeons, and after working awhile with Professor
Owen[2] at fossils and dry bones, and with Professor Tuckett
at the Microscope, I lost no time in starting for India,
having accepted an appointment to the Presidency of
Bombay from Mr Plowden.[3]

Prior to the era of competition candidates were orally
examined by Dr Scott,[4] the Company's physician: this test
passed, I was duly sworn in at the India Office, with a

---

[1] Dr Lionel Smith Beale, surgeon and microscopist, who was an old
student of King's College, where he was later a Professor of Physiology
(1853–69), of Pathological Anatomy (1869–76), and of Medicine
(1876–96).

[2] Professor Richard Owen, Hunterian Professor and Curator of the
Museum, Royal College of Surgeons.

[3] Henry William Chicheley Plowden, of Rust Hall, near Tunbridge
Wells, a Director of the Hon. East India Company.

[4] Dr John Scott of 13 Stratton Street, London, described in East
India Registers as 'Examining physician'.

batch of cornets and cadets, and set sail for Bombay on the 4th of December, 1853.

It was with a feeling of very considerable relief after the responsibilities of the start that I found myself gliding through Southampton Water on board the P and O's ship *Indus*. It was however with far greater satisfaction that four days afterwards I listened to the water softly lapping against the bows of the vessel when anchored before Gibraltar. Those only who know what sea sickness in the Bay of Biscay is, can thoroughly appreciate this soft music in the silence, following the unceasing thud of the engines; neither were the genial warmth and brightness of the sky and colour everywhere lost on me.

To one suffering as I did from sea sickness, the occasional stoppages at different ports were most enjoyable. Malta and Alexandria came in turn: at this latter place all passengers were divided into parties of six and drew lots for order of starting in the vans for the desert and Nile boats (both now institutions of the past). My party obtained six hours in which to see Alexandria; here while riding about on donkeys, sight seeing, I got the first idea of tropical sunshine, and started my first turban, necessary enough even in Egypt, while seeing its lions and standing amazed at reptile life on Pompey's pillar. A ride through the Bazaar, slave market, Palace of the Pasha, to Cleopatra's needle, the catacombs, marble baths, and other notable places, while so full of objects new to me, was to a certain extent disenchanting. There was a hollow gaudiness in the splendour, a depressing influence induced by the powerful sunlight, and an intense disgust created by swarms of flies, unceasing cries of 'backsheesh', filthy streets and filthier inhabitants.

On the evening of our arrival we left in a boat for a forty mile journey up the Mamodieh Canal. A tiny cabin at the end of our craft was given to the ladies of our party. The rest of us sat on its roof watching the sunset behind the pyramids; and after dark, the flitting forms of hundreds of

half naked Egyptians who, by the fitful glare of a score of
torches, hauled our boat along to the mighty Nile, yelling,
singing and shouting in a manner fully according with their
weird demonlike shadows in the torchglare.

A change of boat was necessary when we reached the
Nile; a little more discomfort and an increased yelling was
consequent, and I was scarcely sorry to greet my first
daybreak on the Nile. Then followed breakfast, mainly of
poultry, the well trained sinews and tasteless flesh of which
caused the awakening of one of my early regrets for the
land I had left behind. I had not the consolation of the
ordinary Nile traveller, that in a few short weeks I should
return having *done* the Cataracts – for was I not away on
an absence of twenty years, to return by the Suez Canal,
then a declared impossibility, though projected by the
Moslem conquerors twelve hundred years ago?

The whole sabbath was passed floating between the two
mud banks in solemn and melancholy stillness; an occasional
mud built village or solitary cluster of palms alone broke the
uniform monotonous scenery until we reached Boulac. An
overflow of the Nile had just previously washed away a
portion of the railway which now reduces both distance and
discomfort to those journeying across the desert.

On that Sunday night, a bed at the Oriental Hotel in
Cairo was a luxury and on the following morning a scamper
over the city, making the acquaintance of more picturesque
filthiness yet much that was most interesting, was the
prelude to the start at ten a.m. of my party across the
desert.

Gaze, Cook[1] and others have made all these scenes and
places common enough now, but I doubt if any of their
tourists recollect the old shattered [shuttered?] transit vans,
drawn by four phantom looking Arabs, galled at every

---

[1] Henry Gaze and Thomas Cook, travel agents. The former established the firm of Henry Gaze & Son, which came into being in London
in 1844, three years after the founding of the celebrated Thos. Cook &
Son Ltd, which now has over 400 branches in more than fifty countries.

point, by which we were bumped and bruised now against each other now against the roof or driver's back. Our transit occupied the entire day and following night, with two interruptions for refreshment. Suez being reached, the few beds obtainable were occupied by the ladies of each van as it arrived: I therefore contented myself with the floor beneath a billiard table which, from its appearance, might have amused.

Rubbing sleep from my unrefreshed eyes at daybreak, I recognized the hirsute face of an old fellow student of King's. From him I learnt that all recruits for the Medical Service of the Bombay division of the Indian Army were compelled to serve in its Navy for a period of two years, and he was now undergoing the hated period on board the Honorable East India Company's steamer *Victoria*, then waiting in harbour to convey us and the mails to Bombay. Bengal and Madras were more fortunate in being provided with a line of the Peninsular and Oriental's most comfortable steamers. Fortunate indeed, for the good tub *Victoria* occupied three weeks in her passage, a period which now serves for the entire route from England to Bombay. The scanty cabin accommodation was insufficient for all and I, with three others, were of necessity obliged to choose the softest plank on deck, often awakened in rough weather by a rebellious wave wetting us to the skin, and in calmer seas, masses of fiery soot from the funnel set fire to a railway rug, my only covering. I was moreover initiated into early rising by having to leave my plank at four a.m. daily, for deck-scrubbing, but I solaced myself by escaping the attacks of rats, cockroaches, and tarantulas, with which the old tub swarmed below.

We tarried at Aden and I rode to camp where I met another fellow student of King's who was serving with the 1st Regiment of Bombay Fusiliers,[1] and I entirely concurred with that traveller who observed he saw nothing

---

[1] The 1st Bombay Fusiliers later became H. M.'s 103rd Foot and finally 2nd Bn Royal Dublin Fusiliers (disbanded 1922).

B

green at Aden, save himself, yet, fresh from my wretched accommodation and sea sickness which clung to me ever yet, I was glad enough to visit the old volcano.

Leaving Aden we sailed into smoother waters, and twelve days afterwards, anchored in the harbour of Bombay. It was not yet daybreak, but all anxious to see the land of my choice, I peered into the dim light; a forest of dark masts over all sides was all I could recognise while a Babel of tongues greeted my ears.

The morning gun at daybreak found us all busily collecting our odds and ends of baggage. Friends and acquaintances of some of our party came off the shore in boats, and in those good old hospitable days the slightest acquaintance or introduction insured the newcomer a home until he left the Presidency town. In those days too, the sea lapped the shore where palatial hotels now invite the traveller, and make him as independent as uncomfortable.

Strangely enough, though we had all for some days past become impatient for the termination of our journey, the hour of separation brought its regrets. The calmer water in the Indian Ocean facilitated pleasing acquaintance, [and] moonlight dances on deck to the music of a tolerable band: we read poetry, played cards, gloried in the sunsets, and illumined sea. Oftentimes after dark the fiery track caused by our vessel's passage among the infinite multitudes of hydrozoa was visible a mile in our wake. Perhaps the recent separation from home ties renders the outward bound susceptible to warm attachments, perhaps the want of occupation and novelty of climate aids something; be this as it may, the spot behind the wheel had become hallowed in my memory.

Some sad hearts left the old *Victoria* on that 9th of January, 1854. Some of our party had come out to be married on arrival; the wedding garments were on board! could they hesitate now?

The first aspect of Bombay in those days was enough to dash the courage of the most hopeful; a long line of coast, or rather mudbank, running up the harbour, dotted with cotton boats and other small craft, the buildings behind covered with palm leaf thatch resembling, in the distance, English barns; black and copper-coloured natives either fat to obesity or lean to deformity, scantily clad about the loins, yet with sufficient drapery in the head dress to have clad a family in decency if spread in single sheet. The heat, too, was in character and effect, far different from my antici-pation. Then was the coolest time in the year, and the sun, though scarcely risen, produced a faint sickening sensation. When exposed to its rays, the great quantity of moisture in the air so thoroughly disfavored evaporation that the slightest exertion soaked one's under garments.

The vehicles which awaited us on shore were execrable; but two Broughams existed in the island, and scarce one of the splendid equipages now so common in the Presidency towns could be found.

I had been articled to a physician in Cheltenham, and his brother, then well known as garrison surgeon in Bombay,[1] welcomed me to a tent on the Esplanade, near his residence. The Indian tent, how far different to what I had seen in England; its enormous size, double roof, and walls with passage between, quaint buff coloured lining with seaweed pattern, so familiar to all who have served in India, struck me as an overcapacious and comfortless habitation. Little did I then know how many years of my life would be passed beneath the shade of such an one. Far less too, in that gentle heat, could I imagine how grateful in after years I should become for its ample space and double

---

[1] Dr William Carey Coles (1817–88). (*Diary*.) He is shown in East India Registers as being at that time at the Jamsetjee Jeejeeboy Hospital, Bombay. Served in China, 1842–3. In the *Cheltenham Annuaire & Directory* of January, 1839, a Mr Henry Coles is first listed as a prac-tising surgeon at Pemberton House, Cheltenham. In the Directory for 1849 he is shown as practising with a partner, Mr George Arnott, at 1 Liverpool Place, High Street. In the following year Mr Arnott is listed as a practising surgeon, but Mr Coles is omitted although still under 'Resident Gentry'. It would seem that it was to Henry Coles that Sylvester (not mentioned in the Directory) was articled.

walls when pitched in the ravines of Calpee under its death-dealing sun.

At its door, however, there was no lack of amusement. The sea at high water almost touched the storm rope; my floor mat was spread on its sands thickly strewn with shell and madrepore; strange and gaudy flowers grew in the garden plots, and birds which heretofore I had seen only in museums, or rare collections, screamed and yelled discordantly as they fought for any scrap or crumb thrown from the table. Birds of prey were in those days constantly hovering near Bombay dwellings, and others of far pleasanter habits and plumage were common enough. The former have almost disappeared under the better sanitation of the city which was inaugurated in the governorship of Sir Bartle Frere and carried out very expensively by Dr Hewlett.[1] Under this regime too, in 1860 the shore of back bay, on which I was then encamped, was reclaimed and a large piece added thereto from the ocean, and now a magnificent carriage drive runs along its entire length, and a line of railways is in active operation.

In the year I landed, the shore sloped very gradually to the water's edge and was the general burning ground for the Hindoo dead; consequently for upwards of a mile the sands were strewn with human bones and skulls, some charred, some bleached by long exposure. The sands were, moreover, the favored riding ground for the people of Bombay, and here, amid the funeral piles and burning bodies of a large population, parties of ladies and gentlemen took their morning and evening gallops, the empty skull often flying before the playful Arab's hoof with a hollow reverberation. People who only know Bombay as it now is will scarcely believe that this same shore was then

---

[1] Sir Henry Edward Bartle Frere (1815–84). Administrator. Appointed Governor of Bombay in 1862. He was later Governor of the Cape and first High Commissioner of South Africa, 1877, and was involved in events leading to the outbreak of the Zulu War.

Dr Thomas Gillham Hewlett (1831–89). Author of *The Sanitary State of Bombay*, 1869, and a *Report on Enteric Fever*, 1883, etc.

the general latrine for the native population adjacent.

If I had left many advantages behind in England, I had certainly gained one in exchange, which was an immunity from constant rains. Here in Bombay it falls from July to October and rarely, if ever in other months: January moreover besides being dry is cooler and gayer than any part of the year. There was no lack of charming society and good dinners well cooked. Each diner out took his own servant, and in those days, though proceeding to the house in uniform or black dress coat, it was customary to carry a starched white jacket and substitute it for the warmer and more exhausting garment if so permitted by invitation from the host.

Society was small; the influx of tradesmen and needy merchants had not taken place; a few merchant princes and the Company's military and civil service comprised the whole, a comfortable and close borough! Then too, Government was liberal; a month's leisure was allowed me in which I made myself acquainted with the chiefest features of the service on which I had entered. The weekly public breakfast at Government house gave all the opportunity of an introduction to the Governor, Lord Elphinstone,[1] who was exceedingly popular. How well do I recollect those enjoyable breakfasts, the charm of Lord Elphinstone's manner, his kindly condescention to all.

My credentials, asked for by the Physician General, Dr McLennan,[2] had made a favorable impression on the Medical Board of which he was the ruling spirit, and consequently I found myself gazetted to a favored station, the head quarters of Artillery, but to await the arrival of a batch of recruits expected by the ship *Ascendant* – and this delay was nearly costing my life in this wise. Rising as

[1] John, 13th Baron Elphinstone (1807–60). Cornet, Royal Horse Guards, 1826; Lieutenant, 1828; Captain, 1832; Governor of Madras, 1837–42; Governor of Bombay, 1853—9. He prevented a rising in Bombay during the Indian Mutiny.

[2] Dr John McLennan (1801–74). Author of *Fractures and Dislocations*, 1850.

usual one morning at daybreak to take my accustomed ride
along the bone-scattered sands, I felt a more than usual
lassitude, which feeling increased so fast that by the time
my horse was saddled I was scarcely able to mount, yet
thinking this was a natural effect induced by the exhausting
climate, I rode away from my tent, but before I had proceeded half a mile was so thoroughly prostrated as to be able
to regain it with the greatest difficulty. I felt no pain whatever and sank on my bed powerless: a deadly faintness and
nausea ensued, followed by all the symptoms of severe
Asiatic Cholera. I had no previous experience of the malady
but at once recognised its true character, and so did my
Portuguese servant.[1]

I need not recount the day's suffering I underwent,
chiefly from the terrible thirst and cramps in the limbs. My
memory scarcely recalls any particulars of the event but I
recollect battling with my medical attendants against all
kinds of medicaments, and clamouring for fluids. I suffered
agonies from their counter-irritants and was given up as
past recovery. During the evening, about dusk, I fell into a
sort of stupor which ended in real sleep, from which I woke
about ten o'clock that night and found my Portuguese
servant gently fanning the mosquitoes from my face and
hands, and beyond a racking thirst and great debility, I was
free from uneasiness and able to be carried from the bone
scattered shore inside a bungalow, and slept again soundly.

My narrow escape from this terrible Asiatic scourge discomfitted my existence and diminished my liking for the
country for many subsequent months. I could assign no
cause for my sudden attack save that King Cholera was
seldom absent from the City in those days of insanitation.

Previous to marching for Ahmednuggar, the Head
Quarters of Artillery, I went to Calaba, a small island
joining Bombay by a causeway, and here I stayed with the
Bombay Fusiliers, now H.M.'s 103rd Foot. They had an

[1] Probably Philip de Lima, who, according to Sylvester's diary, was
engaged on 9 January, 1854, on Sylvester's arrival in Bombay.

excellent Mess and Band and were justly proud of a well earned reputation in many hard fought fields. One night I sat at Mess next to Captain Burton,[1] now well known by his many books and travels; every member of the Mess had some capital anecdote to tell of the Haji as he was invariably called after his trip to Mecca and Medina, and with my desire for travel, an evening beside him was one of intense enjoyment. At this period he had just returned from his 'first footsteps in East Africa' and was seeking government sanction to proceed, with a party of officers, on a second visit of discovery: I seized the opportunity to enlist as one of these, and Burton promised to make the necessary application for my services.

Meanwhile, the *Ascendant* arrived and I proceeded to march with the batch of Artillery recruits to Ahmednuggar in the Dekkan, a fifteen days' journey; the recruits numbered one hundred and eighty, seven women, and as many children. Our first day's travel was made in a number of small boats across the harbour to the Panwell river, which we reached about eight o'clock in the evening.

The many and varied forest trees, shrubs, palms, and feathery bamboos which reached to the water's edge on Elephanta [an island in Bombay harbour with rock-cut Hindu temples], and other islands we passed, were full of interest to me. At the small village of Oolwa we saw the encampment of H.M.'s 87th Regiment[2] in which we were informed Cholera was rife, not a pleasing report to one so recently a sufferer.

On the following morning at one a.m. we reached Panwell, and found camel and bullock transport awaiting us.

[1] Captain (later Sir) Richard Francis Burton (1821–90), 18th Bombay Native Infantry, was at that time a Lieutenant, to which rank he had been promoted from Ensign, on 21 January 1846. He did not become a Captain until 3 March 1861. He cannot have performed a great deal in the way of military duties being so much engaged in exploration, travel, and writing. During the Crimean War he acted as Chief of Staff to General Beatson, who commanded the Bashi-Bazouks. Burton translated the *Thousand and One Nights*.

[2] Later 1st Bn The Royal Irish Fusiliers.

We had taken our men from the *Ascendant's* deck and they
now for the first time, after six long months, trod on
Mother Earth and with a wild delight marched three miles
to our encampment. How changed is all this now! The recruit is brought by the colossal new transports through the
canal in thirty days, and in a few hours more is carried to
his destination by rail, the speedy transit depriving him of
the gradual acclimatization ensured by the Cape route, and
the long march on arrival, which helped to fit him for field
duties.

At each halting stage, on frequented routes, a large shed
exited for soldiers on the floor of which they slept. Lieutenant Harris,[1] in command of our party, and I, passed the
night beneath a group of trees, and excepting that I was
awakened by the sniffing of a Jackal close to my face, I was
by no means discomfitted at my first's night's rest on the
bare ground.

Nothing to one unused, and fresh from life in England, is
more enjoyable than the bustle of camp and the busy scene
at daybreak while marching with a regiment in India. We
had as many or more native servants and followers as
European recruits and the work of striking camp in the
fresh cool air at daybreak seemed to give us new energy;
and then on arrival at our new encampment, pitching tents
amongst new scenery and arranging our little surroundings
for the day had its attractions, and made breakfast welcome.

The marvellous cheapness of provisions, poultry, eggs,
milk and other necessaries in those days enabled the poorest
subaltern to indulge in sumptuous meals well cooked by the
Portuguese settlers of Goa who recruit our Bombay kitchens.

As the day wore and sun rose high, the increased temperature rapidly induced that drowsy listlessness and lassitude
which but too often tempt the European to abandon
himself to hurtful habits of yielding to sleep.

During our progress of about fifteen miles daily to the
foot of the high mountain range of the Dekkan, we marched

---

[1] Lieutenant Thomas Marshall Harris, Bombay Artillery.

through low ranges of hills, dotted here and there by miserable collections of huts, among most of which Cholera was lurking. We buried three camp followers and missed one of our Europeans for four days. He was at length brought to camp by some villagers who had found him drunk; he was an Irishman and ready with an excuse. He told us that he had, while wandering on the outskirts of camp, met a tiger, and to escape, ascended a tree under which the tiger, with hungry expression, sat and waited for his descent four long days and nights, and to be sure, as the Company had gone to so much expense in bringing him to India, he did not wish they should lose him. He was therefore compelled to wait until the tiger's patience had become exhausted, when he descended and met these black gentlemen who had kindly shown him the way back to camp. The story was told in an irresistibly comic Irish brogue and was the means of mitigating his punishment.

As our men had to walk the marches, we usually left our encampment soon after midnight and reached the new ground at seven a.m. On moonlight nights it was pleasant enough when once on our way, but the reveille is an unwelcome sound to those unused to such unseasonable hours, neither is the work of packing, in the dark, one's tent and baggage on a refractory camel, a pleasing task when suddenly aroused, more stupified than refreshed, from half a night's slumber. The customary cup of tea at starting, brought by the khitmutghar, mitigates the discomfort, neither does the knowledge that he has sacrificed his night's rest to have it in readiness make it the less refreshing. By many officers this custom of drinking tea before commencing a night march is believed to act as a prophylactic against Cholera and malarious influences generally.

During our ascent of the western ghauts [mountains] the moon was in its full splendour and nothing could exceed the beauty of the winding road now almost unused since the route by rail has been adopted. In many parts the ascent was steep and our path overhung deep and densely wooded ravines some thousands of feet deep; in other places it was in turn overhung by giant cliffs and crags from which grew strange trees and leviathan creepers. The cheetah and tiger, hyena and jackal and other wild beasts prowled in the deep shadows and now and again the solemn stillness was broken by their cries.

After the moon set, I found six hours in the saddle, marching slowly through the dark solitude of these mountain paths, drowsy work. The measured tramp of the soldiery and jingling camel bells helped to produce this effect, and when not talking, we often fell asleep until rudely disturbed by the stumbling walk of our chargers. During our short halt midway in our morning's march we generally slept soundly by the wayside.

The last stage to Khandulla, which is situated on the high plateaux of the Dekkan, was a welcome one in point of climate. We ascended some five thousand feet and were enabled to get a splendid view over the many peaks and ranges we had left below us. The newly risen sun threw a bright golden hue over the deep ravines, at this hour filled with a soft haze which gave them a mysterious depth and charm, peopling them with every strange plant and creature, making one long to explore them – but it is in these very places especially that malaria finds its home. The sportsman knows this full well; the germs of all malarious diseases are found in the hot, close air of these beautifully wooded ravines and valleys at the foot of mountain ranges and, though the hunter seeks his quarry there by day, he is especially careful to avoid sleeping or halting in such spots.

At Khandulla the hot dry wind was a very agreeable change to the sweltering moist heat of the lowlands near the sea and though the temperature was higher, the climate was far more bracing and did much to enable me to forget the narrow escape I had experienced from King Cholera. Bombay residents have now commenced to build bungalows at Khandulla, and by means of the rail, often avail themselves of the pleasant change of climate.

Marching onwards, we passed the Cantonment of Poona, most favoured in point of climate of all Bombay stations. Still further onward we encamped at Seroor, another military station, and the head quarters of the Poona Irregular Horse.[1] The appearance of this regiment on parade is singularly picturesque. Major Tapp was then in command, and Lieutenant Payne Barras, Adjutant.[2] I and the other officers of our detachment were entertained by Lieutenant Barras with whom we went jackal hunting on the evening of our arrival.

On the 3rd of April, 1854, we reached Ahmednuggar and as the sun was becoming very hot under canvas, I was hardly sorry to accept the shelter of a bungalow. This station being the head quarters of the European Artillery, we had the advantage of an excellent Mess and Band. The officers' lines were particularly attractive on account of beautiful gardens, well stocked with oranges, plantains, grapes, guavas, and other Indian fruits and vegetables.

I shared the quarters of an Artillery subaltern, Lieutenant Davis: he was of a moody disposition and held converse with the other world. A disagreeable spirit prophesied his death during the year and he died accordingly, about a month after the message, of Cholera.[3]

Pig sticking, hunting half wild dogs and hares beguiled our evenings; my professional duties occupied about an hour in the early mornings on parade with the guns, and another hour at hospital. During the long hot days I painted with Lieutenant Strutt,[4] read, or wrote to friends in England. Hunting half wild or village dogs with spears I held to be a cruel amusement; they often escaped wounded

[1] Raised 15 July 1817. Later amalgamated with the 3rd Bombay Light Cavalry.

[2] Major Thomas Tapp (1st Bombay European Fusiliers), commanding the Poona Horse. The Adjutant, Lieutenant Charles Payne Barras, was an officer of the 29th Bombay Native Infantry.

[3] Lieutenant Henry Marshall Davies, Bombay Artillery. Born 21 January 1835; died at Ahmednuggur, 17 June 1854.

[4] Lieutenant Charles Henry Strutt, Bombay Artillery. He became a Military Knight of Windsor, 10 October 1901.

and then were in no amiable humour. It was said, I think in joke, one so wounded had become infected with madness and bit our Commandant, who was called among us King Pottinger[1] – be this as it may, he forbade us this pastime.

Mess in the cool evening was very enjoyable. We were a large body of officers; the room was flanked by long verandahs prettily overgrown with flowering shrubs and creepers, and at night lit up with clouds of glittering fire flies; the band of thirty-eight musicians under a German Bandmaster discoursed sweet music; an ample supply of English papers and periodicals made the nights pass swiftly until I was escorted home by a servant, lanthorn in hand. This was necessary on account of the frequency with which snakes occupied the hot and dusty roads.

There were rumours at this time of hostilities with Persia, though they did not actually commence until three years later.

No sooner had the novelty of quiet life in cantonment passed away than I began to seek a change, and having an Uncle in the Nizam's cavalry,[2] procured a month's leave of absence and started in a bullock cart over the dreary waste to Aurungabad on a visit, but was recalled on the morrow, to return to Bombay with a detachment of Artillery for the coast guns, Russian ships having been descried hovering on the coast. I returned at once, but the panic had passed.

A few days afterwards, however, I heard that Burton's expedition to East Africa had been sanctioned and a message from him directed me to be in readiness, but at this

---

[1] Major John Pottinger (1816–77), Bombay Artillery, then Director of the Depot of Instruction at Ahmednuggur. He was the half-brother of the better-known Major Eldred Pottinger (also Bombay Artillery). John Pottinger acted as Major of Brigade in Persia, 1857, and was with the Ahmednuggur Field Force in the Indian Mutiny.

[2] This was Sylvester's uncle, Surgeon William Henry Bradley (1807–81), to whom he refers frequently in his diary. He too was on the Bombay Establishment and had served as Surgeon's Mate and Surgeon in the ships of the Hon. East India Company. He served against the Bheels, 1837–8; in Afghanistan, 1839–40; Nagpur, 1842, and against the Rohillas, 1854. He served in Persia and in the Indian Mutiny.

time I was appointed as Professor of Anatomy and Physiology at the Medical College in Bombay, Curator of the
Museum, and Assistant Surgeon of the Hospital.[1] My inclination was strongly in favour of the African expedition,
my interest was doubtless with the latter, which at length
I chose; and fortunately so, as it [the African expedition]
accomplished nothing, being attacked by the Somalis of the
coast opposite Aden, soon after starting. Stroyan was killed,
Burton and Speke wounded; Hearn too had a narrow
escape.[2]

On the 8th of June, in the height of the rainy season, I
accomplished the journey by Mail cart to Bombay, experiencing to the full the effects of a tropical deluge of rain.
On the 17th of the month I delivered my opening lecture.
The College was a large, handsome building in the Gothic
style but more than half its space sacrificed to ornamenta-
tion, and without a single good lecture theatre; nevertheless
it afforded ample accommodation for the few students
attending in those days when Medical Education was in
its infancy: now, however, it is found extremely inade-
quate.

My class comprised British, Hindoo, Mussulman, Portuguese, and half caste students; they were apt at learning for
the most part, zealous, and endowed with wonderful

[1] In his diary, on 1 June 1854, Sylvester records that he was 'appointed
professor of anatomy and Physiology, Curator of the Museum & Assistant
Surgeon, Jamsetjee Jeejeeboy Hospital'. He had applied for the appointment on 4 May 1854.

[2] Lieutenant John Hanning Speke (1827–64), 46th Bengal Native
Infantry. Discovered Lake Victoria. Served with the Turkish Contingent in the Crimean War. Lieutenant William Stroyan was an
officer in the Indian Navy (Bombay), which he entered on 5 March
1842. He was a Surveyor. Died at Berbera on 19 April 1855. 1st
Lieutenant George Edward Herne entered the 1st Bombay European
Fusiliers as an Ensign and died as a retired Lieutenant-Colonel, 103rd
Foot (the same regiment) on 16 March 1902. He was distinguished for
survey work, mechanics, and photography on the West Coast of India,
the Punjab and Scinde. He served in the Punjab campaign, 1848–9, including the siege and capture of Mooltan, and was at Goojerat, the
surrender of the Sikh army at Rawalpindee, and the pursuit of the
Afghans to the Khyber Pass.

powers of memory.[1] The Museum was well provided with
empty cases and shelves and left me ample occupation for
any time that remained to me after my lectures, demon-
strations, and hospital work were over. My pay for this
work of about eight hours daily was between forty and fifty
pounds per month while with the Artillery it was about
thirty pounds: compulsory subscriptions and donations to
funds were however very heavy.

At this period of my service, intelligence of the Crimean
War reached India and made me regret that I had not
joined the army at home. The depressing climate of Bombay
and monotony of my duties increased my regret on this subject; nevertheless, I worked diligently at my Professorship
and the Museum until January 19th, 1857, when, disgusted
with the treatment I received at the hands of the College
Principal,[2] I resigned and volunteered for service with the
Persian Expeditionary Force then embarking for the
Gulf.

During my three years' residence in Bombay I made a
very considerable collection of dissection specimens and
skeletons of natural history for the Museum, and completed
a descriptive catalogue. I experienced a cyclone and water
famine.

At the time I write, there were about 50,000 inhabitants
in Bombay, dependent on the wells and tanks of the city for
their supply of water. In long, hot seasons following a
partial monsoon, the quantity often ran short, and in 1854
altogether failed. All the inhabitants, European and Native,
were restricted in their consumption, and many of the
latter perished. Many more would have done so but for the
supply brought daily in boats from Elephanta, and by rail
from the Tauna district. The recurrence of such a calamity
is now prevented by the construction of a dam across the

---

[1] Sylvester did not always employ such flattering phrases. In his
Diary in December, 1854, he describes the stupidity of his class as being
beyond all toleration.

[2] Surgeon Charles Morehead (1807–28). He studied in Edinburgh
and Paris, and published *Researches on the Diseases in India* in 1856.

Vehar Valley, by which means an unfailing supply of water is brought by pipes to the city, and since its advent, King Cholera almost never visits it. Most of the old wells and tanks are now filled up, which prevents the use of the polluted water they contained, for even now a portion of the Native community and many Brahmins scriple and indeed altogether decline to drink water which has flown through pipes wrought by the hands of us infidels. To the introduction of Vehar water solely do I believe Bombay is indebted for its recent immunity from that dire scourge, Cholera.

The cyclone I shall not easily forget. I was residing, at the time of its occurrence, at what was then almost the only hotel in the island. It was kept by Mrs Blackwell at Mazugony and called the Hope Hall Hotel. Most of those staying in the building – a large upper storied bungalow – had retired for the night, I to my bedroom on the upper story, open to a verandah in front, which stretched across the entire front of the hotel: behind, my room communicated with a large sitting room in which were hanging several immense glass chandeliers edged with pendant prisms.

The disturbance commenced gradually and first attracted my attention by the wind jingling these glass drops louder and louder until I could hear them break and drop on the floor; my mosquito curtains were rudely torn off the bed while all the lightest articles of furniture were blown down; tiles rattled off the roof; the wind commenced to roar amongst the trees, of which there were many in the pretty gardens which surrounded the hotel.

The noise became so great that voices could no longer be heard above the roar of the hurricane which was soon appalling. Occasionally some object of great weight lent its noise to the terrible uproar and could be heard thumping and crashing through the building: the darkness was profound. In my inexperience of cyclones I verily believed that something or other which Dr Cumming had predicted had

come to pass. I lay still through a storm of furniture and
other missiles which had been hurled on my bed, until a
thump from the mirror made me fear some heavier one
from other flying objects. I then endeavoured to get out of
the room, but was immediately swept off my legs and but
too thankful to bury myself again in what little covering
remained on my bed, and there await the issue. I forget
now what the duration of the danger, but fell asleep as the
wind became silent.

Anything more desolate than the morning scene I can
hardly describe. The whole of my apartment was gutted;
my bathroom and large tub which occupied part of the
verandah had been wafted away; the large foliaceous trees
all around were stripped of every leaf, many thrown down
or stripped of their branches. The water, generally so
bright and blue in the beautiful harbour, was mud coloured,
turbid, and strewn with wrecks. The shores were covered
by boats of all descriptions, and bigger vessels driven ashore.
Among them were many dead; birds of every description,
too, were scattered over the island.

After my resignation at Grant College had been accepted
by Government, there was a difficulty in obtaining my
successor and the Principal used every endeavour to per-
suade me to remain, but, as much as the Force had already
embarked, I was impatient to leave, and knowing then, as I
know still better now, that interest at head quarters is the
only means of getting anything one desires, I obtained an
introduction to Sir James Outram[1] from a relative:[2] Sir
James replied as follows:

My Dear Bradley,
        I have only time to thank you for your note and to say that I
understand Dr Sylvester is to go with the force and that I am too

---

[1] Sir James Outram (1803–63), Bombay Army. Educated in Aberdeen.
First sailed to India in company with a fellow-cadet, later Major,
General Stalker, who was afterwards to be superseded by him as commander of the Persian Expedition. He is best known for the prominent
part he played in the Indian Mutiny.
[2] Dr W. H. Bradley. (*Diary*.)

glad to have the services of so superior a Medical Officer.

In haste,

Very sincerely yours

J. Outram

Bombay, 14th January, 1857.[1]

At once I saw myself in orders for the Rifle Corps[2] and provided myself with the necessary uniform, only to be superceded by a senior a few days afterwards. I went, however, eventually on general duty and sailed in the *Raby Castle* in charge of a troop of H.M.'s 14th King's Light Dragoons.[3]

[1] This letter does not appear in the narrative, but a copy having been found in a collection of Sylvester's old letters and documents in Miss Hodder's possession, it has been inserted, as it was obviously his intention to do so.

[2] 4th Bombay Rifles, already in Persia. This regiment later became the 104th Wellesley's Rifles, and later still, the 1st Bn 6th Rajputana Rifles.

[3] Later 14th Hussars and now amalgamated with the 20th Hussars as 14th/20th King's Hussars.

II

The Persian Campaign, 1857

T HE force, of which I had become a member, was very
successfully dispatched and landed at the Isle of
Karrack in the Gulf, and proceeded subsequently to Bunder
Abbas, thence marching to Bushire, the transport ships
meanwhile coasting to Reshire, where the enemy had
thrown up a redoubt which was taken with a loss, on our
side, of Brigadier Stopford, Colonel Malet, three junior
officers, besides a few soldiers, European and Native.[1] The
steamers were under fire for three hours, but there were no
casualties afloat.

This engagement was followed by a surrender of the
Town which contained about fifty pieces of artillery. So
easy a victory gave rise to the suspicion that the Persians
had contrived this in order to draw our small force further
inland, the better to annihilate it; consequently twenty

---

[1] Sylvester here refers to events which occurred before his arrival in
Persia. Although it was intended that the force should be commanded
by Sir James Outram, the first division had been despatched before he
arrived from London, where he had been appointed to the supreme
command. This division was commanded by Major-General Foster
Stalker, C.B. (Bombay Army), who was senior to Outram, but for a
special brevet which allowed the latter to supersede him. On Outram's
arrival in Persia, Stalker continued to command the division. The 2nd
Division, which arrived later, was commanded by Brigadier-General
Henry Havelock who was to attain such great fame during the Indian
Mutiny.

Brigadier James Stopford, C.B., in command of the 1st Brigade and
Major George Grenville Malet were killed whilst leading their respective
regiments, H.M.'s 64th Foot (later 1st Bn North Staffordshire Regt and
now amalgamated with the 38th, 80th and 98th as The Staffordshire
Regt) and the 3rd Bombay Light Cavalry. Stopford served with the
40th Foot in Afghanistan, 1841–2 and commanded that regiment at
Maharajpore, 1843.

thousand additional troops were dispatched from India
under our Outram, and it was with this reinforcement I set
out, with a promise from him that I should be appointed to
one of the six irregular Cavalry regiments it was contemplated to raise had the war continued. The magnitude of
this force was in a measure necessary as Government was in
ignorance as to how much aid Persia was secretly getting
from Russia, or whether the Persian occupation of Herat
was not in some measure instigated by that country.

No one can tell the relief which I experienced when
freed from the monotonous duties of an Eastern Hospital
and dissecting rooms. I passed the grim looking college as
day broke and embarked from Apollo Bunder [a wharf in
Bombay] on which I had landed about three and a half
years ago. My charge, the squadron of Dragoons, was
drawn up ready for embarkation, and by means of a huge
crane, their horses were lowered into cotton boats, six in
each, and so carried under the bows of the *Raby Castle*
where a pulley from the yard arm hoisted and lowered them
into the hold. By noon we had stowed away the entire
number, seventy-six, without accident, but so closely packed
that, below, the temperature was almost unbearable.

Our troopers and sailors were in the best of humour and
sang in the bright moonlight until one and all lay sleeping
on the deck.

Next day, the commissariat stores having been embarked,
we were towed by a steamer out of harbour and away. We
proceeded north: the weather became exceedingly cold
which ill suited me so seasick had I become, and on reaching
Muscat I was almost too weak to walk through its streets,
which were excessively hot. The town is very pretty when
seen from the ship's deck. The high barren looking mountains which form its background must add to its temperature
as well as its beauty. They are volcanic and enclose a good
sized harbour: those immediately overhanging the town are
surmounted by formidable looking towers; other smaller
masonry works, still more ruinous, are dotted about on

steep crags so that one would imagine either ibex or eagles must man them. These fortifications, erected by early Portuguese mariners are not now in use. The town is little above the sea level and is celebrated for the manufacture of hulwa, a sweet meat well known throughout the East. The Imaum's stables are worth a visit, but being unable to walk so far, I made my way back to the ship with the impression that I had never seen a dirtier or less interesting bazaar.

About the middle of March we anchored in Bushire roads: meanwhile the force had fought the action of Koosh-aub.[1] My discomfort was by no means ended with our voyage as we were four miles distant from the shore and a perfect hurricane of wind kept the vessels tossing and pitching heavily. We had ample opportunity to admire the distant town which had a pretty and formidable appearance.

On the fourth day of our anchorage a few small commissariat boats came beneath our vessel. The high wind still blowing, nevertheless we commenced disembarking, a most difficult business. To the first boat we entrusted our tents and some servants, but no horses. It had scarcely been set adrift ere it capsized and I had the mortification to see my Portuguese servant and tent dashed away by the waves. The former was saved by the life boat, and the tent washed ashore and recovered some days afterwards.

Matters at this time were not going smoothly in camp: General Stalker and Commander Ethersey committed suicide:[2] Outram had arrived, assumed command, and left for Mahmora on the Euphrates with the flower of the force.

The almost bloodless naval engagement and consequent peace which followed were, so far as our arms were con-

[1] Fought on 8 February 1857.

[2] General Stalker committed suicide on 14 March, and Commodore Richard Ethersey, Indian Navy (Bombay), a couple of days later. Outram attributed Stalker's death to anxiety over the hutting of Europeans, and to pecuniary entanglements, and Ethersey's to considering himself unequal to his responsibilities as commander of the naval squadron. To these causes others have added the very trying general conditions.

cerned, a most fortuitous termination to the campaign though fraught with disappointment to the greater number of those engaged, for we had speculated on seeing Teheran, Ispahan, Shiraz, and encamping amid the ruins of Nineveh and Persepolis.

I have written that this speedy cessation of hostilities before we had scarce got a glimpse of the land of the Caliphs was fortunate, and it was so because we were with most insufficient means of transport had it become necessary to march away from the sea coast. The only march of the campaign made by the Persian expeditionary force was a distance of forty-six miles to Brasjoom and Khoosh-aub, and this was undertaken of a necessity without camp equipment or shelter of any kind. The force was absent six days during which time it was exposed to very constant pitiless rain and cold, a state of affairs which would soon render the best of troops ineffective.

Bushire, so imposing from the roadstead, disenchanted me as I walked up its dirty alleys. Its walls and round towers help to give its deceptive appearance from the sea. The rifle regiment to which I was nearly belonging was stationed in the town itself, but the force which Outram had left behind on his departure for Mohammerah was still in the entrenched camp a little more than a mile from the town. Thither I rode over a dreary plain of sand, the sea on one side, and far away in the background, abrupt bold mountain ranges, here and there their highest peaks covered by snow. The camp itself fronted to the town and was surrounded by a ditch about three feet wide, and the sand therefrom thrown up as a parapet while batteries frowned grimly from the angles.

After the action of Khoosh-aub and pending Outram's departure for the Euphrates, life in camp was tedious and wearisome and to the three thousand men and officers left behind to garrison Bushire on his departure, it was doubly so: the eye grew tired of the interminable sandy plain, everywhere unrelieved save by the distant Halilah ranges.

Walking in deep rolling sand was difficult and disagreeable; we had much ado to keep our tents standing
and clouds of sharp cutting particles mingled with myriads
of flies were blown the live long day through the camp. The
flies became a perfect plague, for no sooner was anything
edible exposed than it was thickly crusted by a black mass.
Dirty Persians with dirtier eyes covered with these plagues,
cried 'sweet water' for sale as they drove tiny donkeys so
laden through our lines. Among such clouds of these black
pests it was impossible to escape swallowing an occasional
one at almost every meal and the emetic effect was constant
and wide spread through the camp. A long train of gunpowder mixed with sugar, when spread, always attracted
myriads, and if exploded, blew a cloud of dead bodies into
the air, but mitigated the nuisance nothing.

We were dependant on the commissariat for food and
horse forage as not a tree or blade of grass was visible; the
water moreover was brackish and almost undrinkable. It
caused much sickness, and in my weak condition induced
by the voyage, brought on melena, to which I almost
succumbed. I was, however, tenderly nursed and ably
treated by Drs Batho, Rogers, and MacAlister[1] who removed me to Bushire Residency for the better avoidance of
the extreme variation of temperature twixt day and night
and which we keenly felt under canvas. My own memories
of Bushire therefore are especially dreary having lain there
many days in a state of delirium bordering on death.

Meanwhile, the medical authorities in Bombay, eager to
serve me out for having retired from the Collage, determined to send me to sea for my two years' service in the
Indian Navy, well knowing how severely I suffered on

---

[1] Drs James Ebenezer Batho, Adam MacDougall Rogers and James
MacAlister, all medical officers of the Bombay Army. MacAlister had
served in the Crimea with the Turkish contingent and later (1860)
served in China. East India Registers give Batho and Rogers as being
Surgeons of the 26th Bombay Native Infantry and the Poona Horse
respectively. Both these regiments were in Persia. MacAlister was the
civil surgeon in Bushire. (Sylvester's *Diary*.)

board ship; neither did the knowledge of my present illness consequent on the voyage to Persia alter their determination, but an official certificate of my sufferings at sea, procured from Commander Powell of the Indian Navy,[1] who chanced to be a fellow passenger with me on the voyage out, frustrated their intentions.

On the declaration of peace with Persia I was anxious to return to India as soon as I had sufficiently recovered to walk alone. Some few officers obtained leave of absence and visited Bagdad, Nineveh, and other places of interest. My illness was thus alluded to in the *Times of India*: 'From private correspondence we learn with much regret, that the late professor of anatomy and physiology in the Grant Medical College,—Esqre is seriously ill in the camp of Bushire. It appears that he suffered considerably from sea-sickness during the voyage, – rather a protracted one – and landed in a very debilitated state; for the first week his health improved a little but on the morning of the 1st instant he was laid prostrate by a sudden attack of haemorrhage from the bowels as we understand or something of the kind. It is to be deplored that the treatment which this singularly talented officer had received from his professional service in Bombay rendered such a step as resignation of his late appointment a matter of necessity. For the past three years Mr—has been *nominally* curator of the Grant College Museum; he was in truth that, but in addition was professor of anatomy and physiology and to use the words of one of his colleagues "taught it as it had never been taught before", a teacher of comparative anatomy, an assistant surgeon in the hospital attached, and demonstrator of anatomy, altogether doing for the past three years the work of three, and incessantly engaged from 7 a.m. until four in the Evening!!! His classification arrangement and mounting of the specimens recently sent out to the Grant Medical College by Government is a work which abundantly testifies to his zeal and energy and thorough knowledge of

[1] Probably Captain Frederick Thomas Powell, Indian Navy (Bombay).

the subject, and Government should see to it that such an ornament to his Profession and valuable teacher of its highest branches should not be lost to the service if his life is spared. Drs Batho and Rogers are in constant attendance upon him.'

On the 7th of May I left Persia and embarked for Bombay on board the steamer *Pioneer*. It was becoming very hot during the day and all were tired of the inactive life in camp. There happened to be no cabin accommodation on board our vessel, so that we were exposed to a very ardent sun by day and dews by night, while living on deck. Our first night on board was well nigh being disastrous as we ran upon a sand bank at full speed but succeeded in getting afloat again without further mishap than a loss of the captain's fingers which were torn off by his throwing the lead upon the steamer's screw. Assisted by Lord Seymour and Captain Bruce of the Punjaub Police,[1] both of whom were fellow passengers, I amputated them though with great difficulty in my weak state.

The weather was calm during our entire voyage and I regained some of my lost strength before reaching Bombay, and anxious to be at work again, I hastened to the sanitarium of Mahabuleshwar on the Ghauts about three thousand feet above the sea level as being the quickest means to recover.

The China expeditionary force which was subsequently recalled to Calcutta on account of the Mutiny was then leaving Bombay, and it was suggested that I should go in charge of the Company's steamer *Assaye*. This would have exactly suited my disposition had I been sufficiently recovered, but feeling that another month's sea sickness would be more than I could bear, Captain Bruce and I journeyed to Mahabuleshwar in company.[2] The rarified and

---

[1] East India Registers of 1857–8 give Captain Herbert Bruce of the 2nd Bombay European Regiment (Light Infantry) as Commandant, 5th Punjaub Cavalry, and in 1860 as Chief of Oude Police.

[2] They arrived in Mahabuleshwar on 20 May. (*Diary*.)

cool mountain air, the lovely vegetation, the flowers, fruits, and magnificent scenery gave me a fresh tenure of life. Never can I forget the Paradise it appeared to me after that hot, barren, interminable plain of sand I had so recently left in the Land of the Caliphs.

III

The Breaking of the Storm

THE season on the hills was just closing on our arrival;
many visitors were already hurrying back reluctantly
to the plains, yet desirous to avoid the burst of the monsoon
then impending. During early mornings we were buried in
cloud but as I had yet a few days unexpired leave, I was
anxious to remain on the cool hill summits unless driven
down by the violence of the rains.

It was on one of my last mornings' walks there that,
calling at the Station library for the latest news, I encountered a little knot of officers, each much excited, and
all declaiming vengeance against what I learned was an
outbreak of mutiny amongst the sepoys in Bengal. This was
in fact my first intelligence of the Great Indian Mutiny.[1]
That the cherished sepoys of Bengal should have rebelled,
murdered their officers, seized the arsenals, and set a new
king on the Throne of Delhi was sufficiently stirring, and to
the old officers there assembled, appeared incredible.

Bruce, my companion, who was contemplating a journey
to Cawnpore by Mail cart, lamented the impossibility of
joining his appointment and I felt that my future was hazy.
I may mention that, as the road through Central India was
unsafe for many months subsequently, Bruce proceeded by
sea to Calcutta and grew famous as the head of the intelligence department under Sir Colin Campbell at Lucknow.

I hastened to the plains, and on reaching Poona found
that station in a state of excitement hourly increasing as

[1] It was in fact on 6 June 1857, when in Poona after leaving
Mahabuleshwar, that he learnt of the rising at Nusseerabad on 28 May.
(*Diary*.) Three officers killed were Colonel John Penney, Captain Hugh
Spottiswoode and Cornet Richard Nicholas Newberry, all 1st Bombay
Lancers.

additional horrors done by the swelling number of mutineers reached us. I was forthwith pounced upon as one of the first available officers for duty, and directed, curiously enough, to join the left wing of H.M.'s 14th Light Dragoons, from whom I had so recently parted in Persia.[1] The entire regiment had not yet arrived from that country but its left wing was directed to proceed on service in the Dekkan without delay.

The monsoon had burst with more than its usual fury; rain descended in torrents; my small amount of baggage had not arrived from the Hills. I had sold my tent and chargers on leaving Bushire, but was glad enough to be at work again, more especially as its nature promised ample excitement. I was obliged to disregard the fact that I was still far too weak and bloodless to undergo much exposure.

Borrowing a horse from my friend Tragett,[2] I rode to Kirkee, the Dragoons' station and reported myself for duty: we were mutually pleased to meet again. The bustle of preparation for the march at midnight was everywhere apparent; officers and men were delighted. I purchased a horse of Serjeant Major Hunt and accepted the offer to share the tent of Captain Herbert Gall, who was appointed to command.

Each post from Bengal brought tidings of additional mutinies and fresh atrocities, but as yet the Bombay regiments had shown no symptoms of disaffection, if I except some few troopers of the Bombay Lancers who joined the mutineers of two Bengal Regiments[3] stationed at Nusseerabad; nevertheless we were suspicious of them

---

[1] He had been warned on the 6th to hold himself in readiness to join the 14th Light Dragoons. (*Diary.*)

[2] An entry in Sylvester's *Diary* records: 'Came down at 12 p.m. Arrived at Tragett's bungalow, Poona, at 9 o'clock on the 5th [June].' Lieutenant Robert Thorpe Tragett, 26th Bombay Native Infantry, was Acting Adjutant, Poona Horse, 1859, and Adjutant, 1861, in which year he died.

[3] 15th and 30th Bengal Native Infantry and some of the 1st Bombay Lancers.

and no doubt they were sorely tempted. The very sight of a black face in British uniform provoked threats from the troopers of the 14th and in these I think the officers silently acquiesced. It may be guessed therefore that we did not cordially welcome the 25th Regiment of Bombay Native Infantry when we learnt they were to form part of our force.

On the 8th of June our left wing, in marching order, was inspected by the commander in chief[1] and at 2 a.m. next morning we commenced our march. The rain had ceased for a while and the moon shone brilliantly; we were in the best of spirits, and once on the road the men sang cheerily and were full of speculation as to our destination, for, being required everywhere, we knew not what would be our first service. In the morning we reached Loonee; next day Konderpore. Here the 25th Regt commenced to march in company with us commanded by Lt Colonel Robertson; here too we received the news of further disaffection in Bengal and of the recall of the China expeditionary force to Calcutta.

The rain now descended in torrents so that we gave up marching by night and floundered through mud knee deep, arriving at Nigaree in the darkness. We passed the night without shelter, holding our horses, and as our baggage animals were unable to travel, we reached Ahmednugger in a sorry plight, having been twelve hours a day in the saddle, well soaked by continuous rain.

At this station so many requirements for our services were made that it was difficult to know which was most urgent; all were importunate, and after proceeding twenty miles in the direction of Mhow, we were counter marched in consequence of alarming news brought by Captain H. O. Mayne[2] from Aurungabad, and thither we were directed to

---

[1] Sir Henry Somerset (1794–1862), a grandson of the 5th Duke of Beaufort. Entered the army in 1811. Served in the Peninsula and the Netherlands. 18th Hussars. Commander-in-Chief, Bombay, 1855–60.

[2] Captain Henry Otway Mayne, who raised Mayne's Horse (later the Central India Horse) with which Sylvester was later to serve. Born in

go. The ladies and children had already left, and the officers besieged by the mutinous native troops of the Nizam's contingent were shut up in their Mess house. I can well recollect the dazed feeling which appeared common to us all at this crisis, for in addition to the first accounts of the mutiny, which were in themselves sufficiently alarming, war was declared against China and it was reported that Persia had broken the treaty so recently signed, that the troops in the stations we had left behind us had mutinied, and that those in our company were but watching the most favourable opportunity.

Though we numbered three hundred sabres yet what were we amidst so many foes, and expected to proceed in half a dozen directions during the monsoon when campaigning was never attempted? To be sure, we knew that troops had been ordered from England but events were multiplying so fast that the most hopeful scarce expected they would arrive in time to avail much. I felt thankful I was serving with Europeans; most Englishmen with natives silently distrusted them though they kept up a semblance of faith.

Just as we left Ahmednugger the news of the mutiny at Mhow reached us and there also came a false report that Delhi had fallen with a loss of 17,000 of the enemy. A battery of European artillery commanded by Captain Woolcombe[1] was now added to our strength and by forced marches we left for Aurungabad. Our last stage was forty-four miles, crossing the Godavery river en route. We were

---

1819, Mayne was appointed to the 6th Madras Light Cavalry and was transferred to the 1st Cavalry, Hyderabad Contingent. A. D. C. to Lord Gough in the 2nd Sikh War, and was present at Chillianwallah and Goojerat.

[1] In his *Recollections of the Campaign in Malwa and Central India* Sylvester gives the battery as being the 4th Bn 2nd Company, whereas in *The Officers of the Bombay Artillery* by Colonel F. W. M. Spring (1902) it is stated to have been the 4th Company, 2nd Bn which was commanded by Captain John Dobree Woollcombe (1822–75) until 22 May.

designated the Dekkan Field Force and General Woodburn[1] assumed command.

On entering cantonments, tired, dusty and sleepless, we were joined by the officers of the station and a company of Madras Sappers. Thus reinforced, we marched to the lines of the 1st Hyderabad Contingent Cavalry and ordered them to fall in on parade. Captain Abbott[2] was spokesman to the men under his command. The language should have been persuasive; Woolcombe's loaded guns were pointed at them while our naked sabres glittered in the fierce sunshine. It occurred to me that the men showed no affection for their commandant; a few yielded but the remainder signified their entire disapproval while their leader fired a pistol shot at Abbott. This was the signal for all to break into confusion, and mounting their horses, they fled. As soon as General Woodburn had recovered his astonishment he ordered the guns to throw grape and the Dragoons to pursue. I joined in the pursuit which was very ineffectual; our heavily laden and jaded horses were unequal to the fresher and less weighted contingent horses. Most of the fugitives escaped and we marched some fifty prisoners into camp and disarmed them.

Lieutenant Redmayne and some troopers mounted guard, Captain Leith[3] commanded a small force at the Bridge near the city, and a Court Martial summarily tried Meer Fider Ali who fired at Abbott. His attempt to prove an alibi was unavailing and next morning he was hanged in presence of the force and contingent soldiery. I was ordered to the front to pronounce him dead, an unnecessary precaution as a heavy Dragoon had hung on to each leg.

That night, at dusk, a squadron of Dragoons, two of

[1] Major-General Alexander Woodburn, Bombay Army.

[2] Captain Henry Dyett Abbott (31st Madras Native Infantry), serving with the 1st Cavalry, Hyderabad Contingent. This occurred on 23 June.

[3] Lieutenants Leonard Redmayne and James Leith (1826–69) 14th Light Dragoons. The latter was not then a Captain, and was given his correct rank by Sylvester in his *Recollections*.

Woolcombe's, two of the contingent guns, and some of the 25th Regiment, under command of Captain Gall, marched at dusk on Boldana in Berar.[1] I was in medical charge. A troop of Abbott's disaffected regiment was guarding the treasury and a few Europeans. With an occasional halt to get our meals, we reached Boldana on the third day, experiencing alternately heavy rain and fierce sunshine. By night we groped our way across trackless country and though aided by villagers and torches, oftentimes a halt was necessary, and the services of the sappers were needed before our guns could pass. The route lay through the villages of Chundaya, Chicklee, Jafferabad, crossing the Poorna and Daumam Rivers. After passing the latter stream, rain descended in such torrents[2] as compelled our halting some hours during which time we made bonfires of curby straw [straw of different grains], grouping miserably around them. That night's exposure caused some of our men to sicken and one became seriously ill.

Some part of our way lay through a beautifully wooded country intersected by clumps of huge tamarind and other trees, and it was marvellous how well we slept on the wet ground during the short halts we occasionally made. Our mission was accomplished, the Europeans and treasury rescued. Mr Bullock[3] entertained us sumptuously and thought it advisable that we should remain at Boldana. General Woodburn wrote for our instant return, which order we obeyed, taking the route through Jaulnah. Our infantry were all weary and footsore; my face was so blistered by sun and rain that it cost me much inconvenience. The country at and near Jaulnah was very beautiful and

[1] This party also included two of the Nizam's guns and some of his Infantry. (*Diary*.)

[2] Sylvester had a particularly uncomfortable time as his young horse could not bear its rider's cloak over its back and tail, with the result that he was soaked through. (*Diary*.)

[3] Mr Bullock was the Resident in Boldana and he had already disarmed the disaffected troops so that all Gall's party had to do was to take them away, with the treasure. (*Diary* and *Recollections*.)

appeared teeming with antelope, wild hog, and other game. We often saw immense herds of the former.

On reaching Jaulnah we encamped on the parade ground of the 6th Madras Cavalry stationed there. We dined with the officers that night. The few of that party now living will not have forgotten the glorious hospitality we received. Foremost among our entertainers was Captain Dowbiggin, a brother of the veritable Dowb, and I feel constrained to say that if Dowb was only half as good a fellow, he well deserved the interest manifested in that memorable Crimean telegram.[1]

On the 6th of July we again reached Aurungabad and rejoined the remainder of our force. Accumulated news of fresh disaffection was in store for us. The Nizam and his minister were yet staunch, but seditious placards were posted over the walls of his capital, Hyderabad, calling on its immense population of Arabs and Rohillas to fight for their religion and country; an outbreak was momentarily expected at the large military cantonment of Secunderabad; the mutineers everywhere appeared on the tide wave of success and vowed they should soon drive every European into the sea. At this time it appeared to me that no profession promised so well as the military, and I was with difficulty persuaded from purchasing a Cornetcy in a Dragoon Regiment.

The affair of the disaffected cavalry at Aurungabad had been sadly mismanaged and General Woodburn reported sick.[2] The command for the time devolved upon the next

---

[1] Lieutenant William Henry Dowbiggin, 6th Madras Light Cavalry. Resigned 18 May 1858. 'Dowb' may have been Major Montague Hamilton Dowbiggin, H. M.'s 4th Foot. He was appointed, by telegram, to the staff of General Sir James Simpson in the Crimea, and served as an A. D. C. This may have been the 'memorable Crimean telegram' but why he should have been 'veritable' has not been discovered.

[2] On 7 July, Sylvester was called in to look at Woodburn, when he signed a certificate for the General to go to Poona for a month. On that day he also received a letter from Dr Morehead which contained a 'wigging' for not having reported his departure. (*Diary*.)

senior officer, Major Follet of the 25th Native Infantry.[1] Execution parades followed: some were shot by carbines, others blown from guns in the presence of the entire force. Here for the first time I realized the stolid indifference with which a Mahomedan can meet death; it is one of the most singular attributes of the Mahomedan religion. Its followers often work themselves into a state of fervour which enables them to catch glimpses of Paradise and the black-eyed houries awaiting them when sacrificing their lives for their religion. I watched closely those who were blown from guns and failed to discover any exhibition of either fear or regret. The culprit's head generally flew high in mid air, the body was shattered to fragments, the legs fell beneath the muzzle whilst the arms flew wide asunder.

Intelligence of the mutiny of Mhow, Indore and Mundlaisur hastened our departure, much to the disapproval of the Contingent officers who were to remain behind with those of their regiment who were yet loyal. I confess I should not have cared to be with them; soon after our departure, however, they too were marched on active service. Our destination was Mhow and for some days all went well and we covered the ground as quickly as swollen rivers, nullahs [dry water-courses], and muddy roads would allow.

We reached Adjuntah and visited Major Gill[2] who is so well known in connection with the celebrated caves there, and from Adjuntah onwards our way lay through jungle more or less dense almost the entire distance to Mhow. This route was never undertaken by Europeans in the monsoon, as malaria abounds especially at the foot of the Mhow ghauts [chain of mountains], and in the valley of the Taptee which we were approaching. At the village of Edulabad we were fairly under its evil influence. The air

[1] Major Francis William Follett.

[2] Major Robert Gill entered the 44th Madras Native Infantry in 1824. He copied about thirty of the cave prescoes (full size). Of these twenty-five were burnt in a fire at the Crystal Palace in 1866. He died in 1875.

c

was hot, still, and sultry, the soil rich black loam, highly
cultivated, and for the most part covered with cotton in
flower. A steamy exhalation was perceptible enough, nor
was its more potent influence long hidden.

We gained the bank of the Taptee on the 20th of July
and encamped at the village of Antoolee: here one of the
Dragoons was suddenly attacked by cholera and almost
simultaneously Major Follett and some of his sepoys were
seized. We buried him, and I think most of those affected,
that evening, and at my earnest entreaty, marched on at
pace.

Captain Keatinge, Political Agent of Mundlaisur[1] joined
our camp and the Maharajah Holkar[2] sent us thirteen
baggage elephants, despite the ugly rumours then afloat
concerning his sentiments on British rule. Cholera still hung
upon our track; many natives died; seven Dragoons in all
had been affected; three only had succumbed.

On the 11th of July we reached the large Mussulman
city of Burhampoor and received intelligence of the
Massacre of Cawnpore by the miscreant Nana. We were
now in Scindiah's territory; some of his troops were
stationed here. We disarmed fifty and sent them adrift. Our
next stage brought us to Asseerghur, which is an old Hill
Fort garrisoned by us. It is extremely picturesque being
situated on a hill of trap rock springing abruptly from the
undulating country. Beneath all is dense jungle, hereabouts
extending up the precipitous sides of the fortified hill. It
was with great difficulty we found sufficient space on the
north side of it whereon to encamp. There was a very
scanty supply of bad water and a heavy, steamy atmosphere,
eminently suggestive of fever and cholera pervaded the
camp. The latter disease was still among us and at every
halt we buried two or three of its victims, which dispirited
us all.

[1] Captain Richard Hart Keatinge (1825–1904), Bombay Artillery.
Later awarded the V.C. Chief Commissioner, Assam, 1874–81.

[2] Sir Takorajee Rao Holkar II, Maharajah of Indore.

Some few more of Scindiah's faithless infantry were tried by Drum head Court Martial and three were shot, the less guilty smarting with revenge, and being set at liberty, hastened to swell the ranks against us in Hindoostan. It appeared to me that all should have been shot. No middle course was practicable for we had no spare soldiery available to guard prisoners.

Near Asseerghur, Colonel and Mrs Durand, Dr Henry Wilson and other fugitives, with a party of ladies (escaped from the mutiny at Indore) joined our camp. They had suffered much and the hardships had been too much for Mrs Durand.[1]

On the 27th the force crossed the Nerbudda at Mokka Ka Tur. Our horses swam it without accident. The river here is of great breadth and very picturesque, its banks well wooded and abounding in wild game, peafowl, wild hog, deer, hares, painted partridge, bears, bison and tigers. At length, tired out by incessant marching through unhealthy jungle, across swollen torrents and rivers in almost unceasing heavy rain, we reached the Vindhya chain of ghauts and during the night ascended sixteen hundred and fifty feet.[2]

We were now designated the Mhow Field Force and Brigadier Charles Stuart assumed command.[3] Our ascent of the Vindhya range was marked by a most agreeable change of climate: the air was cooler, drier, and more invigorating though rain still fell in torrents and roared and

[1] Colonel (later Major-General Sir) Henry Marion Durand (1812–71), Bengal Engineers. He arrived in India in 1830. His wife was Anne, third daughter of Major-General Sir John McCaskill. He married again after the death of his first wife which is later recorded by Sylvester. Assistant Surgeon Henry Wilson, was on the Bombay establishment.

[2] At this time Sylvester was still hankering after real soldiering as opposed to military doctoring. In his diary, 26 July, is the entry: 'I am seriously thinking of getting Gall to write home for a Cornetcy for me.'

[3] Brigadier Charles Shepherd Stuart (1804–79), Bombay Army. From Sylvester's *Diary* it would seem that he did in fact assume command earlier than the narrative indicates, as an entry for 10 July reads: 'Brigadier Stuart is commanding, he seems an agreeable enough man.'

dashed in angry cataracts down the deep gorges into the gloomy ravines at the foot of the ghauts. There too was a belt of jungle in its richest foliage: tall huge leaved teaks towered from dense masses of gracefully feathered bamboos. The vegetable world appeared to revel and run wild in the plentiful rain and fervent heat. At my urgent request we did not halt below the ghaut at Burwai; the water was bad. A tiger carried off one of our commissariat bullocks. We buried three other Dragoons, dead of cholera, and two of our officers were sick with fever.

Colonel and Mrs Durand marched in company with us to Mhow. The latter usually passed us on the line of march in a palanquin [a boxed litter] followed by a bevy of native horseman and an elephant. It was not generally known in camp that she was ill beyond recovery.

At Simrool, on the summit of the ghauts, the force was joined by the 3rd Regt of Hyderabad Contingent Cavalry under Captain Sutherland Orr. This regiment came to us with a bad name; it had disputed by sword with Brigadier Colin Mackenzie at Bolaraum;[1] two squadrons however were left in charge of the Ferry on the Nerbudda. Wool-combe's battery horses had suffered severely and we were compelled to send into Mhow for those of Hungerford's[2] artillery, to drag in the guns. So far as soil for encamping was concerned, we were now worse off than below the Ghauts, and were kept awake all night by Leith's troop horses breaking loose and galloping through our tents. Frequently too of late I had seen the reflection of the

---

[1] Sylvester first saw the 3rd Regiment on 31 July. (*Diary*.) Captain Sutherland George Gordon Orr, 23rd Madras Native Infantry, was serving with the 3rd Cavalry, Hyderabad Contingent. Brigadier Colin Mackenzie (1806–81) joined the 48th Madras Native Infantry in 1828. He was present at the conference, in Afghanistan, on 23 December 1841, when Sir William Hay McNaghten was barbarously murdered. He was Brigadier-General in the Nizam's army and was dangerously wounded in the course of a mutiny at Bolaraum, 1855, for which he was considered responsible.

[2] Captain Townshend James William Hungerford, Bengal Artillery. He was stationed at Mhow at the outbreak of the mutiny there, and overawed the mutineers with his guns.

soldiers' lights shine upon the water covering the floor of their tents.

On entering Mhow,[1] the Europeans who had escaped the massacre here by reaching the fort, galloped out to meet us and with the camp followers from the Bazaar, set up shouts of welcome. We passed the charred and blackened ruins of the officers' bungalows which had been burned by the men of the 1st Bengal Cavalry and 23rd Native Infantry. Fortunately, the church, Library and Cavalry Hospital were roofed with slate instead of thatch, as is usually the case in the Indian stations, and consequently escaped destruction. The sheds also, which covered the horse lines of the mutinied cavalry, were intact, and by the help of the canvas tent walls, formed good shelter for our own troopers and the European Artillerymen. Our sick were located in the Hospital and we took shelter in the Mess house. The inside of this building was strewn with the handsome plated ware, crockery, china, and other articles which were unacceptable to the mutineers who had of course marched away to Delhi with their horses, arms and uniforms complete.

Colonel Platt and his Adjutant, Fagan,[2] had been shot by the sepoys of the 23rd; who [Platt and Fagan], as was very generally the case, trusted their men too implicitly and personally entreated them to remain faithful. The officers of the 1st Cavalry were wiser in their generation and kept clear of their troopers, though Dent rode for his life, and Dr Thornton[3] escaped by remaining many hours in a covered drain. More lives would have been lost here but for the fort to which ladies, children and officers fled when firing commenced. The mutineers were too intent on plundering

---

[1] 2 August 1857.

[2] Colonel John Platt (1802–57), 23rd Bengal Native Infantry, with which regiment he had served since 1824. Took part in the Chinese War, 1842. He was killed at Mhow by the men of his own regiment who had shortly before petitioned him not to join a European regiment when he had the opportunity of doing so. In the end they left him dead and terribly mangled. Captain James Fagan was the Adjutant.

[3] Lieutenant Robert Wilkinson Dent and Surgeon Henry John Thornton, 1st Bengal Light Cavalry.

the Treasury and bungalows to molest the Europeans further; moreover, Hungerford's battery, manned by fifty Europeans, was stationed at Mhow. Probably, too, the disaffected men were urgently required at Delhi, and impatient to share in its defence, for that city was now besieged by the Punjab troops. The force of example could hardly have better exemplification than that given by the conduct of some men in Hungerford's battery who broke open the treasure chest they guarded, and stole therefrom fourteen hundred rupees.

We were now within thirteen miles of Indore, the seat of Maharajah Holkar. His troops had mutinied, sacked the British residency and in part joined the rebel forces in Hindoostan; some thousands were yet in the City of Indore. Holkar professed himself still friendly to us but unable to control his army, yet desired us to leave it unmolested as he had promised pardon to those still around him, although they had participated in the attack on the British residency and sacked it. He confessed himself sorry for their conduct and declared that his Treasury had been plundered to the extent of sixteen thousand pounds. I do not think this story was implicitly believed by Colonel Durand who was acting as Agent to the Governor General in Central India for Sir Robert Hamilton,[1] absent in England. Neither was there an officer or soldier in our camp who was not disgusted at the policy then adopted towards Holkar and his army, but he possessed a powerful friend and advocate in the absent agent and consequently, though we had received a reinforcement of three hundred of H.M.'s 86th Royal County Down Regiment, commanded by Major Keane,[2] we were left in a state of inaction, as it was impossible to proceed further with so large a force as Holkar's doubted soldiery in our rear; and

[1] Sir Robert North Collie Hamilton (1802–87). Agent to the Governor-General, Central India (Bengal Establishment).

[2] Major Giles Keane. The 86th joined on 5th August, 1857. (*Diary*.) This regiment later became 2nd Bn The Royal Irish Rifles, which designation was changed to The Royal Ulster Rifles in 1922, after the establishment of the Irish Free State.

thus it was that we halted at Mhow, and though the rest
and shelter was a boon to the troops and baggage animals, it
was an impatient time to us all.[1]

Never shall I forget the luxury I then enjoyed of sleeping
eight hours under cover without the prospect of a march at
midnight in pouring rain. There can be no doubt that many
of our marches would have been far less harassing if we had
made them in the daylight, but our Brigadier belonged to the
old school and he did not then possess the knowledge of campaigning which subsequent months of necessity brought him.

During our halt at Mhow alarms were very constant. A
troop of Dragoons and its complement of officers and men
slept accoutred every night; Woolcombe's guns were
similarly held in readiness. News of Havelock's victories,
hard fighting before Delhi, the arrival of reinforcements in
Bombay from England, Sir Colin Campbell's advent, and
the mutiny of the 27th Bombay Native Infantry reached
us;[2] and on the 28th of August, Mrs Durand died.[3] Many
officers showed what sympathy they could with Colonel
Durand, by attending her funeral. Rain was incessant, the
grave was filled with water, the Europeans had a sickly
appearance and we buried several more who died from
cholera. Many of the Irregular Cavalry horses were lost
from exposure to such unusually heavy rain.

[1] 'I amuse myself in my leisure by painting & writing letters, reading
Morehead's diseases in India.' (*Diary*.)

[2] Fortunately for the Europeans, the Bombay and Madras armies remained steadfast although there were a few cases of disaffection, one of
these being the mutiny of some of the 27th Bombay Native Infantry at
Kolapore. The suppression of this by Lieutenant William Alexander
Kerr (24th Bombay Native Infantry) and fifty men of the South
Mahratta Horse, of which he was Adjutant, provides one of the most
astounding and exciting episodes of the Mutiny. For this action, Kerr
was awarded the V.C.

[3] Mrs Durand died at Mhow on 28 August 1857. Shortly afterwards,
Sylvester recorded in his diary that 'Durand, the political, accompanied
us & a strange Guy he had made of himself by putting on a Black cap
cover for his Wife's death.' This entry he accompanied with a small and
crude sketch of Durand's head (all eyes and moustache) surmounted by
a small forage cap with a black cover and a curtain hanging down the
back and sides.

IV

From Mhow to Indore

NOT until the 20th of October did we leave Mhow, taking with us a siege train which had been prepared in the Fort. A small force under Major Robertson preceded us by a few days and rejoined us at Bellode on the road to the Fortress of Dhar. The rainy season was over and the days were excessively hot. Colonel Durand accompanied us as political agent, and it now oozed out that we might anticipate hostilities on arrival at Dhar. Our little army was in great spirits; there were none sick; all invalids and Europeans had been left under a guard of fifty men of the County Downs within the fort at Mhow.

The march lay across a pretty undulating country innocent of roads and often intersected by muddy nullahs. The eighteen pounders were dragged through these by prodigious efforts. Twenty pairs of bullocks, with the trunks of two or three elephants were often necessary.

At length, at ten o'clock,[1] we were within two miles of Dhar and as we had marched at two a.m., the force was halted and a ration of rum served out. Captain Mayne, who had attached himself to our force at Ahmednugger, rode forward with a few native horseman and on nearing the village had been fired on. This was satisfactory and we prepared for action. The plan of attack arranged previous to marching was to divide our force pretty equally, one column to be commanded by Major Keane, the other by Brigadier Stewart,[2] the columns to march by different routes and show themselves on opposite sides of the town and fort, as near the same hour as possible.

A long steep elevation in our front completely shut out

[1] 23 October, 1857.   [2] Stuart.

the view and over this the 86th Regt advanced as skirmishers, the Staff and main body of troops following. No
sooner had we gained the summit of the rising knoll than a
most lovely landscape, dotted with lakes and hills, lay
beneath us, and about a mile distant was the fort and
village. On its left a mass of trees, further to the left of
which, though not visible to us, was Major Keane's column,
on the right a collection of hills, the flat summit of the
highest crowned by one of the enemy's batteries, together
with a cluster of their infantry, especially brilliant from a
large display of banners.

The beauty of the scene was enhanced by a large sheet of
water which lay deep beneath our position and almost
washed the Fort walls. Columns of smoke were visible as
they towered into the hot sunshine from its bastions, for
their guns had opened fire on both our columns. Their first
shots at us fell short into the lake.

Our line on the ridge was artillery in the centre, Dragoons and Hyderabad Cavalry on the right, on the left of the
guns our infantry and sappers. Thus massed, both the hill
battery and fort quickly got our range and knocked over a
jemadar [Lieutenant] in the ranks of the Native Cavalry.
This provoked a futile reply from Woolcombe's guns, but
the old smooth bore was unequal to the distance. Gall was
therefore ordered to charge and take the hill battery. I
joined in the gallop down a ravine and up the steep hill
slope. The enemy, catching sight of our turbans, fled for
safety to the village, abandoning three guns and a quantity
of ammunition: some of this consisted of hammered shot
and one piece of cannon bore the mark of the East India
Company. There was great cheering from our native
soldiery during this charge and the men of the 25th Regt
were as pleased with the captured guns as children with
toys: they turned them and fired upon the fort.

During these events on this side, Major Keane, on the
north, drove the enemy from his outworks within the
village, and Woolcombe, after upsetting a gun and tumbril

over an escarpment of rock, took the site of the captured battery, and was enabled to shell the fort bastions. The enemy's cavalry hovered about us and killed and wounded some four skirmishers. We then engaged them in swampy ground, with considerable success, but our troopers, too impetuous, pursued too near the village and several were wounded – one with an arrow – the first of the kind I had ever seen.

The enemy had withdrawn into the fort and pettah [extramural suburb often separately fortified] beneath, from whence he kept up a desultory cannonade, and Brigadier Stewart [Stuart] considering we could not interfere further, directed us to encamp in a valley some two miles distant. It was a pretty spot, covered with greensward and abounding in partridge and florican which we put up in numbers while scouring the country around. The native cavalry we had suspected fought really well in hand-to-hand encounters with the enemy's cavalry.

Pickets were thrown out and the next day was passed in inactivity, waiting for our siege guns which had stuck fast in a nullah. The entire force slept armed; a regular plague of fleas tormented us. There was great dissatisfaction among the officers because the village was not taken and held, and the fort surrounded. It was unfortunate that our Brigadier had his spurs to win. Subsequent events appeared to justify the opinion that immediate steps should have been taken to prevent the enemy's escape that night. Our pickets saw distant torches and heard the noise of camels after dark.

During the first day's halt I took a rifle to our pickets and amused myself by firing at the men who could be seen working their guns on the bastions and I also brought away a sketch of the fort. Five elephants were descried in the distance: a squadron of our men gave chase, came up with them in a village, and were fired on. The inhabitants would not give up the culprits and the village was consequently burnt and some of the guard killed. The elephants, together with their drivers and some ponies, were brought into camp and proved a great boon to the commissariat for transport. Having joined in yesterday's pursuit, my commanding officer, in order to punish me, forbade my joining in the elephant expedition. Five thousand rupees, the price paid by the commissariat for these animals was distributed to the Dragoons and men of Orr's regiment who accompanied them.

On the arrival of the heavy guns, every spare hand was enlisted to throw up a sandbag battery for them, on the range which hid us from the fort. It was in action by daybreak, doing good execution, and under cover of its fire we took the village without much opposition. The walls and huts afforded good shelter.

Lieutenants Strutt and Christie,[1] with part of Woolcombe's guns took up position in front of the main gateway of the fort, from which a brisk matchlock fire was constant. A gunner was shot through the chest and Christie through the boot and turban. Country spirit had been found in the village and many of our European soldiery were drunk and committed atrocities among the villagers.[2]

While Strutt's shells into the fort bastions kept the enemy tolerably quiet, Robertson with his sepoys took possession of an embankment on which the Madrassees threw up a breaching battery about three hundred yards from the west curtain [a rampart between bastions] of the fort. Strutt and Christie were the moving spirits here, when the guns were in position. It was heavy and hard work, firing breaching guns in so hot a sun; the fort garrison moreover concentrated its fire on them despite our infantry who, sheltered beneath the earthwork and among the houses, fired at the smallest semblance of a human being at

---

[1] Lieutenant Benjamin Christie (1836–60), Bombay Artillery. Promoted to Lieutenant, 27 August 1858, antedated to 13 June 1856.

[2] These drunken fellows, off-duty men of the 86th and Artillery, with some native troops, killed everyone they met, irrespective of age or sex. Their behaviour on this occasion placed them on the same level as the worst of their adversaries. They had to be stopped by their officers and the Provost Marshal. (*Diary*.)

the fort embrasures. The extreme left of the village, termed the pettah, was so close beneath the fort walls that it could not have been held had we taken it. A few of the enemy were still in possession and kept up an annoying fire on the battery, which induced some of our garrison to approach it at night and set it on fire. This attempt caused it but very little damage and a second essay was made by Woolcombe, Christie, and Strutt, together with a party of their gunners.

The night was bright moonlight and the proximity of their path to the west curtain of the fort made their hazard a dangerous one: soon however, towering flames and unceasing volleys from the fort walls proved the success of their venture, but the enemy, so thoroughly roused, made their retreat doubly dangerous, and volley after volley greeted the gallant party, of whom Christie narrowly escaped death or capture by swimming a portion of the lake.

Under the continuous hammering of twenty-pounder shot, the curtain commenced to crumble, and our videttes and pickets were arranged so as to prevent the enemy's escape. The number of miles, however, to be guarded, rendered this problematical. Alarms of their escape were frequent enough to keep the Cavalry in constant work.

During any respite I often passed a pleasant hour in Strutt's battery, and it always seemed to me that he and his brother officer, Christie, bore charmed lives, until at length an unlucky shot passed through the chest of the latter who for many months appeared beyond recovery. An excellent constitution at length pulled him through, to be destroyed in an encounter with a tiger not long afterwards.

Moonlight enabled the breaching guns to be worked night and day; Hungerford's battery and men were also engaged in the village where Major Robertson was in command. On the 30th of the month the wall commenced to crumble and each concussion of the shot sent up columns of dust and debris, whereupon a white signal of truce was hoisted on the fort battlements. Our guns ceased, and forthwith came a deputation offering to treat with the Rajah of Dhar [an absent minor], for it now appeared our enemy had seized upon his fort, but with what amount of connivance from his guardians Colonel Durand probably knew.

The Brigadier communicated the message from the fort to Colonel Durand who directed unconditional surrender, at which the garrison laughed, but meanwhile made good use of their time in observation from the walls on which they congregated. Soon afterwards a second flag of truce was hoisted: again negotiations failed. Crowds of the garrison flaunted themselves on the bastions and curtains, while others critically surveyed the breach, and doubtless saw how little remained to keep us from coming in. Many in camp considered this parley merely a ruse to inspect the ruined curtain but the garrison had ample means of knowing the practicability of the breach, and without question wished to ascertain the Dewan of Dhar's wishes.

At this Captain Gall enjoined increased vigilance at the pickets, for frequent captures were made of men, who, by means of ropes, had descended the walls, and it was thereby evident there existed a wish to get away. Still the interchange of shots between our troops in the village and men on the bastions was maintained.

On Saturday, prize agents were appointed, the forlorn hope was in orders, its support and all arranged to storm on the Sabbath morning, but there was an ominous silence within the fort which we could not interpret. It was a joke in camp that not a mouse, unobserved, could escape through our line, but whence the silence in a fortification of such magnitude? We could not have destroyed the garrison, and the capture possessed an increased interest as report fixed the amount of treasure at one hundred and thirty thousand pounds, which the Political Agent promised should be prize money.

I wandered to the battery in the evening, to take a last look at the breach, now ready, and it certainly was a rough

way to enter if defended. Late that night, the Brigadier
with his Staff officers, Captains Coley and Macdonald,[1]
thought it well that some cursory examination of the
breach should be made, and two corporals of Madras
Sappers crossed stealthily the open space, while their return
was breathlessly looked for. Step by step was cautiously
made, the breach gained, and stone by stone ascended in
deathlike stillness, the summit reached and there too all
was still, for the garrison had escaped! A general rush then
took place, and in their mortification, the Staff shouted for
cavalry to pursue. In an instant our camp was a very Babel;
trumpet and bugle rang shrill and deafening through the
lines. I awoke, mounted, and in a few moments we were
dashing towards the village, almost riding down the 86th
Regt who had been similarly roused, and were marching
with all haste. On gaining the village, a few words suffice[d]
to inform us on what had occurred, and it appears that an
alarm that reinforcements for the enemy had been seen on
the Mundeesoor road had induced Captain Woolcombe to
send for us. The Union Jack waved from the highest tower
of the fort and the 25th Regimental Band played the
National Anthem as we started in pursuit.

No inexperienced person can guess the difficulty of riding
wildly across country in the moonlight; nevertheless, away
we went, sweeping along like so many phantom horsemen,
yet seeing nothing save occasional articles of clothes which
marked the rebel flight. Unfortunately, too, the cavalry
outposts had been changed that day; neither officers nor
men had become sufficiently acquainted with the ground.
For my own part, my horse floundered shoulder deep into a
bog where I and a few other Dragoons were well nigh
passing the night.

While out on this fruitless raid, a terrific explosion from
the fort was heard, and the same moment a bright lurid

[1] Captains Joseph Charles Coley, 10th Bombay Native Infantry
(Brigade Major), and John Alexander Matthew Macdonald, 3rd Bombay
Europeans.

glare filled the heavens, and this, we learnt on our return, was caused by one of the exploring parties having introduced a lighted torch into a heap of gunpowder which, exploding, blew off the roof of a small building and sadly burnt our Adjutant, Giles, Lieutenant Thain of the Commissariat, and the Assistant Surgeon of Woolcombe's battery.[1]

On my return from the pursuit, though scarcely daybreak, my curiosity led me into the fort. The smell was villainous, not of gunpowder only, but of dead bodies of horses and men in advanced putrefaction. At one of these a dog was busily gnawing. Captain Robertson had already made the discovery that the Treasury was intact and guards were placed over it. When counted subsequently, it was found to be ninety thousand pounds sterling; much of this was in gold mohurs, Portuguese sequins, and rupees. There were besides, a silver howdah [seat to be fixed on an elephant's back], bedstead, cooking utensils, and drinking utensils. All this Treasure was in a small and curiously figure-painted room in the upper storey of the citadel or palace as it was termed. This building was in fact the only comfortably habitable part of the fort, which was very extensive, enclosing many acres of ground within its massive walls which measured eighty feet in height, and were some yards in thickness, their outer part composed of trap rock faced inside with limestone. The entrance, which had suffered much from our shells, was a steep ascent through a tortuous pass, enfiladed from loopholed towers.

The interior of the fort was disappointing and little corresponding with its handsome exterior. I walked around its walls and towers, the view from which was as beautiful as it was commanding. There were twenty-seven pieces of artillery, but many among them useless; six of the largest

[1] Lieutenants James Giles, 14th Light Dragoons and David Davidson Thain, 24th Bombay Native Infantry. The Assistant Surgeon of Woollcombe's battery was Dr Ebenezer Robert Butler. In his *Diary* Sylvester mentions Redmayne as being with Giles and Butler, and at first makes no reference to Thain as being present, but later does so.

were of native manufacture. Old clothes, bedding, 23rd Regimental belts, artillery pouches, caps, bloody apparel, grain, salt, &c, &c, were scattered about. Two Rohillas, terribly wounded, lay in the gateway, and informed us that but sixteen of the enemy, and two women, had been killed during the siege, and that its commandant, Gool Mahomed, with the entire garrison, had escaped through our pickets on the night previous.

It was passing strange that they did not carry the enormous treasure with them as it was contained in four wooden chests, easily accessible. It was said to have been amassed by the extraordinary cupidity of one of the present Rajah's ancestors. Of so miserly a disposition was he that he weighed the grain upon which he fed his sacred birds, lest they might get too much. Having got possession, we loaded it upon seventeen elephants and sent it under a guard to the fort at Mhow, and I have now survived long enough to be able to acknowledge that we actually received it as prize money, though in sadly diminished amount. If my memory serves me, I received four hundred and seventy five pounds. It is however most curious to notice that though so few years have elapsed since these events, yet the chief actors in these scenes are dead. Those who occur to me are Colonel Durand, Major Robertson. Captains Coley, Barrett, Leith, Orr, Mayne, Hungerford, and Lieutenants Thain, Christie, Gowan, Dew, and probably others whose career I could not trace.[1]

The day after the Capture of the Fortress, a large body of Hyderabad Contingent troops, under command of Major William Orr, joined us, and Captain Gall, who, with the cavalry, scoured the country for a circuit of twenty-four miles, traced the fugitives to Mundeesoor where they were preparing to give us battle again.[2] Further search was

---

[1] Captain Thomas Barrett and Lieutenants Lawrence St Patrick Gowan and George Meyrick Dew were all officers of the 14th Light Dragoons.

[2] In his *Diary*, Sylvester records that the Hyderabad Force, of all arms. arrived from Edulabad on 4 November 1857. The officers were invited

instituted for the Dhar jewels, but we discovered none though the palace floors were excavated.

The sick and wounded accompanied the treasure to Mhow and on the 8th of November we marched for Mundeesoor. Captain Mayne, who had accompanied our force from Aurungabad, constituted himself head of the intelligence department and together with Lieutenant Martin[1] and thirty native horsemen, preceeded us. Our road lay through a pretty and fertile country. The inhabitants were present in the villages which were generally well shaded by clumps of mangoe and pepul trees.

On reaching Noyla, the end of our second day's march, particulars of another mutiny reached us: the Mehidpore Contingent, thirty-five miles in our front, had joined the retiring garrison from Dhar, and together with their guns, had gone away to Mundeesoor. Major Timmins and Lieutenant Dysart, officers of the Contingent,[2] escaped into our camp and told us that, on the arrival of the garrison of Dhow at Mehidpore, their Contingent force was ordered out to give them battle; all however was doubtless prearranged; the officers and a few faithful men offered what defence they were able, to save their guns, but as most of their men went over to the enemy, they were compelled to fly for their lives. The surgeon and some other officers were hacked to pieces. Mrs Timmins escaped, disguised as an ayah [Indian nursemaid], to our camp.

---

to dine in the Mess of the 14th Light Dragoons. 'Major Orr, a fine soldierly looking man spoke of my uncle, &c. The Dr his brother very good looking and a fine man but our Orr, Sutherland, is by far ye most handsome.' Gall was called out just as Mess was over.

Dr. John Henry Orr was with the 1st Cavalry, Hyderabad Contingent. Major William Orr was an Artilleryman. All the Orrs were in the Madras Army.

[1] Lieutenant Cunliffe Martin, 1st Bengal Light Cavalry. Escaped during the mutiny at Mhow. Retired as Commandant, Central India Horse, 1888.

[2] Major George Timins (1809–75), 34th Bengal Native Infantry, commanded the United Malwa Contingent from 1841 until it mutinied in 1857. Lieutenant George Sale Dysart, 23rd Bengal Native Infantry 'worked the guns'.

On receipt of this intelligence, Colonel Durand decided to march on Mehidpore, where the rebels had halted. Subsequent information of their advance on Mundeesoor induced him to order the newly arrived Contingent force in pursuit, while we continued our march which was of necessity slow, on account of our heavy guns and bad roads.

Major Orr's pursuit had been successful, and fell upon the rear guard of the rebels while they were exerting themselves to get their artillery across a river. All their guns and ammunition were at once abandoned to us and Major Orr reported that three hundred of the enemy had been killed, and on the 16th of November, Sunday, Major Orr's force rejoined us, bringing their spoil and ninety-four prisoners: among these were some ruffianly countenances. One prisoner was minus an arm, lost at Ghuznee;[1] a few of the Mehidpore officers' servants, and some women and children were also among them. On the following day, all were tried by Court Martial, and seventy-four shot. Some of these men were wounded and one acknowledged that he belonged to the Dhar garrison. and together with six or seven hundred others, escaped through the pickets of the Hyderabad Cavalry. All were blindfolded, and kneeling, received a volley from a company of H.M.'s 86th Regt. Major Orr's casualties, excepting one badly wounded officer, were slight.

On the morning of the 21st[2] we halted about two miles from Mundeesoor and a reconnaissance was made from the rising ground. The enemy could be seen in great force and prominent among them were many banners. During the halt, my charger unaccountably took fright and bolted through a squadron of our men and a long line of troops, knocking over a medicine chest and several footmen. In vain I tried to stop him as he made straight for the enemy's ranks. He fell, but recovered, and at length fell headlong into a nullah from whence I was extricated, stunned, by

[1] Taken by the British on 23rd July 1839, during the 1st Afghan Campaign.
[2] 21 November, 1857.

Captains Keatinge, Woolcombe, and Strutt. I was soon recovered and in the saddle again.

It will have already appeared that our Brigadier had at
least the merit of taking affairs cooly. The order was therefore given to encamp and fight on the morrow. A strong
picket was placed on the height, under command of Major
Robertson: this the enemy came out to attack. He directed
his artillery to open fire, and Lieutenant Dew, with thirty
of the 14th, dashed into a gole [a mass] of three hundred of
the enemy's footmen. Captain Sutherland Orr charged also
with the Nizam's Cavalry. At the noise of firing, the remainder of the force hastened to join in pursuit of the enemy
now fast flying across a considerable stream which they had
crossed to attack us. It was calculated we killed about a
hundred men and captured several standards. A quiet
night followed.

While the recent events I have recorded were in progress, the garrison of Neemuch, about twenty miles distant
from Mundeesoor, was sorely besieged, and here, as in
many military stations, the fort saved many lives. The
Europeans, 2nd Bombay Cavalry, and a handful of British
gunners not only held the fort, but worked the guns and
made occasional sallies. In one of these, after very gallant
behaviour, Captain Tucker[1] lost his life, and as a trophy, his
head was taken by the rebels and hoisted over the gateway
of Mundeesoor.

There can be no doubt that the Neemuch garrison was
for some time in a critical position, for on one occasion the
besiegers, with ladders, attempted to scale the fort. The
ladies, here as elsewhere, behaved heroically and made
ammunition for the cannon on the walls.

On the morning after our affair with the pickets, we who
were not in the secrets of the Staff imagined that Mundeesoor fort and city would be attacked, but an attempt was
made to skirt the city and gain the Neemuch road. This
manoeuvre with our train of baggage animals, commissariat,

[1] Captain Nathaniel Butterfield Tucker, 2nd Bombay Light Cavalry.

and followers, required caution. Occasional shots were fired
at us from the city and a few inhabitants came out with the
intelligence that a large body of the enemy had gone away
over night, but that the fort was strongly garrisoned. At
midday, while crossing a river, Colonel Durand received a
report to the effect that the enemy had raised the siege of
Neemuch and were advancing to meet us. All available
cavalry, under Captains Gall and Sutherland Orr, were
ordered to attack them.

We went away at a smashing pace across country,
through fields of high standing corn, and after a five mile
gallop, sighted a body of men with camels and some few
women; they were, fortunately for them, nearing a village.
As fast as possible we made the best of our opportunity by
cutting up and spearing all we could reach. They were
mostly Veliatees and Mekranees belonging to Heera Singhs'[1]
army, and fought bravely for life. There was desultory
skirmishing with them over some miles of country, for
many were hidden in trees and fields of standing jowarree
[millet]. Leith and Giles of my regiment were slightly
wounded. We estimated the killed at two hundred. The
main body, with their camels, treasure, and standards,
having gained the shelter of the village, defied us to attack
them. Nightfall, the absence of infantry, and jaded condition of our horses obliged us to return to camp, and sore
from yesterday's bruises, I was glad to reach it.

Next morning,[2] at sunrise, we again resumed our march
on Neemuch by crossing the river of yesterday. The enemy
threatened to attack the rear of our column, which contained a number of wheeled vehicles. My regiment stood
guarding these in their passage for hours, under a very
scorching sun and, having seen the last safely across, we
trotted up to the head of the column, thinking our twenty-
two miles into Neemuch would be unmolested. It was not
so, for almost simultaneous with an attack on the head of
our column there came an alarm that the rear guard was

---

[1] A leader of the mutineers.   [2] 23 November 1857.

engaged. The booming of artillery left no doubt that our work was cut out for the day, without going so far as Neemuch, and apart from the unconscious excitement in the knowledge that death was busy about me, and that I should properly be present with each squadron of my charge, now engaged a mile apart, there was terrible excitement along the entire line of unarmed drivers of bullocks, carriers of the sick, of water, and other followers for in truth we were a long line to defend.

Joining the squadron which galloped to the front with the guns, I discovered that the enemy had placed his battery on rising ground, on which were a number of palms and a native hut or two, while his right rested on the village of Goolaria. The position was well chosen for we subsequently discovered a deep sunken road protected his left from cavalry. Our line was quickly formed and a smart fire opened from Woolcombe's and Hungerford's batteries, as well as from the whole line of infantry. Major Orr's force deployed on our left, to support the general attack.

Under the hot fire of our infantry and artillery, the enemy's slackened. Hungerford, with his battery and support of thirty of our men, executed a brilliant movement to the right, enfiladed the rebel line, and almost before our fire had ceased, charged across the deep sunken road amongst the rebel guns. The obstacle threw the handful of Dragoons into momentary confusion, and so hot was the matchlock fire upon them that they were compelled to retire. Martin, who was doing duty with the 14th and led them, was severely wounded. Gall, with the reserve squadron, hastened to the support, the six rebel guns were captured, and the enemy driven into Goolaria.

The entire cavalry scoured the cornfields and plantations of sugar cane around the village. Here we sabred a number of men on horses, ponies, and on foot, escaping heavily laden with plunder, chiefly that of the cantonment of Neemuch, as evidenced in its variety: crockery, glass, military drums, fishing tackle, surgical instruments, musical boxes, books, trinkets, money, and clothes.

We now proceeded to burn all the buildings outside the village, which was surrounded by a low wall. Not until in many cases their long hair and clothes were in a blaze did the rebels break out of the burning huts, to receive a more speedy death. One large tree of great height had several men in the branches and necessitated revolver shots to bring them down. Those hidden in the high sugar cane proved most troublesome, and we had several men and horses wounded while clearing it. Gowan was again wounded in the hand.

During the whole of this work, the enemy kept up a brisk fire on us from within the village, to avoid which some of us sheltered ourselves and horses behind a clump of trees, near to which was a large covered well, and looking beneath its timbers I espied the legs of a rebel, and after despatching him we found four others whom we shot with carbines. These men were heavily armed; one was possessed of a blunderbuss marked Tower 1815. Around the opposite side of Goolaria the country was scoured by the Contingent Cavalry who cut up many of the enemy and were rewarded by considerable loot.

During our engagement with the enemy in front, after many feints, the garrison of Mundeesoor fort actually attacked the rear guard, which had been reinforced at the first alarm. Two field guns kept the rebels at bay while Leith and Redmayne, with a troop of the 14th Dragoons charged, supported by parts of two of the Nizam's cavalry regiments. Unfortunately, however, their impetuosity led them into broken ground where excavations had been made, and water collected, and Redmayne, whilst gallantly leading, was shot dead. The two Dragoons immediately following were also wounded, private O'Neill very severely.[1] Our cavalry retired, leaving Redmayne's body in the hands of

[1] O'Neil was shot through the chest, and the other man, Buchanan, 'through the cloak & the ball was prevented entering him by a button on his drawers.' (*Diary*, where the spelling 'O'Neil' is used.)

the rebels. His charger and accoutrements all fell to them
as plunder, though Captain Abbott recovered his terribly
mangled body.

Darkness stayed our operations for the day: I had plenty
of occupation with the wounded on returning to camp;
pickets were posted round the village to prevent escapes;
some thirty prisoners were executed, and excepting a few
shots fired by nervous sentries, and one alarm, when we
turned out, the night passed tranquilly.

On the next day we buried the remains of poor Redmayne at eleven o'clock, near three small date palms: Gall
read the service for the dead; all who were off duty attended.
This sad business over, the heavy guns were brought to
bear on the village and after a few rounds had been fired
from them, the 86th, 25th, Contingent Infantry, and
Madras Sappers and Miners stormed. It was warm work,
for in addition to a hot sun and brisk matchlock fire, the
enemy had fired the village in many places. It was a grand
sight to see the tall white shakoes of the County Downs and
huge blue turbans of the Madrassees prominent amidst the
columns of fire and smoke. Every now and again a wounded
man limped forth, or a couple of red coats were seen lifting
a burden which had gone beyond hope. Sometimes a handful of the rebels rushed out into the sugar canes behind,
preferring to contend with spear or sabre rather than bayonet. Two hundred surrendered under a flag of truce.

At length, towards nightfall, the work was almost
complete, save at the upper end of the village where a few
desperate men ensconced themselves in a small temple. A
gun and scaling ladders were sent for, but the Brigadier
preferred to leave them. In the morning there was not a
living soul in Goolaria though pickets again surrounded the
village. But for the escape of these men, it might have been
a successful termination.

Neemuch was relieved and Captain Mayne carried in
despatches. Mundeesoor fort and city had also been evacuated by the main body, but a few desperate men were

hidden in the city, and now that our prestige was established, the authorities readily pointed them out. The city of Mundeesoor, and fort, would have given us much greater trouble to capture had the rebels taken up that position. Captain Tucker's head had been removed, and in place thereof we erected those of two arch-rebels. The Contingent Cavalry were sent to trace the route of the retreating rebels, and discovered that they had gone to Naghur, much disheartened by defeat. Tucker's head was recovered and buried; Redmayne's bridle too was found in the fort, which was partially dismantled and in places blown up.

The Political Agent, Colonel Durand, who had without doubt, though unostentatiously, been military director thus far, now ordered our return to Mhow, where, with reinforcements, we were destined to form the Central India Field Force, and happily too the command was transferred. Meanwhile we were designated the Nerbudda Field Force.

December the 6th: on our return march we received a 'Home News' informing us of the advent of Sir Hugh Rose (now Lord Strathnairn),[1] to assume command. On the 9th of the same month, marching daily, we reached Mehidpore, the scene of the late mutiny. It struck me as a most charming cantonment, situated as it is on the banks of the Sipree river and embosomed in splendid trees, altogether as parklike in appearance as any landscape in the East. The bungalows, as usual, had been stripped of their contents and were so many heaps of blackened and charred ruin. On the parade ground was one heavy iron gun which the mutineers had been unable to take away. Belts, buckles, caps, fuzes and such like articles of military equipment were strewn about and nineteen graves, each said to contain several dead, were proof of the brave resistance the officers of the Contingent and few faithful men had made. One of

---

[1] Sir Hugh Henry Rose, later 1st Baron Strathnairn (1801–1885). Born and educated in Berlin, where he received military instruction from Prussian officers and N.C.O.s. Entered the army as an Ensign, 93rd Highlanders. Served in Syria, 1840, with the Turks, and in the Crimea. Field Marshal, 1877.

the officers killed, Lieutenant Mills, was nephew to our Brigadier,[1] and we could not trace the manner of the disposal of the bodies slain here.

Marching now at this season was by no means unpleasant though the mornings were cold and sun very hot during the day. The health of the troops was excellent, the country productive and abounding in small game: roads none. On reaching the large city of Ojein, in Holkar's territory, we encamped with precaution, the events around his court and recent conduct of his army fully justifying it.

On the 15th of December we marched on Indore, speculating as to the kind of reception we should receive from H. H. Maharajah Holkar. Colonel Durand was, I believe, determined that his troops should fight or surrender unconditionally. The Maharajah himself was reported to be absent on a shooting expedition and that he was most anxious for the arrival of his friend Sir Robert Hamilton. The reason assigned for this gentleman's tardy arrival was that he dreaded passing through the Mhow jungles in the unhealthy season.

Approaching the city, some of Holkar's cavalry, clad in French grey, came out to give us, as they said, a friendly greeting; we disarmed them. The inhabitants at the fort and cantonment of Mhow, thirteen miles distant, were now straining attention to catch the boom of our cannon. They fully anticipated the hostilities which without doubt ought to have taken place. Alas! all was to be condoned. I am not sufficiently acquainted with the intrigues then in progress; I can only give the impressions shared by the officers and men of the force who were outside the secret, and these were that a terrible example should have been made of Holkar and his soldiery. It is impossible to believe he could not control them; it was also believed that Sir Hugh Rose, who assumed command of our force at Indore, shared this opinion and smart passages were said to have been inter-

---

[1] Lieutenant George Longley Mills, 14th Bombay Native Infantry. Sylvester's *Diary* states that he was Stuart's cousin.

changed between him and Sir Robert Hamilton who declared that Holkar had disarmed his refractory soldiery and would give up those who had attacked the British Residency on the 19th of December. Our presence being distasteful to Holkar, the force again returned to Mhow.

During our encampment near Indore we had seen the roofless houses of the cantonment, the battered walls of the Residency, and desecrated church; all however went unpunished when Colonel Durand relinquished his powers to Sir Robert Hamilton. Near the broken altar rail in the Church someone had inscribed on the walls, the [10th] verse of the 19th chapter, 1st Book of Kings.[1]

[1] 'They have forsaken thy covenant, thrown down thine altars, and slain thy prophets with the sword; and I, even I only, am left; and they seek my life, to take it away.' (As quoted by Sylvester in *The Campaign in Central India*.)

V

From Indore to Jhansi

ON the arrival of Sir Hugh Rose, he at once inspected our
forces on parade, visited the hospital tents, and spoke
kindly to many of the wounded. He held a Durbar [a
reception or levee also applied to the body of officials at a
native court] at which each officer in turn was presented:
certainly his pale, thin and delicate appearance did not
suggest the endurance, energy and ability to command,
which he afterwards displayed in so eminent a degree.

The force remained at Mhow until the 30th of the month
when its return to Indore was directed. Suddenly the
mystery was solved: at 2 a.m. next morning Sir Hugh Rose,
tired of the policy adopted with Holkar's court and constant
excuses from his Durbar, determined to surround the city.
This we had done by daylight, when Sir Hugh and some of
the force entered and proceeded to collect and bring into our
camp all the men he could find belonging to Holkar's army.
So far as I recollect, about three hundred were found, but
as no evidence could be got of their guilt, it would perhaps
have been exalted butchery to have executed them. Some
few, against whom proof was obtained, were hanged, others
blown away from guns. In camp it was generally [believed
that] even this small punishment had caused very considerable estrangement between the political agent and
Major General commanding.

Every department was now busy with preparations for a
second start. Our baggage was reduced to the minimum,
wheeled vehicles were forbidden, an enormous siege train
was ready, reinforcements had joined, and our designation
was again changed to Central India Field Force, consisting
of two Brigades. Brigadier Stewart retained command of the

first, and Colonel Stuart of H.M.'s 14th Light Dragoons[1] was appointed to the second, which was for the most part made up of newly-arrived troops. This Brigade was at Sehore in readiness to move, and thither, on the 8th of January, Sir Hugh Rose proceeded, escorted by a troop of Dragoons and the Hyderabad Contingent battery.

While we were in readiness to commence our march on Jhansi, Major General Whitlock[2] with a splendid force of all arms was at Jubbulpore, with the avowed intention of reaching that city before us. Had we known something of the character of our leader at this time we need not have been apprehensive for the laurels we won at Jhansi some months afterwards. It is scarcely an exaggeration to say that General Whitlock's magnificent force accomplished nothing save the capture of the largest booty of the campaign.[3]

It so chanced that I had a relative in that force who very frequently wrote to me during the almost parallel marches we made to the Jumna.[4] There was but the most indirect postal communication whereas our letters were interchanged by relatives of native soldiery traversing the country between us in a few days. I recollect the burden of those letters was that General Whitlock would never ride save on a mule which could not be persuaded to go forward, and that he was likened to a bad revolver, always going round but never going off. The sequel will show that in this case the race was to the swiftest and Jhansi fell to us.

[1] Sylvester here spells the names incorrectly and adds to the confusion created by the two Brigadiers having similar names. The first of the two, Brigadier C. S. Stuart of the Bombay Army, has already been mentioned (note 3, p. 67); the new arrival was Colonel Charles Steuart of the 14th Light Dragoons who had served in the Punjab Campaign, 1848–9. He was present at Chillianwallah (where he received a sabre wound) and at Goojerat. He commanded a Brigade of Cavalry in Persia, 1857.

[2] Major-General George Cornish Whitlock (1798–1868), Madras Army.

[3] At Kirwee on 6 June 1858. This seems to have been a perpetual source of irritation to Sylvester.

[4] His uncle, Dr. W. H. Bradley, with the 2nd Cavalry, Hyderabad Contingent.

Meanwhile however, nothing could exceed the impatience with which we awaited our orders to march, and it became well nigh unbearable after the departure of Sir Hugh Rose. We feared lest that we might be left behind, and I went so far as to apply for another regiment.

On the 18th of January, Brigadier Stewart's[1] published dispatches of Mundeesoor arrived in camp and went far to render him still more unpopular with Her Majesty's regiments. Having served entirely with native troops, he had nothing in common with European soldiers and their officers, among whom it was the habit to estimate lightly 'sepoy generals', and so long as the anomaly of a double army exists, so long will this habit continue. I do not for a moment by this remark reflect on the admirable way in which the native elements of our force had conduced to our success, but it was obviously unfair to give them the entire credit.

On the 29th, the siege train, six miles in length when marching, arrived in charge of the 5th Company, 14th Brigade, R. A. On the 3rd of February the Head Quarter wing of H.M.'s 86th Regt. joined, together with the 21st Company of Royal Engineers. Thus reinforced, we left Mhow two days afterwards.

During our inaction the Major General opened the ball at Sehore by executing one hundred and fifty of the Begum's Contingent; thence, with his second brigade and Hyderabad Contingent he marched to the relief of Saugor where a hundred and seventy-one Europeans were besieged. The stronghold of Ratghur, held by the enemy, lay in his route and received first attention. On the 24th of January, at 5 p.m., the enemy was seen in position on the banks of the Beema river, west of the fort. Cavalry and Horse Artillery were brought into action, and after a few rounds, he was driven within the fortifications. Our loss was one Dragoon, one native officer, and an apothecary seriously wounded. Operations ceased with nightfall.

[1] Stuart.

On the morrow following, Sir Hugh with his staff and a cavalry escort spent the entire day in a reconnaissance. Ratghur was but a type of the hill fortresses scattered throughout the Dekkan and Central India: most of them are built on the summits of trap or other igneous rock, rising almost perpendicularly from the plain. This circumstance alone renders them almost inaccesible if provisioned and defended. The precipitous sides are for the most part clad in impenetrable jungle, while the surrounding country is deep forest; such is Asseerghur, Chanderi, and such was Ratghur. Generally, however, a spur of rock, narrow and steep, affords a communication with the plain below. Major Boileau, Madras Engineers,[1] advised a spot such as this, found at Ratghur, should be chosen for breaching. Meanwhile, the brigade, and troops of H.H. the Begum of Bhopal invested the hill.

On the 26th, part of the force drew the attention of the garrison to [the] town end of the fortress while the 3rd Bombay European Regiment and Engineers placed the heavy guns in position. The double enceinte commenced to crumble under the continued hammering. To keep down the enemy's fire on the battery, the Madrassees threw up a site for mortars. The town was taken and its temple occupied by Lightfoot's battery.[2] Report numbered the garrison at not more than six hundred, chiefly Velliattees, Mekranees and Bundeelas,[3] but these did not comprise the enemy's forces, for just as the breach became practicable, two thousand men attempted to raise the siege. Our outposts and videttes engaged them but from the wooded nature of the ground, and difficult bed of the Beema river, their action was paralyzed. Fighting was carried on in

[1] Major Archibald John Maddy Boileau, Madras Engineers.

[2] Captain John Granville Lightfoot (1823–78), Bombay Artillery. Was present at Mooltan and Goojerat in the Punjab Campaign, 1848–9. Hon. Colonel, 1862. Died in Mauritius.

[3] Velliattees: literally 'foreigners' from the N. W. Frontier of India; Mekranees: from Mekran in Beloochistan; Bundeelas: a tribe of Rajputs from Bundlekunde.

single combats, in which the Hyderabad Infantry under Captain Hare and some troopers under Lieutenant Westmacott[1] joined. The enemy recrossed the Beema and were pursued by Sir Hugh to Chunderapoor.

The episode of Dhar was re-enacted here; a feint was made at the main gate, guarded by the 3rd Europeans, while the actual escape was made at a sally port, and thence down the walls and cliff by ropes, the exit through that part of the line held by the Begum's troops. Oddly enough, Lieutenant Strutt, who was one of the first to discover the evacuation at Dhar, was the first on this occasion to make the discovery here, and walked in, much to the displeasure of Sir Hugh, but chagrin under such circumstances was natural.[2] Cavalry were ordered in pursuit and cut up twenty. Some few animals were found in the fort, grain, water, but no treasure. Curiously enough, the grey Arab charger taken from Lieutenant Redmayne, after his death at Mundeesoor, was recovered: it had received a shell wound in the face. At the auction it was purchased for the Major General.

Besides those cut up in the pursuit, nearly a hundred prisoners fell into our hands. Among these were men of importance; Mahomed Fazil Khan, on whose head one thousand rupees had been placed by Government, was captured by a servant of Captain Need,[3] who received the reward. Kamdhar Khan, a jagheerdar [holder of assignment of revenue], and he, were hanged over the gateway.[4]

A battery and troop of artillery, three troops of the 14th Dragoons, a complement of European and Native Infantry, and the Madras Sappers, proceeded cautiously through

---

[1] Captain George Hare (20th Madras Native Infantry), serving with 5th Infantry, Hyderabad Contingent, and Lieutenant George Richard Westmacott (23rd Bengal Native Infantry) serving with 4th Cavalry, Hyderabad Contingent.

[2] 'Strutt was put under arrest for taking the fort without orders.' (*Diary.*)

[3] Captain Arthur Need, 14th Light Dragoons.

[4] 31 January 1858.

twelve miles of Jungle to the relief of Saugor. Approaching
the village of Borrodia [we][1] were received by a brisk fire,
by which some of our horses were killed. Captain Forbes, in
command of some of his regiment – the 2nd Bombay,[2] and
a portion of the 3rd Bombay European Regt, made a
dashing charge and cut up a considerable number as they
were retiring on their position in the village. The enemy
ventured to place his guns there also, and succeeded in
getting them out of that hazardous position when he fled at
the close of day. He did not, however, retreat until an
assault had been made: it was led by Colonel Liddle[3] while
Lieutenant Strutt shelled the fort. Among our killed and
wounded was Captain Neville of the Engineers[4] who had
recently joined the Divisional Staff. Lieutenant Pittman,
R.H.A.,[5] with whom I made my first march in India,
narrowly escaped with his life, a round shot having grazed
his shoulder.

The night proved cold and wet, and after the fatigues of
the day the Major General returned to Ratghur.[6] The
rebels, discomfited by two signal defeats, retired to Jilla and

[1] It is evident from entries in his *Diary* that Sylvester was not himself present on this occasion, as in the cases of many of the incidents
recorded by him.

[2] Captain (later General Sir John) Forbes of Inverernan (1817–1906).
He entered the 3rd Bombay Light Cavalry (not 2nd as stated by Sylvester) as a Cornet on 1 March 1835. He led the charge of the 1st and
3rd Squadrons when they broke a square of 800 Persians at Khooshab.
He was present, with the staff of King Victor Emmanuel II, at Solferino,
1859.

[3] Lieutenant-Colonel John Liddell, 3rd Bombay Europeans. Sylvester
has the correct pronunciation of the name, but the wrong spelling.

[4] Captain Glastonbury Neville, R.E., who joined only the day
before. He had served in the Crimea.

[5] This would be Lieutenant Richard Pittman (1831–67), Bombay
Artillery, who had served with the Bashi Bazouks in the Crimean War.
The Bombay Artillery was amalgamated with the Royal Artillery in
1862, which would account for his being described as being in the Royal
Artillery.

[6] In view of his later admiration for Sir Hugh, it is of interest to note
that, on 8 January 1858, Sylvester entered in his *Diary*: 'I am afraid
Sir Hugh is a failure.'

two other strongholds, Muriaoli and Bhopyle. The defences of Ratghur were laid waste, after which the force marched triumphantly to Saugor[1] and passed some days in revelry and rejoicing. The cantonment of Saugor, thanks to some misunderstanding among the mutineers of the Bengal infantry stationed there, was not destroyed.

Preparations were now made to march on the fort of Garrakotah. Lieutenant Prendergast of the Madras Engineers[2] destroyed the rebel defences of Nowrowlee, and Captain Hare with some of the Contingent troops marched to the fort of Tanoda, with like intent.

Leaving a troop of H.M.'s 14th Dragoons and two companies of the 24th Bombay Infantry at Saugor, the force, in two marches, reached Bussuree, two miles distant from the rebel position in Garrakotah. Two branches of the Sonar river run close beneath the fort, so near in fact that the inner, in point of defence, served as a moat for some distance, and where absent, impenetrable forest took its place. On arrival, the 3rd Bombay Cavalry under Lieutenant Dick[3] had a successful affair with a rebel picket, and on an attempt to possess the village, the enemy disputed it. After a few rounds from the Horse and fort artillery, the 3rd Europeans assaulted and carried it. All night long, however, the mutineers made futile attempts to retake it.

On the day following, as at Ratghur, the Major General and staff proceeded to reconnoitre and invest the place. Without doubt, many of the escaped garrison of Ratghur were here in arms against us, and, afraid of the cordon being drawn around them a second time, escaped by Paunch Ghaut towards Dumoh. Pursuit under Captains Hare and Need was again successful. Need was a good

---

[1] 3 February.

[2] Lieutenant Harry North Dalrymple Prendergast, Madras Engineers. Served in Persia, 1857, and in Abyssinia, 1867–8. For saving the life of Captain Dew on 21 November 1857, and other deeds, Prendergast was awarded the V.C.

[3] Lieutenant William Abercromby Dick, 3rd Bombay Light Cavalry, Lieutenant-Colonel, 1870.

D

swordsman, and out of a hundred killed, he slew five with his own hand; moreover, with cavalry, it is the lead which is all important.

After destroying so much of the fortifications as to render an assault easy in case of its re-occupation, the force left Garrakotah and returned to Saugor, in order to organise the Commissariat.

The 1st Brigade, during these latter events, was steadily moving up the Agra trunk road, with the enormous siege train. On the 26th of February we reached Goonah, a station, previous to the mutiny, occupied by troops of Scindiah's contingent. As usual in his territory, the houses had all been destroyed by fire, and his soldiery gone. In their place we now found Captain H. O. Mayne with sixty Sikhs of the Gwalior contingent who, like their countrymen in the Punjab, were faithful throughout. These sixty men were the nucleus of a regiment afterwards formed and still existing as the 1st Central India Horse.

Our entire march from Mhow had been pleasantly cool, through a gently undulating but well cultivated country; wheat, flax and opium crops were fresh and green, and the heat by day quite bearable; every day however it became more oppressive and often gave us an earnest, though a faint one, of what was in store. After leaving Goonah we left the trunk road and marched into the heart of Bundle-kunde, to Easanghir, the whole country belonging to the Maharajah Scindiah.

Intelligence received by Captain Keatinge, who still accompanied the force — now as political agent — caused the Brigadier to change his plans and march on Chanderi, six miles short of which place, at a village called Koorsara, the force halted while Captain Gall, Captain Fenwick, R.E.,[1] and myself, with a party of Dragoons and Irregular horse went forward to reconnoitre. Our track lay through dense jungle that scarcely admitted us to pass in single file. Columns of smoke towered in the air from the high ground

[1] Captain Thomas Fenwick, Royal Engineers.

as we advanced, thus signalling our approach to the enemy. At length, entering a deep and densely wooded valley, through the end of which an occasional glimpse of the distant hill fort was distinguishable, a volley of musketry greeted us, compelling our retreat.

Next day, with infantry skirmishing among the dense jungle, we again reached the spot in force, and they, even with their red coats and white headdresses, were completely hidden. The enemy was still there though further in advance, occupying the ruins of buildings on the left slope of the valley. From these they were driven by the artillery fire through a tract of jungle beyond where they took refuge behind a loopholed wall intersecting the valley. This outwork checked our advance momentarily as our field pieces were useless to breach it. A rush from the infantry gained its summit, the Engineers pulled it down in part, the force marched through and encamped behind a sand-stone ridge of hills which commanded the fort. A picket was left at the wall and another at a deserted village near our camp. The night passed quietly.

Nothing could be more picturesque than the site of our encampment, encircled by jungle clad hills and huge forest trees amongst which flights of green parrots screamed angrily, as though displeased to see us in their solitudes. In our front the hills were disposed in a horse shoe shape, and through the curve, which was about a hundred feet in height, a tunnel existed, bored in the solid rock. Probably it had been made by order of Ghiassudin, King of Delhi, as an inscription over its entrance stated that by his direction the lofty gate of Goomtee and Kerolie, near one of the many beautiful tanks of the town, had been made. Through this extraordinary opening we could, from our camp, see the fort high up on a rock.

The morning after arrival, the Brigadier proceeded, with the infantry, to clear the entire ridge, which was done with little trouble. From the summit we gained a panoramic view of the country on every side. Immediately opposite was the fortress, crowning a precipitous forest clad rock about the height of that on which we were standing. Between us was a densely wooded ravine behind the camp. At first sight the fort appeared wellnigh impregnable, but a more minute acquaintance discovered a spur which led to one of the curtains, but on either extremity of this spot a loopholed bastion, mounted with artillery, suggested a difficulty. So close were we to the rebel garrison that with an opera glass their dresses were plainly distinguishable. Round shot fired at us passed over the ridge into camp, some part of which it necessitated us to remove.

Chanderi had often been a bone of contention: forty years previous it had been taken by Baptiste,[1] one of Scindiah's generals, and advantage was taken of the road he then made, to get our guns on the heights. During the independence of Malwa it surrendered to Mahmood Khillji after eight months' siege; in 1526 a Rajpoot wrested it from Ibrahim, King of Delhi; two years afterwards, Baber took it by escalade but together with his army, was massacred by the besieged. It was obvious that of late years it had lain quiet, for we disturbed a panther from his lair, flights of wild duck wheeled overhead, and monkeys trooped about the branches.

Many days were needed to get our howitzers and breaching guns in position on the ridge, so exposed was it to the fire from the fort: much of the work indeed was in consequence carried on by night. It might be imagined that in a hilly country, covered by jungle and with roads not better than cattle tracks, cavalry would have an easy time. It was not so; constant reports of hostile reinforcements, combined with Captain Gall's energy,[2] kept us constantly in the saddle. Once, on leaving camp, the enemy retook from Scindiah's troops, into whose care it had been committed,

---

[1] A French officer in the service of the Nizam of Hyderabad in the 1790s.

[2] It is evident, from entries in his *Diary*, that Sylvester was inclined to consider Gall to be over-energetic and over-zealous.

the temple and crenellated wall of Futtyabad, thus cutting off our return and necessitating our ascent of a precipitous ridge, running the gauntlet of the enemy's fire.

At this time, our information, whether pertaining to the enemy or of our 2nd Brigade under Sir Hugh Rose, was of the scantiest description; we were confined for space in camp, and our cattle and followers were often molested while out foraging. On the 10th of March, the twenty-four pounder guns were drawn up Baptiste's road by elephants: it was necessary that they should go over the crest to the slope facing [the] enemy. Every relief therefore, or convoy of ammunition, crossed under a heavy fire. Sandbag batteries, rifle pits and such-like works were constructed under great difficulties, and the heat during midday was intense. The noise, and clouds of smoke and dust stirred by the breaching added to the fatigue contingent on duty here, and though it sadly taxed the endurance of the newly-arrived Artillery, yet it was by far the merriest spot in our camp. One sad loss however was sustained by us in the person of Lieutenant Moresby of the Artillery,[1] struck on the head by a round shot.

On the 14th, Lieutenant Dowker[2] with thirty horsemen rode in from our 2nd Brigade, bearing dispatches from the Major General, then thirty-three miles distant, en route for Jhansi. Even so far away our guns were heard, and Sir Hugh sent the Contingent force under Major Orr to intercept anybody of our garrison that might attempt escape. That they would attempt it no one doubted, both from previous experience and the fact that an underground passage existed from the rock to the city beneath, whereby the rebels supplied themselves with provisions and water and made constant raids on our camp followers.

On the 16th,[3] the head quarters and three hundred of the 86th joined us. A more splendid body of men it would

[1] Lieutenant Richard Moresby, Royal Artillery.
[2] Lieutenant Howard Codrington Dowker (22nd Madras Native Infantry) serving with the 1st Cavalry, Hyderabad Contingent.
[3] 16 March.

be difficult to conceive; far different indeed to the puny
creatures now filling the ranks of the British Army. Their
equal in fighting could not exist; the moment shots were
heard, the whole sick in hospital, who were of course
permitted in these times to retain their rifles, started at
once for the fray: an instance of indiscipline undoubtedly,
but one I secretly encouraged for at this time they were
under my medical charge as well as the Dragoons. During
the evening of their arrival, the order book contained the
details for storming, and I discovered that I was to turn
infantry soldier for the occasion and accompany one of the
parties, Assistant-Surgeon Cruikshank[1] the other.

At 3 a.m., while yet very dark, we struck our camp, and
left it in charge of Major Gall, for he, with Major Robertson,
Captain Woolcombe and others, had received brevet rank
for Mundeesoor. The two storming parties formed up
beneath the tunnel or Kattee Gattee as it was called. The
Royal Engineers, part of the 25th and 86th regiments made
up the party for the breach while the remainder of these
corps, under Captain Little,[2] composed the second party
who were furnished with instructions to make an attempt,
at some other spot, to scale the fort with a view to withdraw
the rebel attention from the breach, but to enter the fort if
practicable. These instructions appeared to me to afford
little prospect of an exciting morning, and as I had the
misfortune to be attached to this latter party, I made a
mistake in the darkness and confusion and discovered myself
with the other.

If our attempts to cut off the retreating garrison at other
forts were unavailing, it was still less likely success would
attend any endeavours here: no attempt therefore was
made.

After forming up with as little noise as possible, and

---

[1] Dr John Cruikshank (1833–97), Bombay Establishment. Severely
wounded at Jhansi. Sylvester met Cruikshank on 8 February when the
latter, who had last seen Sylvester in Persia, was surprised to find him
blooming. (*Diary.*)

[2] Captain Alfred Butler Little, 25th Bombay Native Infantry.

waiting in silence for the first streak of dawn to light our path, at the preconcerted signal of a horrible volley of shells, rockets and grape hurled upon the breach, we uttered a yell which must have echoed over many a deeply wooded ravine and hill top, and rushed down the gorge which separated us from the fort, Gosset of the Engineers[1] leading. Those watching in the breach must have had their nerves sadly shaken, but yet not paralysed, for they in turn dealt us a terrific volley. Fortunately, however, we by this time had reached an obstacle far beneath the range of their guns, and save the unpleasant whirr of a storm of ammunition overhead, we were in no way hurt.

The obstacle at the foot of the breach was a huge trench into which some of the stormers fell head foremost. Scaling ladders bridged the obstacle in an instant and without apparent effort we ascended the breach. Of this I recollect but little save that owing to the long-necked cavalry spurs screwed to my heels, I lost one boot in the rugged way. The foremost of the County Downs who entered ran along the fortifications, taking gun after gun, pitching the affrighted few they could catch over the heights, or bayonetting them in a frenzy of zeal to avenge. One word and one sentiment animated the European soldiery then – that word Cawnpore! that sentiment Revenge!

Hardly had the foremost of Gosset's party gained the breach when a magazine blew up, carrying seven of the 86th into the air. Some were killed, others terribly burnt; their uniform, shoes excepted, was scorched away. These events appeared to have consumed but a few moments of time, but in reality perhaps we were half an hour, which I judge because that it was broad daylight when I could calmly look around me and see the fugitives who had reached the sally port in full flight through the jungle below. Some of these were killed by Major Orr's force in waiting. A number of rudely-manufactured guns fell into our possession, but little else.

[1] Lieutenant William Butler Gossett, Royal Engineers.

We descended and marched through the deserted city, once containing fourteen thousand stone houses and twelve thousand mosques until brought by Maharatta to a splendid and picturesque architectural ruin. It was St Patrick's day: the band played appropriate tunes as we tramped through the echoing street to camp. Captain Keatinge was the only officer badly wounded; part of the hilt of his sword was shot into his hand and a spent ball struck his chest. The loss among our rank and file was comparatively slight. The party I had so basely deserted were said to have been into the fort simultaneously or before ours which assaulted the breach. Captain Fenwick and men of the Royal Engineers burst the guns and dismantled the fort, which was given into charge of a party of Scindiah's soldiery, under a Shah Subah [governor of a province].

A dispatch from Sir Hugh directed the 14th Light Dragoons to march forthwith and join him, leaving our sick with the artillery. We set out at four in the afternoon, and after proceeding six miles, gained a more open country intersected by a splendid river, its course marked by trees, shrubs, and rushes of emerald green, contrasting pleasantly with the sombre sienna tints surrounding. We halted here and lay some hours on its banks, watching long-legged cranes, wading birds and kingfishers of every hue, which swarmed in the waters.

A few hours stolen sleep while waiting the passage of our baggage animals was very refreshing, for the constant harassing work by day and alarms by night had told on us all. Happy is it, however, that we cannot know the future, for that was the last refreshing sleep we enjoyed for many a weary day.

The next evening we reached Tolbeit.[1] The Major General and 2nd Brigade had left the day previous, our orders being to overtake him. We marched continually, snatching an hour's sleep by the roadside, or a hasty meal, during stables. Every step appeared to take us into a hotter

[1] 20 March 1858.

and more sterile country; large interminable plains with granite boulders sticking out like cromlechs [standing stones] replaced the brighter forest clad country we had left behind us. Where cultivated, the corn stood yellow and dropping, ripe for the sickle, but the villages were deserted and there were none to gather in the harvest.

Dark and late at night on the 21st we came in sight of the camp fires of the 2nd Brigade before Jhansi. A feeble cheer from our men marked the end of a most fatiguing march.

While Sir Hugh and the 2nd Brigade halted at Saugor, Major Orr's force had hung on the scent of the Garrakotah fugitives and traced them to the hilly districts of Shaghur, Marowra, and Multowa. A range of wooded hills separates these districts from Saugor: it is practicable for guns at three points. The Major General determined on Mudden-pore, while Major Scudamore[1] was directed to make a feint of marching through Narrat, for there the rebels, expecting the Brigade, had made rude though formidable prepara-tions of defence. During the morning a party of cavalry reconnoitred the approach to Narrat but was fired upon from a fort and village three miles from camp, and returned.

During the afternoon, Major Scudamores's force ad-vanced, assaulted, and carried the village at the point of the bayonet. The 3rd Bombay Europeans under Major Mac-donald were mainly instrumental in this and captured fifty-two prisoners besides leaving fifty of the enemy dead; the remainder escaped into the jungles from the west side of the fort.

Sir Hugh arrived at the pass of Muddenpore with a strong advanced guard and was at once under fire of its defenders, estimated at nine thousand men, chiefly Bundeelas and Velliattees with a few Bengal Sepoys. Their position was on the left side of the rocky and precipitous

---

[1] Major Arthur Scudamore (1816–80), 14th Light Dragoons. Was present at Ghuznee (with the 4th Light Dragoons) and at Chillianwallah and Goojerat. Major-General, 1875.

gorge, among dense shrubs and brushwood. The Hyderabad battery advanced and opened fire but was obliged to withdraw from the precise and heavy matchlock fire. Infantry, chiefly the 3rd Europeans and Hyderabad, skirmished along the hill side and dislodged the enemy's sharpshooters entirely from the glen, driving them into another hill where they were shelled by the Bombay Artillery. A more decided loss, however, was inflicted on them by a charge of the Grenadier and Nos. 1, 2 and 3 Companies of the 3rd Europeans.

A general advance of the entire body of Infantry and Hyderabad Cavalry then followed and drove the rebel force to Muddenpore village, where they had six guns. A few rounds from our artillery caused them to retreat again through the jungle, to the fort of Sooree: the Hyderabad Cavalry, following, succeeded in cutting up a few. During [the] night they evacuated this place also, leaving their guns, grain, tentage, cattle and ammunition. It was said they had gone to Shaghur, the Rajah of which place had commanded them.

The barrier of the Tihree country having been forced, the 2nd Brigade marched to open ground and encamped. On the 5th of March, Morowzo was reached, and the fort, a strong one, partially surrounded by water, was annexed to the British possessions under a salute of twenty-one guns. Its Rajah, who was disaffected towards us had flown, and though reported to be in hiding ten miles away, was sought unsuccessfully. Tolbeit, a beautiful fortress, was also found abandoned. From thence the Brigade reached Jhansi without further hostilities.

VI

Jhansi and the Betwa

WE were naturally pleased to be again immediately under command of the Major General who had thoroughly beaten Whitlock's force in the race for Jhansi notwithstanding many vexatious delays. It was also an ascertained fact that the enemy was present in great force; that he had made equally large preparations; the mutiny too which had taken place here had invested Jhansi with a peculiar interest,[1] and having arrived we hoped for at least one night's rest.

The feeble cheer then which broke from our troopers when they first sighted the camp fires before the city is readily accounted for, and we marched in without a challenge and picketted our horses alongside those of the right wing. Whether they recognized any old acquaintances I cannot say. It was some time before we received a greeting, but at length Dew's cheery voice was heard, and from him we learnt that the 2nd Brigade had now encamped; that [the] greater part of the Dragoons were on outpost duty; that all were badly off for provisions, wood, everything in short, and that for three days they had not undressed. This intelligence was so far consoling as shewing how little better they had fared than ourselves. We had arrived too late for any duty that night, and after a very frugal meal, we lay on the ground and slept soundly.

[1] This mutiny occurred on 4 June 1857, the regiments concerned being the 12th Bengal Native Infantry and the 14th Irregular Cavalry, but the moving spirit behind it was the Ranee, a brave woman of ability. She hoodwinked Captain Alexander Skene (68th Bengal Native Infantry), the Political Agent, who, with the Europeans, took refuge in a fort in the city. On a solemn promise that their lives would be spared, they surrendered, and were then tied up in two rows, the men in one and the women and children in the other, and were butchered.

I was all curiosity at daybreak, and was up with the reveillee. The country, as far as I could see, was a hot inhospitable looking plain, devoid of trees or vegetation but relieved here and there by granite rocks and bald, woodless crags. Its redeeming feature was the splendid fortress, huge and frowning, looking formidable even at this distance of two miles. The city beneath it was hidden by rising ground.

We had, however, barely time to acquaint ourselves with the feature of the country before orders directed our advance to the city, where cavalry was urgently needed. On our way we passed the remains of the old military cantonment, completely destroyed. Even the woodwork had been taken as fuel from the bungalows, the gardens trampled down, the blackened walls of the sepoys' lines almost washed away by rains. The few trees which had shaded the graves of our countrymen were uplifted and the stones, removed, left no history of those sleeping beneath. The bells of arms [a bell-shaped hut for storing the arms of native regiments] and Star Fort, where Mr Skene so bravely defended himself and wife, were of solid masonry and uninjured.

As we drew near the city we became a mark for the enemy's round shot and our Horse Brigade replied. The Major General and Engineer staff were indefatigable, selecting sites for batteries and outposts, and by the night of the 23rd,[1] twelve miles of city walls were invested. One large outpost of Dragoons, on the distant side of the city, was commanded by Major Gall, another, opposite the water palace, by Captain Thompson.[2] Captain Forbes of the 3rd Bombay Cavalry was in command of one, of his own men, while Captains Murray, Abbott, and Clerk,[3] were present with outposts of the Hyderabad Cavalry.

[1] 23 March 1858.

[2] Captain Pearson Scott Thompson, 14th Light Dragoons.

[3] Captain William Murray (46th Madras Native Infantry) serving with the 4th Cavalry, Hyderabad Contingent, and Lieutenant Henry Clerk (8th Madras Native Infantry) serving with the 3rd Cavalry, Hyderabad Contingent.

For the most part, the enemy confined himself to his defences within the strong walls of the city, or to temples and buildings in the proximity, though we occasionally took prisoners at the outposts, but as they were not required in camp, we summarily disposed of them. The view of the city from the outposts and batteries was very imposing, for above it, massive merlon [the raised parts of battlements] crowned walls and bastions, mosque, minaret and tower, with ample and beautiful foliage, were seen, but most impressive was the huge dark fortress whose gigantic walls had been piled a hundred years ago, in the zenith of Maharatta power. Here, under the shelter of the crimson flag of mutiny, report said, the Ranee, young unwedded,[1] and jealous of power, sat watching the puny figures below, who were so many tiny shadows of her end. During the many long hours, we on picket duty watched and wondered what she said and what she did to those best-favored among a band of chieftains, and imagination ran wild in the fervid heat.

My special duties, however, did not fetter me entirely to the outposts, for when others sickened I had to take their duty also, and on the 24th I was directed to proceed to the 'right attack'. This consisted of a number of twenty-four pounder guns [and] huge mortars in four large rock and sandbag batteries, under a scorching sun and heavy fire. It was close to the Oorcha road. One tiny hut, the habitation of a devotee, afforded a few square yards of shade, but no protection against round shot from the east walls which occasionally went through it. Here too I passed the night, sleeping undisturbed though eight-inch mortars and siege guns roared all night.

In the morning I was directed to proceed to the 'left attack', about a mile and a half distant. My way was through the garden where the massacre had occurred, the only trace of which remaining was a woman's skeleton bleached by the sun, but the head was gone.

The 'left attack' was situated on a ridge, from which pro-

---

[1] She was a widow.

jected huge granite boulders – our only protection from a
heavy and constant fire proceeding from an angular outwork of the enemy, distant three hundred yards. This outwork, called by Sir Hugh the Mamelon [a rounded hillock,
reminiscent of the Mamelon at Sevastopol], consisted of a
half-bastion continuous with the city ramparts. It was
crenellated and mounted six pieces of ordnance. The ground
on which the Mamelon stood was much higher than the
adjoining walls: in front it sloped abruptly to a deep
masonry trench, and behind its battery within the walls
was a *chevaux-de-frise*.

So exposed was our position in the 'left attack' that
casualties were very constant, especially amongst bullocks
and mules bringing in ammunition. The granite boulders,
our only shelter from the Mamelon fire, became so hot in the
sun at midday that we could with difficulty sit behind them.
Captain Ommaney of the Royal Artillery[1] and Captain
Hare with the Hyderabad Contingent infantry, and field
pieces, had held this ridge from the first, supported by the
3rd European Regiment, sheltered by some temples and
trees on the right, close to the scene of the European
massacre. While crouching behind these blazing rocks I
could plainly distinguish the features of the sepoy garrison
and hear their voices. During the night they repaired their
damaged embrasures by logs of timber.

Sir Hugh Rose's plan of capture was now evident. Our
'right' and 'left attacks' were placed opposite the enemy's
strongest positions which, when breached, were to be the
points stormed. Cavalry were disposed on the distant outskirts of the city, while the camps of the two Brigades
would guard the cantonment side. These were about three
miles apart, far beyond the enemy's range of fire, and save
the sick and wounded with thirty Dragoons for protection,
were almost empty.

The 1st Brigade I had quitted at Chanderi arrived on the

---

[1] Captain Francis Montague Maxwell Ommaney, Royal Artillery, in
command of the artillery of the 1st Brigade.

25th. At this date the enemy's fire had been something diminished and some of their heaviest guns silenced, yet the Ranee's heavy pieces on the fort continued to annoy us. Repeated orders enjoining increased vigilance were sent to the various outposts which had been strengthened, and a signal telegraph was erected on an adjoining hill, to indicate direction of an escaping enemy.

I was now released from battery duty and thankful for the prospect of a night in camp, to which I returned, but long before midnight we were suddenly ordered to strike our tents and march to the protection of those of the 2nd Brigade which, under Sir Hugh, had proceeded to the Betwa river some six miles away. Tantia Topee[1] with ten thousand men, was said to be approaching, to raise the siege we had laid to Jhansi. The night was long and wearisome for we all stood expectant, and day broke without a sign of the truth of the report.

We had no sooner encamped in front of the 2nd Brigade than an order came to move near the old jail, and a second time, at evening on the 31st, all troops in both camps were ordered to march, but in different directions. The Major General bivouacked not far from his camp; our Brigade, by a circuitous route, marched towards the Betwa and lay under arms all night. Again, save a little unbidden firing from our native infantry which wounded a Dragoon, we passed it hot and wearily.

Harrassed as we were at this juncture and unaware of our critical position, the morning commenced to dawn on mutterings of impatience, when suddenly the sound of heavy fire in the direction of the 1st Brigade fell upon our ears. Tantia's force had indeed arrived and the chiefest elements in it were the men of Gwalior, flushed with their victory at Cawnpore, over Wyndham.[2] The besiegers and

---

[1] Tantia Topee (1819?–59) was a Mahratta Brahmin in the service of the Nana Sahib. The most able of all the rebel leaders.

[2] Major-General Sir Charles Ash Windham (1810–70). Led the unsuccessful attack on the Redan, Sevastopol. 8 September 1855. With the

besieged scarce awaited daybreak ere their pickets fell back
and the dark masses of our foe advanced over the rising
knoll in front. For days previous General Whitlock had been
expected, and now that our extremity had arrived, where
was he? At this moment he would have been a very
Blücher at Waterloo, for the greater portion of our troops
were on duty around the city and I know nothing which
transpired during the campaign that I can adduce to show
so well the dash of our leader as the fact that, without
calling a single man away from the outposts, he accepted the
challenge with comparatively a handful of men. I say comparatively because Tantia, prior to his execution, deposed
that the force under his command at the Betwa numbered
twenty thousand with twenty-five pieces of cannon.

These pieces of artillery Tantia drew up in line, supporting them with masses of infantry and about seven
hundred horse. He appeared to threaten our left, and
advancing within six hundred yards, unlimbered and
opened a heavy fire. Our opposing line numbered fifteen
hundred men all told and were thus disposed: in the centre
of the first line were the heavy guns supported by parts of
the 3rd European, 24th, and Hyderabad Infantry regiments;
on the right a troop of 14th Dragoons and one of Hyderabad
Cavalry, with the Eagle troop of Horse Artillery;[1] on the
left, Lightfoot's field battery and a squadron of the 14th.
The reserve consisted of Woolcombe's and Ommaney's
batteries, supported on the right by H.M.'s 86th Regt and
a few Dragoons, and on the left by a troop of Hyderabad
Cavalry, and some companies of the 25th Native Infantry.

Our guns replied to the enemy's artillery, and the in-

64th (now part of the Staffordshire Regiment), the 82nd (now part of
The Lancashire Regiment), the 88th (later 1st Bn Connaught Rangers,
disbanded 1922), part of the 34th (now part of the King's Own Border
Regiment) and the Rifle Brigade (now 3rd Green Jackets), he suffered a
defeat at Cawnpore at the hands of Tantia Topee with a numerically
superior force.

[1] 1st or Eagle Troop, Bombay Horse Artillery.

fantry on both sides kept up a tremendous fusilade. The engagement now became general along the entire line. At that early hour there was little breeze and the smoke hung heavily. The artillery from both our flanks advanced to crush the enemy's gunners by an enfilading fire; on the right, however, one of the guns of the Eagle troop was knocked over and disabled, which gave the enemy a temporary advantage. They greeted it with cheers and redoubled their fire, which so galled our close infantry ranks near the heavy guns that the men were ordered to lie down.

The turn which events had taken induced Sir Hugh to take more decided action, and he directed the Hyderabad Cavalry, under Lieut Clarke to charge the enemy's battery. This was done, but Lieutenant Clarke was not well followed, and had to retire severely wounded after three unsuccessful attempts.[1]

The battle was now speedily decided by the intrepid conduct of the 14th Dragoons. Sir Hugh, at the head of Need's troop, dashed into the enemy's left, while Prettyjohn and MacMahon[2] led their troops into the right of his line, and doubled him up. This was a magnificent sight, and in a moment Tantia's ranks were in confusion. Shaken and disorganised, he commenced a disastrous retreat.

The irresistible attack of the Dragoons had hurled the rebel host back on the Betwa. Occasional groups rallied, and when hard pressed, fought desperately for life. Our troops continued to advance, and caused them to abandon six guns and ammunition waggons, besides twelve cannon of

[1] Should be 'Clerk'. In his *Diary* Sylvester records how, on hearing the sound of heavy firing, he rode out of camp with the intention of joining Gall and the three troops of 14th Light Dragoons at the outposts but on the way he met a sowar who entreated him to 'come and see Clerke, wounded. I did, as hard as I could ride, he had led his men to the enemy's guns which were loaded by grape & his Regiment was terribly cut up and he was shot through the loins not dangerously so I sent him into camp.'

[2] Captains Richard Buckley Prettejohn and William M'Mahon, 14th Light Dragoons.

brass, taken in the charge. Unexpectedly, however, our
cavalry came upon a second or reserve force of the enemy,
which opened on them with shot and shell. Our Horse
Artillery replied and again they were shortly in full flight.

Our infantry were now distanced by the pace and the
cavalry and horse brigade took up the pursuit, overtaking
the fugitives at the river, the rugged bed of which embarrassed their passage. Here, having the aid of their infantry, and shelter of a small village, they in a measure
rallied, and made great efforts to carry off the remainder of
their guns, ammunition, elephants, and baggage animals,
but much of it was left in the bed of the wide but shallow
stream.

The ardour of the cavalry led them across the river into
the burning jungle beyond where it had been fired by our
shells. Captain Need, who had been leading, was surrounded
in the stream, and but for the timely assistance of his
brother officer, Leith, would have been cut to pieces, as his
charger stood affrighted, and refused to move; nine sabre
cuts on his horse and saddlery marked his peril. The
Victoria Cross was awarded Captain Leith, but the valor-
ous Need who led the way throughout, remained un-
decorated. This was much commented upon in camp when
we had leisure to fight the Battle of the Betwa[1] over again.

The 1st Brigade, hearing heavy firing on their arrival
at a village called Boregaum, and discovering no trace of an
enemy at the adjacent ford of Kolwar, commenced a hasty
march to Sir Hugh's assistance, when they unexpectedly
came upon a number of rebels making for the ford, whereupon Lieutenant Giles, with thirty Dragoons, cut them up,
but in so doing, one Dragoon was killed, five were wounded,
and ten casualties occurred amongst the horses.

Immediately after this occurrence, the Brigade came to
the small village of Khooshabord which about three thousand of the enemy had occupied, with six pieces of cannon.
These opened on our skirmishers, but a few rounds from

[1] Fought on 1 April 1858.

Bombay and Royal Artillery guns caused the enemy to commence a retreat, whereupon the County Downs, and 25th Bombay Native Infantry, under Colonels Lowth and Robertson, dashed forward and carried the position with the bayonet. Cochrane of the 86th,[1] who behaved with conspicuous bravery, and lost three horses beneath him, was awarded the Victoria Cross.

The enemy now retired from the village, fighting, and Giles, again with his thirty Dragoons, reduced by six men and ten horses, dashed at them, ably seconded by some Contingent horse, but he was powerless against dense masses of matchlockmen. The ground, unfortunately, was impracticable for guns, and our infantry were too exhausted to pursue.

This was one of the numerous instances during the campaign in which five hundred efficient light cavalry could have dealt a decisive blow to the rebellion. Six guns, two elephants, some camels, treasure, ammunition, and two standards fell into our hands, and it was calculated that fifteen hundred rebels had fallen in the two engagements.

During the day, as my regiment was distributed wherever needs were greatest, and as I was most required where blood was most freely shed, I had a grand opportunity of seeing the most exciting part of the work, and by an arrangement of mutual accommodation with Dr Mackenzie, who was senior officer in the 1st Brigade, and late the distinguished head of the Madras Medical Service,[2] I was enabled to be on the scene of action, rendering immediate aid to the wounded, while he paid more deliberate attention to them in the field hospital.

There cannot be a doubt, an able commandant in the fort would have directed an onslaught on our 'right' and 'left

---

[1] Major George Henry Robertson (25th Bombay Native Infantry), Lieutenant-Colonel Robert Henry Lowth (86th) and Lieutenant Hugh Stewart Cochrane, Adjutant of the 86th.

[2] Surgeon William Mackenzie, M.D. (1811–95). Inspector-General, Madras Medical Department, 1861–71.

attacks', dismantled our works, burnt our camps, and crushed our 2nd Brigade by assailing its rear. Major Gall maintained the garrison was deterred from this course by a false attack he made on a distant part of the city wall on which he directed Captain Field's[1] battery to fire; and I, judging that he had been attacked, galloped to his outpost, bearing tidings of the Battle of the Betwa.

The noise of Tantia's opening volley was the signal for the camel-hearted garrison in Jhansi to redouble their efforts, which were more those of demons and fanatics than soldiers, for, though as a matter of fact they fired both fast and furious, yet it was wild as their cries, and scarce less appalling than their drums and music.

On the second of April we rested, and saw with pride Tantia's twenty pieces of artillery parked in front of the divisional staff lines. Shortly after midnight we were warned, without trumpet or bugle, to fall in quietly for the assault. It was arranged that the 1st Brigade, told off in two storming parties, consisting chiefly of H.M.'s 86th, Royal Engineers and 25th Native Infantry, with reserves and supports of the same corps, should advance from the 'left attack' as follows: the first, under Colonel Lowth, to enter the breach at the Mamelon, the second party, under Major Stuart,[2] to escalade the wall between that and the fort. I was directed to join the latter.

The 3rd European Regiment, Hyderabad Infantry, and sappers, were to assault from the 'right attack', all to start at a signal of three guns from Captain Ommaney's battery: further, the order directed that, as Sir Hugh Rose had no knowledge of the interior of the city, it was desirable for the troops to make for the Ranee's palace after entry.

Some hours of suspense were occupied while the troops were arranged and marched to their respective positions. At length, in half day, half moonlight, the signal guns broke the awful silence, and with a deafening yell, the stormers

---

[1] Captain Thomas Spencer Poer Field, Royal Artillery.
[2] Major William Kier Stuart, 86th.

swept forward. Those for the Mamelon breach encountered
but little resistance and one half the party moved to the
right, clearing the inside of the walls towards the 'right
attack'. The remainder moved to the front, clearing the
houses in their progress, reaching an open space near the
fort gate. Here they killed a number of rebels who were
escaping to the fort for shelter. Unfortunately, the 86th, in
their ardour, rushed at the fort gate, under a murderous fire
from its walls. The bullets fell like hail and as the party had
no support, and the men were falling fast, the 'retire' was
sounded and all fell back, carrying the wounded and dead:
one of these was recovered from the very gateway.

Nothing could have been more unfortunate yet more
fearless than this rush of the County Downs across an open
space under the fire of two thousand men in the fort. It cost
the lives of two officers and three men, while upwards of
twenty were wounded. It was here that Dr Stack[1] was shot
dead and Dr Cruikshank was severely wounded, while doing
their duty.

The signal roused Major Stuart's party while lying down
behind the battery, and with scaling ladders, under command of Lieutenant Edwards, R.E.,[2] they rushed to the
walls against which the ladders were placed successfully. In
a moment, Ensign Dartnell,[3] with some of the County
Downs, had gained the parapet where the resistance was
desperate. Every description of missile; stone, grenade,
rocket and stink pot was hurled at them, while the impetuous rush below broke the top bars of the ladders, and so
impeded the ascent of others, that for some seconds Dartnell and his gallant few were unsupported, and he was almost cut to pieces. By protecting his head with his folded
arms, however, he saved his life, and his wounds were the
first that engaged my attention.

[1] Dr Thomas Stack, M.D., Surgeon of the 86th.

[2] Lieutenant James Bevan Edwards, Royal Engineers.

[3] Ensign John George Dartnell, 86th. Wounds received at Jhansi:
four sword cuts (severe) and a bullet wound. He later served in the
Zulu War and in the 2nd Boer War.

The ladders righted, the stormers poured over the wall and drove all before them. Hurrahs and shouts of triumph rang through the city where the bayonet was doing its deadly work.

The stormers by escalade from the 'right attack' were unfortunate indeed, but unquestionably the signal was over late. It was close on daylight before they sped over the two hundred yards of open way between the battery and eastern walls which teemed with defenders: nevertheless, across a field, down a road, ran the sappers, Hyderabad infantry, and 3rd Europeans, falling fast under a hail of bullets. They seek a moment's shelter and draw breath under a mass of ruined buildings, and with a deafening cheer gain the walls, and there, amid a storm of missiles, the ladders are placed against the ramparts. Save one, these miserable failures were all too short! Up that one Lieutenant Meiklejohn[1] and a soldier of the 3rd rushed to their death, for the enemy literally hacked them to pieces; Bonus[2] beaten off another. Lieutenant Fox[3] was shot down on the top of a third, together with six of his sappers, and Lieutenant Dick[4] dragged upon the ramparts and killed.

This unexplained inefficiency of the ladders threw the stormers into confusion, but not yet despair; a Lieutenant of Engineers fired a powder bag against a postern, to effect an entry, and amid the smoke and flying splinters, the stormers essayed a last attempt, only to find themselves baulked by a wall of masonry; and now, dispirited, they moved back to the rifle pits. But the successful troops, having worked to their right and cleared the walls, at length made entry easy, though progress towards the palace was disputed inch by inch. Dismounted horsemen fought with tulwars [curved native swords] and the enemy fired heavily into

[1] Lieutenant Hugh Robert Meiklejohn, Bombay Engineers.

[2] Lieutenant Joseph Bonus, Bombay Engineers.

[3] Lieutenant Francis Robert Fox (14th Madras Native Infantry) serving with the Madras Sappers and Miners.

[4] 2nd Lieutenant William George Douglas Dick (Bombay Engineers) serving with the Bombay Sappers and Miners.

the streets and had to be dislodged from the houses. Colonel Turnbull of the Artillery, while directing the street fighting, was wounded by a ball in the hip and lived but a few hours.[1]

When at length the Ranee's palace – where Sir Hugh had directed the troops to make for – had been reached, a tremendous struggle took place in the courtyard: the rebels could not escape, and fought for their lives. In a room on the left, some soldiers of the 86th were blown up. In the stable yard the hand to hand combat was terrible. It was full of native troopers who cut down several of the 86th and so maddened the remainder that a deadly *mêlée* ensued, which was terminated by Sir Hugh setting the place on fire. With the exception of two who perished in the flames, the whole of them charged and were shot, while thirty horses came into our possession.

Day was now advanced: a chain of pickets was thrown across the city from the palace to the northern wall, securing us one half, but this half yet containing concealed fighting men. A Union Jack appropriately fell into our hands and was hoisted on the palace by Captain Darby[2] who had been one of the severely wounded beneath the fort.

It was a disappointment to all that the Ranee had not been found in the palace, but she sought shelter in the fort at an early period of the day's attack. The fort and a great part of the city was still in the hands of the enemy. The heavy guns on the former had never ceased firing since daybreak, and street fighting went on until dark.

Matters in camp and without the city walls had not been stationary; cavalry and artillery were in their saddles,

[1] Lieutenant-Colonel Sydney Turnbull (1811–58), commanded the 1st or Eagle Troop, Bombay Horse Artillery. He was present at Mooltan and Goojerat, 1848–9. Sir Hugh Rose reported of him: 'In the despatches I have recorded the excellent service performed by Lieut.-Col. S. Turnbull, particularly in the general action of the Betwa, always exposing himself to the fire of the enemy, in order to choose the best position for his guns. This devoted officer was as useful to me as commandant of Arty. as captain on a Troop. His premature fall prevents his receiving the reward which was his due.'

[2] Captain Charles Darby, 86th.

waiting the opportunity which presented itself about three o'clock in the afternoon. About this hour, between five or six hundred of the garrison sallied out, apparently with the intention of going to Tehree, but being perceived by our cavalry pickets, they mounted a large isolated rock, on the sides of which were many shelf-like ledges affording a standing ground. On these the enemy stood in clusters and groups, but exposed fully to our fire.

Major Gall at once rallied the flying camps; Captains Murray and Abbott arrived with their cavalry, Gall was accompanied by a squadron of his regiment, and Woolcombe brought up his battery. Wanting infantry, Major Gall sent to General Rose who dispatched two companies of the 24th under Lieutenant Parke,[1] and seventy-five men of the 25th regiment. Gall dismounted and placed the infantry, 24th in front, 25th in support.

Among the enemy who ascended the rock were seventeen horsemen; these too proceeded as high as the horses could be urged to go, and as the wretched animals could not again be persuaded to descend, all were killed, together with their riders. Major Orr came up late in the affair and assumed command on his side of the hill.

During the first part of the attack, the enemy made an excellent defence and caused us many casualties killed and wounded: among the former was Lieutenant Parke of the 24th. At length, recognizing their position hopeless, some implored mercy, others blew themselves up with their own powder flasks, but the showers of shrapnel from six guns only ceased, to permit our infantry to ascend and clear the rock,[2] which was barely done before darkness stayed the hand [of] vengeance which fell heavily for the massacre in the Jaken Bagh [the garden in which the massacre of the Europeans took place after the mutiny at Jhansi].

At dawn the day following, a desultory fire went on between our infantry – now well sheltered in various build-

---

[1] Lieutenant Atherton Allan Park, 24th Bombay Native Infantry.
[2] Known afterwards as 'Retribution Hill'.

ings – and the sentries of the enemy who were plainly visible on the city wall about a mile distant.

In order to clear the remainder of the city, the Major General, with the 24th Native infantry and a few of the 3rd Regiment, moved along the outside of the city walls while Brigadier Stuart, his staff, and a small party of the 86th crossed to the portion of the city yet held by the enemy. A few were killed by the 3rd and 24th soldiers, but for the most part they retreated to the fort: here, through the loopholes and from the towers a slack fire was maintained, and their flag still hung on the battlements.

It was the impression that, in so strong a position, the rebels would yet make a considerable stand, and projects were discussed for reducing the fortress. On the second night, however, after the siege, much small arms firing was heard at the outposts: that under Major Gall's command thrice drove back a body of the enemy attempting escape, and in the morning Lieutenant Baigrie[1] and a picket of H.M.'s 86th, opposite the fort gateway, noticed it open wide, and being unmolested, they walked in and found the fortress empty. The red flag now gave place to the Union Jack amid three British cheers.

During the siege, much curiosity was manifest to see the interior of the palace, fort, and city, as full of interest. The palace, which had been so fiercely defended, was prettily situated near water and shaded by handsome trees; its walls externally were decorated with paintings after the fashion of Egyptian temples, representing war and the chase, processions and royal fêtes. In shape the building was square, enclosing a courtyard and facing a narrow street. Inside were found pet animals in great variety: deer, antelopes, gazelles, dogs, monkeys, pigeons, parrots and cockatoos. In the yard, in a chaos of disorder were clothes, uniforms, fire-arms, swords, horse and elephant gear, cooking utensils, grass, grain, and horse litter.

---

[1] Lieutenant Robert Baigrie, 3rd Bombay Europeans. Served in the Punjab, 1848–9, the Crimea, and Persia, 1857. Died 1877.

The staircase leading to the Ranee's and state apartments was mean, low, and narrow but, the first storey gained, presented a singularly handsome appearance, especially to our eyes, accustomed to dingy tents. The chief apartments occupied the entire facade of the palace front and consisted of a state or durbar room and two sleeping apartments besides an inner room where doubtless the Ranee retired from the cares of state. Its ceiling was of plate glass mirrors, the panels of the walls carved and gilded, and also covered by mirrors and paintings. The floor was spread with one huge cushion of cotton wool covered in crimson velvet, and one felt it a sin to drag one's spur armed heels over it. The state room was also beautiful, and lighted by four spacious windows. Its floor was covered by English carpets and Persian rugs; huge glass chandeliers, chiefly purple in colour, hung from the ceiling. Chairs, tables, couches, pictures and ornaments were abundant.

The sleeping rooms, fitted up by one no novice in luxuries, were handsomely decorated after the Eastern fashion, scarlet and gold prevailing. The shallow bedsteads, scarce a foot from the floor, were of solid silver their pillows and coverlets of gaudy satin and kinkob. Articles of female apparel lay strewn in disorder; bodices and the full short skirts of Musslemani women were thrown in piles on the floor, together with more costly articles of jewelry.

Outside in the streets, the smell of dead bodies and the bloated carcasses of bullocks, horses, and other animals was sickening: one day's exposure in the heat we were then enduring was sufficient to induce decomposition. A wounded boy who fell into our hands told us that the enemy had burnt from forty to a hundred bodies every night, which were mainly those killed by our shells.

As I only once, and that for a few moments, went inside the fort, it is impressed on my memory as a mass of dungeon-like rooms, passages and courtyards. It was of immense capacity, but had not been provisioned for a siege. The view from its flag tower was most extensive, and afforded

a panoramic view of our camp and the surrounding country
for miles. The entrance was steep and tortuous through
many gates, and each division of the passage enfiladed by
that above. The walls were everywhere thickly loopholed
for matchlockmen, and armed with jingals, wall pieces, and
traversing guns. One huge dismounted cannon lay in the
gateway.

The greater part of the interior of the fortress was
occupied by the citadel, surmounted by the flag tower, and
on the upper parts of this building the destruction worked
by our constant fire of shot and shell was immense. In
many places the latter had torn through roofs and floors,
penetrating every nook and hiding place. Here, in enormous dimly-lighted rooms, was piled the greater part of the
property taken from the British during the mutiny and
despoliation of the military cantonment. Nothing short of an
inventory could convey an idea of the variety of articles
lying there in cartloads – books, desks, stationery, children's
toys, medicine chests, guitars, telescopes, cooking utensils,
furniture, Rowland's Macassar oil, wearing apparel, and
every article of common use among Europeans in Indian
cantonment life.

We were forbidden to loot, by a most peremptory order,
and Prize Agents were appointed, but in these matters it
was permissible to select some small trophies of the siege.
Soldiers and camp followers, by stripping the dead, in
many cases reaped a rich harvest. A considerable amount of
treasure was found in the palace and search was made for
more, but never a rupee came to its captors as Prize Money.

Descending from the citadel into the fort, another
reason of the garrison's sudden evacuation was visible: the
large water tank was dry.

Outside the fort, huge stacks of wood and hay were
burning, many of the houses were yet on fire, and other
fires were kindled on which we piled their dead, but the
city was by no means safe; hidden and half-starved sepoys
were often brought to light and during the after part of the

day on which the enemy escaped, a large number of desperate men were discovered in a block of houses capable of good defence. One of these men was said to be a great favorite of the Ranee. It was the work of many hours to dislodge them, notwithstanding five-inch shells were dropped through the roofs. Worse than all, it cost us dearly; Captain Sinclair, Hyderabad Contingent was killed, and Lieutenants Simpson, Lewis and Fowler[1] severely wounded. This was easily accounted for as the interior of the houses was dark in comparison with the bright glare outside, and our men and officers, while peering through the roofs or floors, were excellent marks for the rebels within. During the whole of the period, the outposts and pickets were still surrounding the city, and cut up all who preferred to attempt escape.

The inhabitants of the city for the most part had of necessity abandoned it to the mutineers. Some of the unlucky few who remained necessarily fared badly, and unfortunately a few women and children were wounded, but in all cases they were tenderly cared for by our troops.

Sir Hugh Rose was said to be wroth at the escape of the Ranee and garrison, and there was some unpleasant recrimination amongst the cavalry when the question of whose pickets she forced was discussed, and there can be no doubt that it was annoying to all, and gave, to say the least, an unhandsome appearance to the Ranee's conduct; she might have obliged us as the Emperor[2] did his opponent at Sedan. I hardly think, however, her guilty life would have been spared. The moment Sir Hugh discovered the flight, which was said to have taken place at nine o'clock the night proceeding, he gave pursuit, but in vain.

On the 12th of April, the outposts came into camp and

---

[1] Captain John Sinclair (39th Madras Native Infantry) serving with the 3rd Infantry, Hyderabad Contingent; Lieutenants Ralph Fitzgibbon Lewis and George Fowler (86th) and Lieutenant George Bowen Cassan Simpson (23rd Bengal Native Infantry) serving with the 4th Company, 2nd Bn Bombay Artillery.

[2] Napoleon III.

Major Robertson was appointed commandant of Jhansi, and to remain with the sick and wounded, retaining a wing of his regiment and a hundred Hyderabad Cavalry.

One sad duty remained before bidding the place farewell: it was the discovery of the remains of the Europeans killed in the outbreak. The spot indicated was the Jaken Bagh, and the Engineers commenced to search, and shortly discovered. From their appearance it struck me that they had lain some time unburied; the flesh and hair were dried upon them, and the body of a child still had portions of clothing adherent. Service for the dead was performed by both Protestant and Catholic priests, and I believe a memorial now covers the grave of seventy-four Europeans, whose murder was avenged by a loss of three thousand we destroyed during the siege.

VII

On the Road to Calpee

Now that operations were concluded, a reinforcement of medical officers joined, and I was displaced from the 14th Dragoons, with which regiment I had served through many eventful months. This change placed me on general duty, which is to be everyone's slave, but having foreseen this event, I secured the appointment to one of the two cavalry regiments General Beatson[1] was appointed to raise in the districts of Hyderabad. There was, however, no possibility of traversing seven hundred miles of disaffected country to join; moreover, Sir Hugh was unwilling that I should leave the Central India Field Force. I would rather

---

[1] William Fergusson Beatson (1804–72), born in Rossend Castle, Fife, had an interesting career. First posted to the 2/25th Bengal Native Infantry, as an Ensign, in 1820. Served in the British Legion in Spain, 1835–6; received the Cross of San Fernando. Later commanded the cavalry of the Nizam of Hyderabad. During the Crimean War he organized the Bashi Bazouks and was attached to the staff of Major-General Sir James Yorke Scarlett who commanded the Heavy Cavalry Brigade. Appointed to command the Umballa Division, 1869.

On 27 April 1858, Sylvester wrote to his brother Edward (curate of Deene, Warwickshire) informing him that he was doing duty, temporarily, with the Horse Artillery. He also informed him that he had been appointed to 1st Beatson's Horse, 'commanded by the General of that name who was the Bashi Bazouk hero of the Crimea, it is to be immensely crack. I don't know what pay but I fancy good, the worst part of the business is it will cost me about £200 in uniform to start with & as much more in horses. The bridle alone costs 16 guineas. The Helmet is like the Life Guards but with a green plume. Alcolic [or alkalak] or coat green loaded with gold lace, overalls full dress scarlet & gold stripe, undress buckskin breeches & jack boots. As I shall have to send home for it you will have an opportunity of seeing it when ready. I dare say now this is all very well but a frightful expense, it will however pay in the end.'

have remained as a soldier in the ranks of the 14th than
have left them.

On the 16th,[1] tired of inactivity, I went some miles from
camp, antelope shooting, in company with Captain Rice,[2]
well known in the Indian Army for his exploits tiger
shooting. Two days afterwards [I] was in orders to proceed
with a force of all arms at midnight, under command of
Major Lowth. Three of Woolcombe's guns, fifty Hyderabad
horsemen, a wing of the 3rd Bombay Cavalry, and a wing
of the 25th Infantry composed our party. At Bedora we met
Colonel Weatherall Captain Cockburn,[3] and an escort en
route to join Sir Hugh. He informed [us] that the fort we
were advancing to attack was empty. We returned to
Jhansi, while the 3rd Bombay Cavalry marched to Goonah
in order to meet the 71st Highlanders, expected to join our
force.[4]

Simultaneously with our dispatch to Bedora, Major Orr,
with the Hyderabad force, was directed to clear the road
from Jhansi to Chickaree, and from thence northward to
Goorserai and Kotra.

A third force, under Major Gall consisting of a squadron
of his own regiment, Lightfoot's battery, some companies of
the 3rd Europeans, and a handful of Hyderabad Cavalry,
proceeded on the Calpee road as far as the village of Lohar,
nine miles north west of Koonch. Here the hostile villagers
betrayed one of the cavalry outposts to the enemy and the
troopers had to cut their way out. In consequence of this,
Major Gall surrounded the village before daybreak on the

[1] 16 April 1858.

[2] Captain William Rice, 25th Bombay Native Infantry. 'A man who
has written an 18 Rupee book on tiger shooting.' (*Diary.*) *Tiger Shooting*
was published in 1857.

[3] 'We met Colonel Weatherall, Chief of the Staff & Captain Cockburn,
late A.D.C. to Lord Elphinstone.' (*Diary.*) Colonel Edward Robert
Wetherall served in Canada, 1837–9, the Crimea, and China, 1857, and
died in 1869. Captain Thomas Hugh Cockburn, H. M.'s 43rd Light
Infantry.

[4] Later 1st Bn The Highland Light Infantry and now amalgamated
with the 21st and 74th as The Royal Highland Fusiliers.

5th of May, and sent to its chief, Monohur Singh, an order to surrender: this he did, together with one hundred and fifty followers.

The garrison of Lohar [which Sir Hugh Rose in his dispatches wrongly calls Sohar and Loharea] preferred fighting, and took possession of a small fort. Two guns and two howitzers were consequently placed in position outside a ditch and second line of works surrounding it. These opened fire while Lieutenant Armstrong[1] with two companies of his corps (the 3rd Europeans) took advantage of a small outwork near the ditch, and from thence advanced to the gateway of the fort, forcing open the two doors guarding it. A third however was closed, and defended, to open which Lieutenant Bonus, Bombay Engineers, repaired to the village, and finding an old forge bellows, charged it with sixty pounds of gunpowder, hung it on the door and fired it. This opened the way for the stormers, led by Lieutenants Donne, Newport and Rose, while Fenwick[2] made a false attack on the south side.

In this gateway ensued one of the bloodiest hand-to-hand engagements of the whole campaign. Donne and Newport were compelled to retire, wounded, and Major Gall, dashing in to support the latter, was knocked down, and excepting Rose, was perhaps the only assailant who never for a moment repassed the gateway. Armstrong was also felled by a stone and Rose received a spear wound in the breast. Here as elsewhere, the officers appear to have borne the heat of the combat, for among the rank and file but one was killed and twelve were wounded. Fifty-seven of the garrison lay dead in the gateway alone. In the fort, one brass cannon, fifty small arms, together with drums, bugles and uniforms

---

[1] Lieutenant William Augustus Armstrong, 3rd Bombay Europeans, employed as Postmaster to the Central India Field Force, though unsuited, being a man of action and always in a fight.

[2] Lieutenants Frederick Clench Donne and William Henry Newport, 3rd Europeans, and Lieutenants Wellington Rose and Peregrine Powell Peart Fenwick, 25th Bombay Native Infantry.

bearing mountings of the 12th Bengal Infantry[1] fell to the spoilers.

Before the departure of Sir Hugh and his Brigades from Jhansi, Lieutenant Strutt, one of the prize agents, held daily auctions of the jewelry, shawls, turbans and other valuables found in the palace. Colonel Liddle of the 3rd Europeans, and a wing of his regiment, was left to garrison the fort and city instead of Major Robertson, who came on.

On the 1st of May, the 1st Brigade, under Sir Hugh, marched for Calpee, but various and contradictory reports were circulated, both as to the situation of the enemy and also as to General Whitlock's position. By some he was made to have marched on Calpee: I had received a letter recounting the capture of Banda and Kirkwee, with the now famous prize money.

On the evening of the departure of this brigade, I was transferred to the 2nd, to assume charge of half a troop of Horse Artillery, Ordnance details, and a wing of the 24th Infantry. Rain fell and a brief respite was given from the fierce heat. We followed the Major General at two a.m. the day after he left Jhansi, thoroughly weary and tired with its sterile plain. Just as we are about to leave our camp ground, one of the sepoys of the 24th regiment stabbed his corporal with a bayonet, and with his musket and forty rounds of ammunition, escaped to an adjoining rock where he was captured but not before he had wounded three others.

Our first halt was at Burragaun, an almost deserted village. The Major General with the 1st Brigade was about fifteen miles in advance. Nothing eventful marked our daily progress except the intense and cruel heat of the climate. The nights were close and suffocating and the sun burnt with a force which at times appeared unbearable. Bright metal articles beneath the shade of a double roofed tent were almost painful to handle, and our cloth uniforms

---

[1] The 12th Bengal Native infantry, together with the 14th Irregular Cavalry, mutinied at Jhansi, 4 June 1857.

E

could hardly be borne. Soon after sunrise the hot wind commenced violently sweeping thick clouds of dust through our camp and tents, increasing out thirst and sufferings.

The whole country was flat and sterile, its surface many inches thick in light coloured almost impalpable soil. A single row of small neem [margosa] trees grew by the road side; otherwise no shade was to be found. Here and there a few dried up cactus plants or bushes of camel thorn scattered the plain, and how sustenance was found for the enormous train of ammunition and baggage animals accompanying us I cannot conceive. It is small wonder that they perished in numbers by the way.

This intense heat caused the European soldiers so much sickness and distress that it became necessary to march at night and this deprived us of sleep. Often times we were compelled to lie down at six o'clock in order to gain three hours as the reveillee sounded at nine. Sleep by day, even if duty permitted, was so disturbed by the sensation of fulness in the head that few attempted it, and in some cases, heat apoplexy was induced.

There were no broad streams nor finely shaded banks such as we had enjoyed in Malwa and Bundlecund. Water was confined to wells, eight or ten miles apart; these, moreover, were narrow and deep and the supply limited: this scarcity appeared to increase at every stage. The scene at a well was distressing: thousands of parched men each eagerly waiting his turn to drink from the leathern bucket as it came to the surface, longing too, as I have often done, to thrust in head and all. Neither did the coveted draught assuage the agonising thirst, because the water was earthy and hot. I know not how many miles of road we occupied when in column of march, but the pace did not average two miles an hour and duty on the rear was almost fatal to Europeans as it kept them all day in the sun.

A few days after leaving Jhansi, the 71st Highlanders joined us. They were sensibly clad in twill uniforms with

covered wicker helmets.[1] A batch of English newspapers
brought the information that Brigadier Stuart had received
the Companionship of the Bath for Dhar and Mundeesoor;
Gall, Woolcombe, Hungerford, Orr and Robertson had
received a step in brevet rank. The followers of Esculapius
got nothing; they belonged to the Indian Army.

On the 5th of May the two Brigades met at a village
called Pucha, and the following evening we left our camp
ground at ten. It was reported that, sixteen miles in advance,
the enemy was in force. We accomplished that distance by
daybreak, having been afoot the whole night, nor did it
require a professional eye to discern that the men were for
the most part dead beat; therefore a halt was given and
liquor served out! Anything more calculated to bring about
the terrible suffering which followed can scarcely be conceived. Doubtless a very temporary feeling of satisfaction
was produced, but the thirst and depression must have been
suffered in a very increased ratio. However, the advance
sounded, we passed one or two small villages, left the road
and struck across ploughed fields.

Shortly, in our front, and distant about a mile, the town
of Koonch was visible. As seen from the plain, it appeared to
me about two miles in length and very full of trees, chiefly
neem. At one extremity, the citadel of an ancient looking
fort, surmounted by a red flag, was a prominent object.

We now ascertained that the enemy had placed a battery

---

[1] In *The Campaign in Central India* Sylvester thus describes the
arrival of the 71st: 'On the 3rd of May the Head Quarter Wing of the
71st Highland Light Infantry joined us, with their Band and Bagpipes,
and the sound of these at starting, and on gaining our encamping
ground, was the only cheering thing which happened during the 24
hours. Their dress and equipment was almost perfect – a loose holland
blouse and overalls of Kakee dye, and a light shako-shaped hat, with
cover and curtain of the same colour. The 3rd B. Europeans were
dressed much in the same way, but wore a forage cap, and pugry, which
afforded little protection, and hung dabby and flabby down the neck.'

In his *Diary*, on 4 May, he wrote: 'The 71st Highlanders joined us
yesterday, Head Qr. Wing, a splendid fine set of fellows dressed in a
lavender suit calculated for ye climate, their band too was excellent.'

of guns across the Calpee road which led to Koonch, and hence the detour now made across the fields. Not only was the red flag an indication of the presence of a rebel force, but Major Gall's reconnaissance discovered that a very large body of troops consisting of Sepoys from Calpee, Bundeelah matchlockmen from Jhansi, and cavalry from Kotah, were under the personal command of Tantia and the Ranee.

The position of our three forces was well chosen. Sir Hugh, with the 1st Brigade, being on the opposite side to ourselves, was not in sight, but shortly after our arrival, Major Orr's force appeared on our right and was seen through a very remarkable mirage, and though not a drop of water existed, save in the usual deep and narrow wells, yet we were mocked by the appearance of a beautiful lake of water beyond which Major Orr's force appeared as a column of giants, all crooked and tremulous through the heated air. Our cautious Brigadier mistook them for the enemy and prepared for action.

All along our front extended the city, around which ran a low wall of sun-dried bricks. Behind this defence the rebel infantry were visible, with guns. In our front the 71st Highlanders were advanced in skirmishing order, but at too great a distance to receive harm. They, and the remainder of our Brigade stood for hours inactive under a terrible sun, and in a dust laden wind that appeared to have escaped from the infernal regions. At length, one by one were stricken down by the sun until a perfect panic seized the regiment; seven died at once, numbers of others, chiefly from this unfortunate regiment, were carried to the rear, insensible. Here, fortunately, a small village and two wells existed, with a moderate supply of water. The utter inability of a newly-arrived regiment to stand exposure to sun at this season was fully demonstrated.

While this brigade remained inactive, the Major General, on the opposite side of the town, commenced a heavy cannonade against the rebel cavalry which were visible among the trees of the outskirts. It was soon apparent, how-

ever, that the policy of the garrison was to retreat, and
Major Gall, with a few Dragoons, entered the gardens on
the south side of the town and saw their main body moving
off. Tired of sitting among the passive soldiery of the 2nd
Brigade to which I had so recently been attached, I rode
and joined Major Gall who crossed our front. He desired
me to carry an immediate entreaty for guns, which I did,
but to no purpose; Sir Hugh, however, on learning that the
enemy were moving away, organised an immediate assault.

Advancing with the County Downs and 25th regiment
in skirmishing order, supported by Horse and Field batteries
with Dragoons on the flank, and a line of reserve com-
prising Dragoons, Woolcombe's battery, and a wing of the
86th, the capture of Koonch was the work of half an hour,
and the British colours were planted by Major Stcuart[1] on
the fort.

Major Orr, who had fought his way from his encampment
at Aite to the village of Omree, and drove back a large
cavalry and artillery force that had gone out to oppose his
advance, sent his infantry to storm the wall and gardens of
the town in his front. This had the effect of driving out
some of the enemy, whom Lieutenant Dowker charged, but
Major Orr's men were unable to maintain their vantage
ground and retreated before overpowering numbers; this
too before the eyes of the 2nd Brigade who received no
order to advance to their succour. Moreover, this temporary success emboldened the enemy to open a heavy fire
of shrapnel on Major Orr's guns.

The Major General's advance from the north side of the
town drove the entire body of rebels into the open plain:
there were some thousands. I could scarcely believe in the
reality of the vision, so seldom had the rebels left their defences on any former occasion. Cries for cavalry and artillery
were on every lip; these arms responded to their utmost but
alas! the constant want of sleep, indifferent food, and whole
days of exposure to a death dealing sun had beaten us also.

---

[1] Major William Keir Stuart, H. M.'s 86th.

Ten horses had died in one battery, and though the Highlanders suffered in far the largest proportion by sunstroke,
almost every other corps shared in less degree, and twice
during the day Sir Hugh Rose was gravely affected.

Notwithstanding this however, Pitman, with his guns,
and Crowe,[1] with the half battery to which I was attached,
dashed at the main body of the retreating army and poured
showers of grape upon them, but their dense masses were
never broken for a moment. It was a pity the artillery of the
1st Brigade were not available half an hour sooner, but they
had to gallop through the town to the scene of action. The
order to cease firing was however given, and the Contingent
Cavalry and Dragoons charged, but the ground was broken
into rough clods, where the rebels stood and maintained a
splendid front with fixed bayonets, and some hesitation at
the critical moment seized the cavalry, many of whom, and
a considerable number of horses, were killed and wounded.

Again the guns opened, and a second time the cavalry
charged, yet still the rebels maintained a steady front,
facing about while retiring. Most of them wore their
scarlet tunics and dhoties [loin cloths] in the place of
trousers.[2] The Dragoon troops, led by Blythe[3] and Mac-
Mahon, fought brilliantly and cut up a great many. A
large number of officers, notably some of those on Sir Hugh's
staff, used their swords to great advantage, but none made
cleaner cuts than the sepoys,[4] who were said to be those who

---

[1] Lieutenant Thomas Carlisle Crowe, Bombay Artillery. Served at
Mooltan, 1848–9, Persia, 1857, and in the suppression of the Fenian
Raid, Canada, 1866.

[2] 'The Dragoons charged, I was carried with them, on coming up to
ye enemy they received us steadily and well, they were all sepoys with
government muskets, bayonets, belts, cartridges &c &c, the number of
their regiment (71st) for ye most part.' (*Diary*.) A large part of the
71st Bengal Native Infantry mutinied at Lucknow on 30 May
1857.

[3] Captain William D'Urban Blyth, 14th Light Dragoons.

[4] To show the force with which the sepoys could cut with their sharp
swords, Sylvester records (in *The Campaign in Central India*) the case of
Line Serjeant Wilson who had his bridle arm completely severed above

burned General Wyndham's camp. Being in the thick of the *mêlée* I found ample employment and was knocked over by a troop horse falling against me.

There can be no doubt that in this affair too much haste was made in charging before the guns had done their work, or a much larger harvest would have been reaped with the sword. A cavalry officer, writing to me after the event, says 'history does not record an instance of devotion superior to that displayed by Tantia's rear guard at Koonch – I should like to see a monument erected on the spot where they fell, all rebels as they were – but for the innocent blood of women and children that they had shed'. The conduct of their cavalry was the entire reverse, and here, as throughout the campaign, they never fought. Tantia himself appreciated the gallant conduct of his troops in this masterly retreat, and one of the last orders written by him, and afterwards found by us at Calpee, testified to their bravery and assured them that a few more repetitions would exterminate the infidel British. The book in which these orders were written possessed other curious entries of command.

All who were able, belonging to the mounted branches, followed Tantia's army for some miles on the Ooraii road, but could not prevent their carrying off an eighteen and twenty-four pounder gun, yet amongst the miscellanies which lay scattered in their track was the body of a fair and handsome woman which some thought might perchance be the body of the Ranee.

Darkness with its usual suddenness closed upon us before we could find our tents, or even food, and it was with much difficulty I obtained water for myself but insufficient for my horse. I had almost completely abstained throughout the day, and consequently suffered little in comparison with

---

the elbow. On the other hand he records seeing the blunt sword of a dragoon bounding off the skull of a sepoy, and in another case, of a dragoon cutting a man across the face with sufficient force to slice the top off his head, yet scarcely cutting the cheek bone.

those who yielded to the pangs of thirst, and far less than the unfortunates who swallowed arrack [liquor] at daybreak. Thoroughly tired, I, as many others, fastened my bridle around my arm, laid on the ground, and went through the form of sleeping until daylight when the hot wind, which had roared the entire night, abated for a while.

The day after the affair at Koonch was passed quietly in camp; rest was imperative especially for the large number of sunstricken, and for the burial of yesterday's dead. On the day following,[1] Sir Hugh and the 1st Brigade marched at 2 a.m. We were ordered to halt, but it was not in peace; the heat was terrible and about 3 p.m. the horizon darkened as though for a thunder storm, and what appeared to be huge banks of clouds came up suddenly; advancing, however, we saw they were made up of yellowish dust such as covered the plains hereabouts. On it came, faster and faster, higher and higher, like a huge curtain dividing the universe. Here and there it was preceded by sudden gusts which at frightful pace whirled in eddies along the soil, tearing up all before it. There was something awe-inspiring to us – comparatively so many pigmies – in the majesty with which it rolled onward and with terrific roar first overhung as a moving mountain range, and then overwhelmed us.

It was as though some vaporous form knit together its atoms, for the monster came upon us in the bright daylight with an edge quite sharp and well-defined. The tired cattle crouched at the roar and were terror stricken; down came our tents until not one remained on all the field; the noonday glare, before so unendurable, became darkened, and every object appeared as if seen through a yellow fog; neither did vision extend for many yards. The impalpable dust with which the air was laden almost choked us, and we nestled on the ground. I, fearing harm from a fall of my heavy tent pole, lay beneath a bullock cart until the force of the wind abated and I could maintain the erect position against it.

[1] 9 May 1858.

In about twenty minutes large drops of rain fell, each one so refreshing that they seemed as pearls from heaven, and now the atmosphere cooled suddenly and so remained for the night. This brief respite from the heat was balm to the wounded and sick, many of whom had been injured by their tents falling upon them. Its influence on all was marvellous and the heavy rain which fell so increased the weight of our tents that we could not march as ordered until the day following. The 2nd Brigade had also been compelled to halt at Hurdowi where there was a large fort which had been evacuated by the enemy, and its chief – a man of note – surrendered.

At length we left Koonch at 2 a.m. on the morning of the 11th for Ooraii, distant eight miles. It was a larger village than those in these parts and the blackened ruins of three European bungalows testified to the mutiny of two companies of sepoys which had been stationed here. A pool of muddy water, however, proved a luxury.

While enjoying a comparatively unlimited supply of water, a messenger from Sir Hugh ordered us to advance another eight miles to the village of Banda on the Calpee road, across which the rebels had dug a trench and placed a battery in waiting for us, and had we carried out this order, and diverted the enemy's attention, Sir Hugh's brigade would have turned his defences by a flank march and joined Colonel Maxwell[1] who was resting across one of the fords of the Jumna river, not far distant from Cawnpore. Sir Hugh and the 1st Brigade was already at Succalee in furtherance of his design.

The men were asked if able to march the distance required and all assented though their pale, haggard, faces told their inability. Nevertheless, each man filled his water can, and, the water carriers taking as much as they could carry, the advance sounded, and we were again tramping the dusty road. Owing to a fatal blunder, we never reached

[1] Lieutenant-Colonel George Vaughan Maxwell, 88th Foot.

Banda, but instead, about midday, saw through the mirage the tents of the 1st Brigade appearing like distorted woolpacks in a lake of water. In short, the place before us was Succalee.

The temperature that morning was 100° at sunrise, and became so distressing that the Europeans fell out by the wayside and as one after another was struck down by the sun, the remainder became terrified, and their fears were increased by remembering the effects of the sun on their comrades at Koonch. It was impossible to carry so many; the transport for the sick was overfull already, and the native carriers unequal to the burden. The water we carried was soon exhausted and excepting at one well by the road side, none was found on the line of march. Here the scramble for water was painful to witness; natives and Europeans alike appeared equally distressed. Numbers had fallen out by the way, and the Highlanders could go no further. This regiment was consequently left at the well and came in after sunset as best it could. The rest of us struggled on, and after some distance, crossed a dry river bed, and here, by digging holes in the sand, a small quantity [of water] was obtained.

At noon, when the tents of the 1st Brigade were seen, our Brigadier decided upon encamping, but the only well contained but insufficient muddy water, and a raid upon a miserable collection of mud huts procured but a few earthen vessels full. Those of us who were mounted scoured the country for wells, and at length one deeper than the rest was found and we pitched our tents. The sufferings of our beasts of draught and burden cannot be conceived. Over this one well it was necessary to place a guard to preserve order, and prevent waste. We were scarcely better off for forage and our rations were not enviable.

In the morning, the 1st Brigade marched again to Etora, and we, although directed to accompany, were unable to move our sick, yesterday's march having proved so disastrous. A day's halt, however, enabled us to join Sir Hugh, but under a new leader,[1] our Brigadier, Colonel Stewart,[2] having reported sick, and from that time took no further part in the campaign, but on reaching England in due course received the distinguished honour of the Bath!

On the 14th of May both brigades were together; the supply of water was hardly more plentiful; much distress continued; the country a dry, dusty plain without a blade of vegetation and scarce a tree; the villages all built of sun dried bricks, in colour like the plain around us. But as we approached the Jumna the dead level became cut up by ravines which, close to the river, were of great depth and intersected each other so that they were impracticable save to wild goats or light infantry.

[1] The command of the 1st Brigade now developed on Lieutenant-Colonel Robert Dennistoun Campbell, 71st Highlanders, who had served at Ghuznee (4th Light Dragoons) and in the Crimea (71st).

[2] Steuart.

VIII

Calpee

A T 3 a.m. on the morning of the 15th,[1] the Major General
and his brigade, together with Major Orr and the Contingent Force, again left us, and with little annoyance from
the enemy, reached Golowlee. Here these two forces encamped. The right of our 1st Brigade rested on the deep
ravines about a mile from the river Jumna, and both faced
Calpee which was six miles distant, eastward. Major Orr
was on Sir Hugh's left, and while Golowlee was immediately
opposite the 1st Brigade, the village of Teree was in front of
the Contingent troops.

On the following morning, at 3 a.m., we marched from
Etora to join the remainder of the force on the Jumna. It
was daylight before we were clear of the village and after
we had proceeded three miles, the enemy in great force was
visible on our left. There can be no doubt that he was
chagrined to find himself outwitted and outflanked, now
that we had turned the formidable defences constructed
across the main road to Calpee. It is quite possible too, he
may have had intelligence of our recent sufferings from
sunstroke, and concluded we were about to cross the Jumna
to Hindoostan proper.

It would be greatly interesting to have a book on the
mutiny, from one who took a leading part against us, and it
is a pity we did not extract more particulars from Tantia
before we sealed his fate. However, whatever the enemy's
conclusions were, he came on with a bold front and evident
determination, on seeing which, Colonel Campbell of the
Highlanders, commanding, halted and closed up the line of
march.

[1] 15 May 1858.

It is most difficult to write anything which could convey a description of our *impedimenta*: long strings of laden camels, ponderous elephants, thousands of bullocks laden with round shot and shell; bags of grain, spare stores of every description; led horses; trains of mules; huge pieces of cannon; unwieldy mortars; pontoon bridges; scaling ladders; sick in dhoolies [litters for carrying sick or wounded soldiers]; sick in wheeled ambulances; sick on camels; sick on foot; and, worse than all, an immense number of wheeled vehicles of the worst possible description, many broken down and all drawn by galled and exhausted cattle tended and driven by timid natives or unwilling agriculturalists pressed for service.

Some miles of these was always an anxious charge for the officers on rear guard. Fortunately, on this occasion one was in command who was equal to the occasion: it was Major Forbes. With him were one hundred and seventy of his own corps, the 3rd Bombay Cavalry, a weak troop of the 14th Dragoons under Lieutenant Beamish,[1] two guns, two hundred Hyderabad Cavalry, a company of the 3rd Europeans, one of Bombay Sappers and one hundred and sixteen of the 24th Native Infantry under Lieutenant Estridge.[2]

When the long baggage train arrived at one of the worst parts of the road, intersected by a ravine, Major Forbes saw the enemy in possession of Etora, from which we had marched. Here some of our followers who had strayed and remained behind, were killed, and their carts looted. A very considerable amount of commissariat stores and private baggage was lost.

The enemy gained courage as he advanced with a strength of apparently about six thousand men, of whom a large number were mutineers of the Bengal Cavalry, and apparently not much disorganised. There were clad in uniforms of grey, green, and yellow; equipped in fact as when in our service. Amongst their artillery were two heavy guns,

[1] Lieutenant William Henry Slingsby Beamish, 14th Light Dragoons.
[2] Lieutenant George Tyler Estridge, 24th Bombay Native Infantry.

drawn by elephants. Many of the infantry were in British uniform and retained the regulation musket.

When our rear guard was within three miles of camp, the enemy unlimbered and opened a precise fire at about six hundred yards: the consternation amongst the timid camp followers added considerably to Major Forbes' critical position. One of their shots killed four of the 24th sepoys; another, two of the Bombay Cavalry and some horses of the 14th Dragoons. Others were wounded and many were the hair breadth escapes. Hurrying on the line of baggage to his utmost, and maintaining a bold front to the enemy, combined with the unflinching steadiness of his little force, Major Forbes arrived in camp, fighting the whole distance.

It was at first thought the line of baggage had been brought into camp intact; afterwards, however, it was discovered that much had been lost. During the day, too, about three hundred bullocks, while seeking forage, were carried off by the enemy. Here again the mutinied cavalry of Bengal showed themselves a cowardly crew. There can be no doubt that they held our rear guard at their mercy, and this they knew, for twice they showed a disposition to charge, but feared.

The noise of heavy cannonade and rolls of musketry fire induced Colonel Campbell to occupy a small village, Muttra, which would have been a strong position to fall back upon in case of necessity, and moreover kept the enemy out of it. The report of heavy firing was not lost on Sir Hugh Rose who tore down to the rescue with the 1st Brigade. The enemy also received reinforcements and attacked Muttra, and now indeed the action became general along our entire front, for the site of the camp of the 2nd Brigade was on Major Orr's left, and facing Muttra. Thus the three forces faced Calpee and each had in its front a village, and the three villages were Golowlee, Diapoora and Muttra. Two purposes were thus served: the wells of water were secured and the shelter of the villages were so many strong positions for our infantry.

It was almost dark before the enemy ceased to molest us, but we maintained our position without striking a single tent although on several occasions the round shot rolled amongst them; nor did we suffer much from their fire, but very grievously from the sun. The sick were brought into camp in a continuous train. It is impossible to say what effect the ardent sun had upon the enemy, but unquestionably it affected the native element with us. Much of the evil perhaps might be set down to the unsuitable manner in which we clothe our native regular troops.

In the quiet evening we rode our horses a mile and a half to a well in the rear, to give them the deep draught they had earned, and we envied those of the 1st Brigade whom, a similar distance traversed, brought them to the plentiful waters of the Jumna.

On the 17th, mortars were placed in position before the tents of the 1st Brigade, to shell the ravines, and not far distant, yet beyond rifle range, we could discern the enemy's sentries posted on high ground. About 3 p.m. they again brought out their heavy guns and annoyed us by round shot which rolled among the picketted horses of the 14th. Little damage resulted but again the entire force was exposed to the sun.

Soon after dark, an officer of the 3rd Cavalry[1] reported that the enemy had turned our flank and captured two guns of the strong picket in out left front. Some truth was lent to the report by the hot haste with which a body of Hyderabad Cavalry galloped in. This was all a mistake; the gunners had not left their guns, neither had they been molested.

During the two following days, very frequent attempts were made by the mutineers to re-take the village of Muttra, but it was strongly occupied by the Highlanders, 24th Native Infantry, and Bombay Artillery, while the

[1] According to Sylvester's *Diary*, this would be Lieutenant Arundel Thomas Spens who served in the 3rd Bombay Light Cavalry from 1853 until he left the regiment, as a Major, in 1876.

Dragoons and Hyderabad Cavalry guarded the plain in front. The consumption of water during our two days' occupation had dried up the well in rear of our camp and rendered the water at Muttra too muddy for drinking purposes. It was therefore with great delight that we were permitted to move about two miles towards the river, at daybreak on the 19th.

Since our arrival at Muttra, we had often heard the distant sound of artillery, which we discovered to proceed from General Maxwell's camp on the opposite north bank of the Jumna. From his position he was able to throw shells into Calpee fort. Some of his staff had forded the river and communicated to Sir Hugh that not more than five hundred of the enemy were present in Calpee, all for the most part being in the ravines in our front.

An additional number of medical officers and water carriers had been required from Cawnpore, now but twenty-six miles distant.

The *reveille* sounded at 3 a.m., and by daybreak all our baggage was started before we left the ground. Major Orr's Contingent force had also moved before us, so that, crossing his old lines, we rapidly reached our new ground, and those of us who were able to get away sped over the rugged sides of the deep ravines which, for a mile in breadth, break up hereabouts the right bank of the river. The soil is a light coloured dry mud and calcareous glomerate which radiated the heat powerfully, and down amidst the deeper ravines, where the air stagnated, the temperature was terribly oppressive.

I cannot easily forget the relief I experienced at the sight of the broad stream at my feet, and it required some moments to believe it was real, and what wonder, after the deceptive mirage of Koonch! Not the least pleasing part of the sight was the swarm of thirsting men and animals drinking without stint. Returning up the precipitous banks, a loose horse, in galloping past, sent my horse and myself headlong down many feet. We were both bruised and cut considerably. On reaching camp I learnt that, after leaving our last encamping ground, and in consequence of the loss by death and the enemy of so many baggage animals, insufficient remained to move camp and therefore a number of the Highlanders' tents remained on the ground.

[A large blank space has been left in the manuscript at this point, except for the words, in pencil, 'Gall's tale'. It would seem that the narrator had intended to insert the account of some happening, given to him by Gall, but had never done so.[1]]

The heat abated some few degrees by our proximity to the Jumna, but the hot winds continued. At 3 a.m.[2] Sir Hugh Rose crossed the Jumna to direct Colonel Maxwell's co-operation with him up the opposite side of the river during our advance on Calpee. In our path along the broken ground which divided us from Calpee, was a village strongly held by the mutineers. It was of course a matter of importance to dislodge them, and General Maxwell was instructed to shell the village across the river at the time of our march on Calpee.

At about one o'clock in the day, thus carefully selecting the time most trying to us, the enemy attacked the mortar battery which I have described as existing in front of the 1st Brigade. Reinforcements of the 86th, 24th, and 25th Infantry regiments were hurried out of camp and drove him back, but with a loss to fighting strength on our side of ten men wounded and thirty sun-stricken. Lieutenant Jerome of the 86th was struck on the forehead by a spent ball from a great distance, and Lieutenant Forbes[3] of the 25th and Etheridge of the 24th were struck down by the sun. At dusk, the mortars, with some field guns, were left under the usual guard of 3rd Europeans and 86th Infantry.

[1] 'Gall's Tale' may have concerned the burning by him, of the Highlanders' tents, for which he received a 'wigging' from Sir Hugh Rose. Gall was furious as this was delivered in front of Abbott. (*Diary*.)

[2] 20 May 1858.

[3] Lieutenants Henry Edward Jerome, 86th, and John Foster Forbes, 25th Bombay Native Infantry.

The road from the Jumna to Cawnpore, and thence down the Grand Trunk road to Calcutta, was now safe, and many of our sick and wounded, together with the late Brigadier Stuart,[1] proceeded to England. My thermometer, in the shade of a double-roofed tent, rose to 115° daily.

Early on the 21st, reinforcements came across the Jumna from General Maxwell's brigade: these comprised two companies of his own regiment, the 88th,[2] some of the Rifle Brigade mounted on camels driven by Sikhs. It was indeed refreshing to see new faces and new uniforms.[3] We were all so jaded and debilitated by the excessive heat it is scarcely an exaggeration to say we were all more or less unequal to much exertion. There was, moreover, a common impression among us that spies, wearing the tin badges of our followers, frequented our camp and kept the enemy informed. I cannot however think such information as they could glean availed much, for none save those in the immediate confidence of the General commanding were in possession of any knowledge of his intended action. We however received intimation of theirs, and on this day we knew that in the morning was to be made their great attempt to drive us into the Jumna, under oath sworn on its sacred waters: we were therefore prepared.

Early on the 22nd, the whole of the sick, wounded, and baggage of both brigades were accumulated round the bazaar and commissariat stores, under guard of cavalry and infantry of the Contingent, four guns, and a wing of the 24th. At 8 a.m. Brigadier Stuart posted himself in the mortar battery with half Woolcombe's guns and some men of the 3rd Europeans. The remainder of our force was disposed as follows, in readiness to accept the challenge, and never having met a reverse, I think all were confident of success.

A long line of skirmishers (County Downs) under Colonel

---

[1] Although the name is here spelt 'Stuart', the reference is to Colonel Steuart, 14th Light Dragoons, and not to Brigadier C. S. Stuart.

[2] The Connaught Rangers (disbanded 1922).

[3] All dressed in clothes of a lavender hue. (*Diary*.)

Lowth stretched from the mortar battery to the river; on the left of the battery, reaching into more open ground, was stretched a wing of the 25th in skirmishing order; and supporting them were a troop of the Dragoons and one of the 3rd Bombay Cavalry, though the ground was bad for horsemen.

The main body of our troops was thus disposed. Centre of line; wing of 25th, half Woolcombe's battery under Lieutenant Strutt, and 21st company R.E. Left centre: Lightfoot's troop of Horse Artillery, squadron 14th Dragoons, a Royal Field battery, 71st Highlanders, and 3rd Europeans. Extreme left: the Hyderabad Contingent force, 88th Infantry and Rifles mounted, and here, as the ravines were shallower and ground more suited to cavalry, Major Gall with some of his regiment and Captain Abbott with his sowars [Indian cavalrymen], advanced in front of the heavy guns.

Soon after nine a.m. the enemy, true to his vow, advanced from Calpee and our videttes commenced to fall back, firing. The number advancing was not easily ascertained on account of the very broken nature of the ground; we could however discern that their cavalry and artillery were on the right of their line, avoiding the ravines on their left. A heavy cannonade took place on both sides, which so filled the ravines with smoke that the combatants could scarcely distinguish their foe, yet with quick perception the mutineers saw that the weakest point of our line was the mortar battery where Brigadier Stuart had stationed himself from the commencement. At this crisis, besides the artillerymen with the mortars and half Woolcombe's battery, there were present a few of the 3rd Europeans under Ensign Trueman of that regiment,[1] Serjeant-Major Graham, and the Brigadier.

Infuriated by opium, hemp, and more than probably by the Commissariat brandy taken from us on the affair of the rear guard, the enemy came on with great *élan*, and but for

[1] Ensign Thomas Trueman, 3rd Bombay Europeans.

a dashing charge of the mounted Rifles, led by Sir Hugh down a ravine in front of the mortars, the little band now mentioned must have been sacrificed and our line broken through. Our right and the enemy's left were now in contact and he broke and fled amid the cheers of the riflemen. Volleys of grape and musketry added to his confusion and flight.

All now joined in pursuit but our infantry were too prostrated to go far. The medical officers that day had a difficult task, not among the wounded, for they were comparatively few, but so many afflicted by sunstroke taxed our energies to the utmost, the more so as shade and water, above all remedies necessary, could not be had. General Maxwell had placed his artillery in readiness and opened with good effect as the enemy retreated on Calpee.

We knew that the rebel army had staked its almost only hope on this last throw, and having failed so signally and yet too with so many advantages, it would be unlikely to rally quickly. This belief induced the Major General to follow up the defeat and end the campaign by taking Calpee: no orders, however, reached us until late at night. These were for the Sabbath, for on a Sunday[1] we marched on Calpee.

All troops were directed to carry a day's cooked provisions, the cavalry and artillery to start at three in the morning, taking the road towards Jaloun, by which it was expected the garrison would escape. The infantry were to march up the river bank, taking the cavalry baggage, the remainder of the force, including the artillery park, bazaar, commissariat and hospital stores, sick and wounded, to assemble in front of Golowlee under a force commanded by Captain Hare.

This programme was carried out, the infantry in one long line, sweeping the ravines, the cavalry and artillery some distance in rear, as reserve. The 86th, as yesterday, swept the ravines on the river bank; the centre of the line

[1] 23 May 1858.

was commanded by Brigadier Stuart, and its left by Colonel Campbell who led his Highlanders.

Sir Hugh Rose, with a second column which included the Hyderabad Contingent, advanced considerably to the westward, moving along the Calpee Road. Accompanying him were Major Gall and Captain Abbott with Dragoons and native horse, as also General Maxwell's mounted Rifles.

The movement commenced soon after three in the morning. No opposition was encountered until the half-way village of Rehree was reached, and here a few shots were fired, notwithstanding the shells from Maxwell's mortars fell into it. Further on a panther and two hares were killed, and large columns of the enemy, heavily encumbered with baggage, could be seen retreating hastily.

The force under Sir Hugh met with no resistance, and the fort and city were reached and occupied. The former was a mere quadrilateral walled enclosure with corner towers, the walls loopholed with merlons. Its situation on the highest point of a very steep precipitous bank was commanding. Deep beneath was the river, the only refreshing object on which the eye could rest, for on every side, and across its banks, nothing but the wearying, dusty plain, cut up by ravines, could be seen. Attached to the river's brim, beneath the fort, were the ferryboats, until now in rebel possession.

Entering the fort by a drawbridge spanning a dry moat, a muddled arsenal met the eye. There was little save munitions of war: fifteen guns, a larger mortar and howitzer, conical piles of British shot, brass shell, muskets, firearms of many descriptions, tents, palls, band instruments, bugles, drums, pouches, packages of cartridges, sepoys' uniform tunics, Glengarries, armourers' tools, and about sixty-thousand pounds of gunpowder. Pity it was for them that no brave spirit of the Willoughby mould[1] had stayed to

---

[1] On 11 May 1857, during the revolt in Delhi, Lieutenant George Dodson Willoughby, Bengal Artillery (together with Lieutenants

light the fuze which would have buried many of us, and the fort, in the Jumna. Amongst the piles of uniform were some stripped from Wyndham's soldiery, bearing 88 and 92[1] on the regimental buttons.

Close beside the fort were the charred remains of officers' and armourers' bungalows, but a very large warehouse and shed remained. In this the troops crowded for the grateful shade. A fair sprinkling of neem trees, planted near the European residences, had been cut down.

The town, not far distant from the fort, was on the right bank of the river, which when full, is one mile across, but at this dry season the stream was narrow and ran beneath the bank on which we stood. The sandy bed, uncovered by water, was in places cultivated with water melons. Looking on the opposite bank, the tents of General Maxwell's force were visible, but the town itself was deserted. Tantia was said to have warned the population to leave if they valued their lives. Here and there in the deserted streets, pigs and pariah dogs disputed over putrid bodies; many of the houses were ruined by shells and all were empty.

While the infantry sheltered themselves in the ruined cantonment, General Rose directed the cavalry and artillery to pursue the retiring enemy on the Jaloun road. He was again too much affected, by the exposure, to lead, and thus, unfortunately, was not an eyewitness of events out of which arose circumstances scarcely conducive to the maintenance of that concord which up to now had mutually subsisted between officers of the European and Native cavalry.

George Forrest and William Raynor of the Veteran Establishment, Conductors John Buckley, George W. Shaw and John Scully, Sub-Conductor Crowe and Serjeants Edwards and Stewart) defended, and finally blew up, the powder magazine. Of this gallant band, only Forrest, Rayner and Buckley got clean away to Meerut, and were awarded the V.C.

[1] Probably '82'. The 92nd Highlanders were not with Windham whereas the 82nd were. This supposition is supported by the description of the buttons given by Sylvester in his *Diary*. They bore the Prince of Wales's feathers, as might be expected in the case of a regiment designated 'The Prince of Wales' Volunteers'.

Five weak troops of Dragoons, Lightfoot's battery, the 3rd Hyderabad Cavalry under Abbott, and fifty under Lieutenant Dowker, all under Major Gall's command, started from the 'Eighty Tombs', and shortly came up with the rear of the rebels who vacated some temples in disorder. A few fought, but for the most part their retreat became a disgraceful flight. Cutting the traces of their artillery horses, they abandoned their guns, ammunition, wheeled vehicles, camels, six elephants, forty bullocks, and an endless variety of arms, uniforms, grey regimental cloth,[1] cooking utensils and clothes. The fugitives, judging from the regimental buttons cut from the bodies of those killed, belonged to eleven Bengal Infantry regiments and to the Gwalior Contingent.

Unquestionably, much time was occupied by the cavalry in capturing the elephants, and in this work the squadrons were of necessity a good deal broken up, or perhaps an attempt could have been made to close with a body of cavalry which crossed our front at about four hundred yards, and passed into a village where a few halted for a moment and then galloped off with the rest.

The enemy's footmen had however been severely punished; Lightfoot disorganised a large mass with spherical case, and of these, Need's troop of Dragoons killed two hundred. Giles and Beamish greatly distinguished themselves. Captain Abbott outstript his men in the pursuit; his light weight and well-chosen path, the hard road, was an advantage which Gall, Barrett and Need, with their squadrons in broken ground, did not possess. Besides six guns the enemy at once abandoned, Lieutenant Dowker captured two, and Captain Abbott one – a British nine-pounder.

At length, Major Gall sounded the rally and collected

[1] The Light Cavalry of all three Presidencies were clothed in jackets of French grey, the Artillery being in dark blue, the Infantry in scarlet, and the Rifles in dark green. The sepoys of the Infantry still wore the scarlet coatee which, in 1855, had been replaced by the scarlet tunic in the British army.

together some two hundred men, but Abbott reporting his horses too exhausted for further pursuit, it was therefore abandoned. Even yet, Lightfoot was shelling stragglers on the Gwalior road, and Need's troop busily disposing of them. Water being available, the order was given, and while Major Gall's horse was drinking, bridleless near an enclosure, it was seized and almost carried off by four of the enemy.

Major Gall now crossed over to Lightfoot, intending to dispatch the trophies into camp and continue the pursuit, but the artillery horses were unequal to it. At this juncture Captain Teed arrived with a squadron of native cavalry, but even this reinforcement was of no avail as the fugitives had now sheltered themselves in villages, while their cavalry was ten miles away. Some reports, injurious to the Dragoons, were made to the Major General in reference to this pursuit; reports as discreditable to him who made them as they were unfounded.

At the ninth milestone on the Jhansi road, the Dragoons, having been fourteen hours in the saddle, turned their horses' heads for camp, in the belief that all the enemy's guns had been taken: it was however subsequently found that one or two had been taken with them.

Flown again too was our Joan of Arc: better so we thought as it was reported that Sir Robert Hamilton would not have permitted her execution had we caught her. We were informed by two camel drivers belonging to Captain Abbott, who were captured and taken to Calpee, that the Ranee and Banda Nawab left in palanquins the night previously, having suffered much consternation from the bursting of a shell from Maxwell's camp close beside her.

Captain Hare, with his regiment of Contingent Infantry, was placed in charge of the fort, and the force encamped at the 'Eighty Tombs' and though the ground was intersected by ravines, and clouds of blinding dust filled our camp, yet there was good water in plenty.

The day following our occupation of Calpee, the sick and wounded (about four hundred) came with the ordnance and commissariat from Golowlee, and General Whitlock, after having captured the hoards of treasure at Kirwee and Banda, had actually reached the Jumna, but some sixty miles lower. It will be recollected that we were not allowed to participate in the enormous prize which literally fell into his hands, though he was supposed to have cooperated with us, and for all we endured in the Central India campaign, we received never a farthing in prize money!

A column of observation was dispatched on the rebel track, but few amongst us thought much about them in the bustle of sending our European sick and wounded across the river to Cawnpore. No one doubted that our work was finished, and many like myself were desirous to join other appointments rather than remain doing garrison duty at Calpee, with regiments in which they were strangers and could feel no interest. General Beatson had already completed his two irregular cavalry regiments, for – it was stated – service in Oudh. I was all the more anxious therefore to join as all the mutineers were now congregating in that territory and indeed the Calpee garrison was supposed to have crossed the Jumna and gone there also.

Many were the speculations as to our future distribution: no part of the force appeared to appreciate the prospect of garrisoning Calpee, neither was this remarkable for all the troops were alien here. During the days of suspense, which were greater to none than to me, a few hours heavy rain fell and the consequent cooler temperature was an especial mercy to the sick, and doubtless saved many a life.

A report was circulated in camp that Sir Hugh Rose was directed to remain with the force, but declined, and on the 31st of May his determination to leave us was evident as his camp equipage and horses were for disposal, and my fears were set at rest. After accompanying the 3rd Europeans to Jhansi, I was free to proceed to join General Beatson. H.M.'s 14th Dragoons and 86th Regiment were directed to march on Gwalior and I took a farewell dinner with the regiment.

On the first of June the effect of the rain had passed away; the extreme heat returned. It was again 110° in my tent. News from Whitlock's column was brought me by a native: that force was directed to garrison Calpee and march at once. This caused much rejoicing. Sir Hugh Rose issued his farewell order, and at one a.m. on the fourth the reveille for the return march of the Hyderabad troops to Dekkan was a gladsome sound to me, as I accompanied them. The moon was shining gloriously on the Jumna and my heart was light as I looked on it for the last time.

Our way lay over the old camp ground, rife enough with stenches, and then over the track of the pursuit; the swollen corpses, hideous and rotting, were ghastly enough in the moonlight. We also passed that piece of road which the enemy had so cunningly prepared for our march from Etora. It was a spot well chosen, for on either side the road was a ravine, which they had converted into a rifle pit. The trench, cut through the road itself, was strengthened by an earthen breastwork, but the guns which had yawned over it were in our possession, and the gunners going fast to the earth from whence they came.

Eleven miles brought us to Atta, our first halting ground. It was pleasant once again to leave the din of camp and breathe purer air. Already the inhabitants were returning to their homes and neglected fields: the British rule was something more just here than a thing of the past. To have sweet water enough and to waste was a luxury, yet somehow I had a presentiment that I should be recalled and every footstep approaching my tent startled me, but no! my fears were groundless. Day passed and the repose was thoroughly appreciated by all. Trumpet and bugles sounded 'watch setting' and we slept under orders to continue our journey, at two next morning.

My fears abated and I slept soundly and on waking it was broad daylight; the sun was already hot on my tent, all had been a dream; it was not true that I had left the force. This was my momentary waking impression, but I rushed to the next tent: it was Dr Burns'.[1] Here in a moment I learnt that in the night the Contingent force had been ordered to halt and await further orders. A faint hope remained: these orders might be to go on, but why should I delay? Two others like myself, Fenwick and Bonus of the Engineers, had availed themselves of the Contingent as an escort and we consulted together. I was for attempting to traverse the thousand miles alone: their prudent counsels prevailed and fortunately so. The country was everywhere unsafe; Major Orr had just had an affair on the high road in advance of us with a Thakoor [a chief, baron or lord, especially among Rajputs] and two hundred and fifty men, of whom he killed a hundred.

Captain Abbott resolved to set our conjectures on the cause of the halt at rest by dispatching a camel to Calpee. He quickly returned with the intelligence that Scindiah's army had mutinied after being joined by the Calpee garrison, and had now occupied the fort and city of Gwalior! We could scarcely credit this new phase of the mutiny because Major Robertson and the 14th Dragoons should by this [time] have actually reached Gwalior, calculating from the date they left Calpee.

On the 6th of June we moved two miles; here we received a messenger from Sir Hugh who, with his force, was four miles distant and proposed joining us on the next day, but as he asked us 'what news' we still refused belief in the Gwalior story. The day following, no room for doubt remained. We marched at one in the morning to Attaria and joined Sir Hugh who had resumed his duties and brought with him the cavalry, Madras Sappers, and horse brigade, leaving the siege train and Royal Engineers, together with the wings of the 3rd European and 24th Regiments to hold Calpee until the arrival of H.M.'s 5th Fusiliers,[2] expected.

---

[1] Assistant-Surgeon George Alexander Burns (1833–83), 5th Infantry, Hyderabad Contingent.
[2] Now The Royal Northumberland Fusiliers.

IX

Gwalior

From the troops accompanying Sir Hugh we now learned the sequence of events which had followed the capture of Calpee. Major Robertson's column of observation, which had followed the rebels, comprised a wing of his regiment, a troop of Dragoons, squadron of 3rd Bombay Cavalry, one hundred and fifty Hyderabad Cavalry, and No. 18 Light Field Battery. On the 29th he was further reinforced by a squadron of Dragoons and a wing of the 86th.

This force, having reached Srawun, about thirty miles distant from Calpee, discovered that the fugitives had not taken the direction supposed, across the Jumna, but on being reinforced by mutineers from Bareilly, were at Indoorkee on the Scinde river, in the dominions of the Maharajah Scindiah,[1] and though this much was known to Sir Hugh Rose, no suspicion was awakened that Gwalior was threatened. It was but natural to suppose that the Maharajah could control his own army, nor could anyone suppose that army, having remained quiet so long, should revolt now that the tide had turned so decidedly against the rebels; nevertheless it was even so.

Scindiah's army, on the arrival of the Ranee and her troops [disorganised by their retreat], fired a few shots, which doubtless by pre-concerted arrangement were so many greetings of welcome. Scindiah, however, professed to have gone out to Bahadurpoor in order to give battle to the Ranee, and on being deserted by his army (all save a few faithful Maharattas), he narrowly escaped with life, by flight to Agra.

---

[1] Jeeajee Rao Scindiah, Maharajah of Gwalior (1835–66). Placed on throne in 1843.

I can scarcely say much credence was obtained in camp by this tale, nevertheless the ugly fact remained that we, worn out by toilsome marches, sunstroke and bad food, had again to contend with, it was estimated, forty thousand men in possession of an almost impregnable stronghold, and not only had the enemy swollen by such vast numbers, but Scindiah's jewels, treasury, arsenal, and immense stores of provisions (laid up for us) had fallen into their hands. In addition, huge banks of clouds, now visible at each sunset, were the harbingers of the monsoon, and exposure to constant rain and sudden depression of temperature, consequent, would without doubt bring cholera, fever, and dysentry among us.

While encamped at Attaria, Major Robertson sent in additional particulars of the revolt, upon the first intelligence of which, the Major General had dispatched Brigadier Stuart with the 1st Brigade to his support, for Robertson was powerless in case attacked by such overpowering numbers, and now both he and Brigadier Stuart were awaiting the Major General and more troops, at Indoorkee.

[At this point there is either a page of manuscript missing, or Sylvester has inadvertently numbered the following page incorrectly.]

Next morning[1] we advanced to Jaloun, a large but wretched looking place with scarce a building of any note. The day was so far memorable to me as the anniversary of my joining the 14th Dragoons at the commencement of the present campaign. Since then we had, according to the Major General's farewell order, 'marched a thousand miles and taken a hundred guns', and it appeared that we were necessitated to take a hundred more, and so we struggled night after night through the small hours, on our way to Gwalior.

At the Pahooj river the inhabitants told us that the rebel army had crossed, about six thousand strong; of these two thousand were horse. Perhaps this was an exaggeration, and

[1] 8 June 1858.

perhaps they exaggerated when they told us that Tantia was two days in the Maharajah's camp before his troops rebelled.

Somehow, the marches we were now making were apparently more tedious than ever. The country was in all respects similar to that around Calpee: light, dusty soil, neither trees nor stones, the towns and villages of sun dried brick, all suggestive of poverty and oppression; no roads, and the beaten tracks, even for vehicles, so intersected with ravines that our patience in long hot nights was sorely tried, while thousands of our impracticable bullock carts were driven through them. The night on which we reached Indoorkee these obstacles to military progress in India were started at seven in the evening: the force marched four hours afterwards, only to find some hundreds jammed in a ravine between high sand dunes. Here Sir Hugh, irate beyond measure, descended in their midst, vowing dire vengeance on the drivers and, calling for fire, made a show of burning the whole convoy.

Indoorkee was a wretched collection of mud huts and a mud fort on a fine stream of water, the Scinde river. The heat here was intolerable and one of Hare's soldiers died of sunstroke. I recollect Lall Singh burning long and brightly that evening not far from my tent; I thought he would never go out [Lall Singh, Red Lion. This may refer to the sun or to Hare's dead sepoy on his funeral pyre]. At Amyne[1] we were twenty-four miles distant from Scindiah's capital. Sir Robert Hamilton was with us: it was his opinion that Scindiah's troops were unwilling to fight and had revolted because their master had refused the rebels passage through his territory. Here we read for the first time Sir Hugh Rose's lengthy dispatches of the operations before Jhansi, and as it is said every drummer boy at Waterloo considered he had mainly contributed to victory, a similar idea may have accounted for the many disappointed expressions among the group of eager listeners at Amyne.

[1] Reached on 12 June.

We now caught up the Column of Observation and the 1st Brigade. Bengal troops had garrisoned Calpee, and the liberated remainder of our force was but seventeen miles behind at Mahona. The medical staff was prostrated; not one remained able for duty: I was therefore again ordered back from Amyne. Hitherto I remained proof against exposure and fatigue, but this was the last straw that broke the camel's back. I reached Mahona, alone, for all my requests to be allowed an escort were refused by Captain Macdonald, Assistant Quarter Master General. On arrival I was so prostrated that it was with difficulty I could attend to the sick.

Just before reaching Gwalior, Sir Robert Napier (now Lord Napier of Magdala)[1] arrived to assume command of the force, but as Sir Hugh still remained, Sir Robert reverted temporarily to the 2nd Brigade.

On the 16th of June we came in sight of the huge rock fortress of Gwalior, and on this side, about three miles distant from the fort, was the British cantonment of Morar, prettily shaded by trees. Roofs of bungalows and a steeple peered out from among them. If an incentive to fight was wanting, at least the prospect of shelter offered something.

The enemy was present in the cantonment of Morar, in what force we could not ascertain as much of his force was hidden by houses and trees. Our force was arranged in two columns, led respectively by General Rose and Sir Robert Napier, all our artillery being in the first line which advanced with the Highlanders, 86th, 25th, Hyderabad Infantry and Madras Sappers skirmishing. Our baggage and hospitals were in rear, protected by the second line under General Napier, who advanced *en echelon* from the right.

Silence was soon broken by the enemy's powerful battery

[1] Brevet-Colonel Sir Robert Cornelis Napier (1810–90), Bengal Engineers. Severely wounded in the Sutlej campaign. Present at Mooltan and Goojerat. Chief of Staff with General Outram at first relief of Lucknow. Commanded 2nd Division in China, 1860. Commanded Abyssinian Expedition, 1867–8. Raised to the peerage, 1868. Field Marshal, 1883.

which was shortly rendered untenable by our strong brigade of artillery in the front line. In the broken ground, the enemy disputed the line of skirmishers, and cost us the life of Lieutenant Neave and six of his corps[1] – the Highlanders – and while every inch was disputed with the infantry, the treacherous nature of the ground over which the cavalry advanced cost the lives of several; in fact, the Contingent horse suffered heavily.

Before our determined advance, the enemy retired towards the city, pursued by the 14th and Hyderabad Cavalry. Gowan, with a troop of Dragoons, did great execution, and in two hours from the advance, we had won the cantonments – an invaluable shelter – for strange to say, they had been very little injured, and much of the wood and forage stored by the Maharajah was untouched. The sight of a well-kept cantonment, with its houses, gardens, church and road, shaded by an avenue of trees, was both humanising and refreshing; neither did it necessitate being as prostrate as I then was, to appreciate it. The church had been in part despoiled, but we cannot reprobate the heathen for that, since a large section professing Christianity would imitate their act if permitted now in England.

My work being over, I established myself in a small summer house in one of the gardens.[2] Near me was a well of cool water, and parching with drought at my feet were flower beds of pomegranate and jasmine, fig, lime and guava trees. It was curious to imagine where now was the hand that had tended them. Most of the force, when encamped, had succeeded in gaining the friendly shelter of a roof or tree to shade their tents.

Other forces had not been idle during our advance on Scindiah's capital. Brigadier Smith,[3] with the Rajpootana

---

[1] Lieutenant Wyndham Neave, Serjeant Hugh McGill, one corporal and two privates, 71st Highlanders. The others are unknown.

[2] At this time Sylvester was suffering from jaundice and was messing with the 3rd Europeans. (*Diary*.)

[3] Lieutenant-Colonel Michael William Smith, 3rd Dragoon Guards.

1 *Deputy Surgeon-General John Henry Sylvester, a self-portrait painted after his retirement*

2 *Lieutenant-Colonel
Richard Herbert Gall,
14th Hussars,* 1862

3 *Maharajah
Scindiah,* 1861

4 *The Jaken Bagh, Jhansi, scene of the massacre of 8 June 1857*

5 *Jhansi Fort*

6 *The Oorcha Gate, Jhansi. The 3rd Bombay European Regiment assault the city on either side of this gate*

7 *The Fort at Dhar*

Major-General William Fergusson Beatson, K.S.F. (Spain)

9 *'Rather solemn at X'mas, 1861'—Assistant-Surgeon J. H. Sylvester.*

10 *Lieutenant James Leith, 14th (The King's) Light Dragoons, winning the Victoria Cross by saving the life of Captain Arthur Need*

11 *Encampment at Ahmednuggur of General Woodburn's Brigade, 13–18 June 1857. From a sketch made by Assistant-Surgeon J. H. Sylvester for the* Illustrated London News

12 *Gwalior Fortress*

13 *View of Bazaar and Church, Simla*

14 *Umbeyla Campaign: camp of the 3rd Sikhs in foreground*

15 *British and Indian officers, 11th Bengal Cavalry, Peshawur, 1862. Sylvester is standing in the centre of*

Field Force marched from Sipree to Kotah-ke-Serai, four miles south-east of Gwalior; Major Orr, with the Hyderabad force, had been directed to proceed to Maharajpore, an old battle field fourteen miles to the south-west;[1] Lord Clyde had dispatched a field battery, a wing of European infantry, two hundred Sikhs, and two squadrons of Meade's Horse[2] from Agra to the north, and thus, with our advance eastward, the enemy's reflections when on the high summit of the rock of Gwalior, could scarcely have been congratulatory. Fate however ordained that the Rajpootana Force should bear the brunt of the battle, and be in at the death of the Ranee of Jhansi.

It was the second day after our capture of the cantonments that this force, while preparing to encamp in hilly and broken ground, was attacked by the Ranee's army. Brigadier Smith at once withdrew to more advantageous ground and accumulated his baggage and hospitals near an old fort.

The action was commenced by a heavy fire from the Ranee's artillery. It was replied to by Smith's artillery, and the enemy driven on the broken ground. H.M.'s 95th Foot under Colonel Raines, and the 10th Bombay Infantry under Colonel Pelly[3] advanced impetuously, drove the enemy behind his breastworks, and took these by a charge, following up the retreating enemy. After proceeding to the summit of a distant ridge, the pursuit was checked by the presence of a large body of the enemy, both cavalry and infantry,

[1] Sir Hugh Gough defeated the Mahrattas at Maharajpore on 29 December 1843. In this battle, Captain (later Sir Henry) Havelock, the hero of Lucknow, distinguished himself.

[2] A regiment then recently raised by Captain (later Colonel Sir Richard John) Meade (1821–94), 65th Bengal Native Infantry and Brigade-Major of the Gwalior Contingent when it mutinied in June 1857. Meade's Horse was later absorbed by Mayne's Horse.

[3] Colonel Julius Augustus Robert Raines (who had served in the Crimea) commanded the 95th Foot, which later became the 2nd Bn The Sherwood Foresters. Colonel Pelly of the 10th Bombay Native Infantry has not been found, but there was a Captain William Parris Pelly in that regiment.

F

with guns in position, not far distant. The shot and shell from these guns of the enemy reached the ranks of the 95th, and some attempt was made by the rebel artillery to enfilade them, but this was frustrated by the Bombay Artillery, and Colonel Raines led the infantry across the Gwalior road to attack the scarlet clad cavalry of Gwalior, but again as always on prior occasions, they retreated on Phool Bagh, near the city, suffering however some loss from a volley delivered during their hesitation.

Brigadier Smith had now gained the heights commanding the extensive plain in front of the city, a plain often used by the Maharajah's army as a parade ground. Nothing could have been more inviting for a charge, and across it dashed a squadron of the 8th Hussars,[1] from the mouth of a narrow pass to the Phool Bagh, a distance of two miles, traversing the heart of the enemy's camp. In this gallant affair, two guns and a quantity of tent equipage fell into our possession; and more than all, the Ranee of Jhansi died, it is said by a carbine shot,[2] and though there is I believe some doubt on the manner of her death, yet the most authentic evidence now exists that she was killed, and burnt after the manner of Hindoos. Perhaps, if Macaulay's New Zealander quits his seat on London Bridge, to visit India, he may read this gallant woman's deed sculptured by her kindred, in marble, for though we properly execrate her memory for espousing a cause which permitted the masacre of innocent women and children, yet we must recollect the mutineers were waging a war of extermination, by no means so great an offence in Asiatic eyes as in ours.

The leaders of this splendid charge were Colonel Hicks and Captains Heneage and Morris.[3] They, together with a

[1] Now amalgamated with the 4th Hussars as the Queen's Royal Irish Hussars.

[2] Fired by a man of the 8th Hussars. It has also been said that, after being struck by the carbine bullet, she was cut down by the sabre of another Hussar. Accounts of her death vary considerably.

[3] Lieutenant-Colonel Thomas William Hicks (1808–92), Bombay Artillery, the officer in charge of the Artillery of the Central India

number of the troopers, suffered greatly from the heat:
Captain Heneage was recovered with difficulty. No sooner
did the enemy recover from his consternation, consequent
on the Hussars' attack, than he rallied his forces and again
threatened Brigadier Smith's brigade, but content with his
laurels, he withdrew to an amphitheatre of hills, and
encamped.

The day following these events,[1] Sir Hugh, leaving the
2nd Brigade in Morar cantonment, marched at sunrise, to
skirt the city to Kotah-ke-Serai. During the entire route,
we could hear the enemy's guns to the left of the position
of Smith's brigade. At night, having accomplished half the
distance, we bivouacked on the banks of the river Morar,
and on the morrow, after a junction having been effected
with the Rajpootana Force, arrangements were commenced
to take the city, and the Maharajah Scindiah arrived from
Agra.

The enemy still held the ridge on Brigadier Smith's left
and, as a canal intervened, the Madras Sappers under
Lieutenant Gordon[2] speedily bridged it; neither could
anyone, after seeing these men work under a broiling sun,
doubt their vast superiority in physical endurance over the
sepoys of Bengal and Bombay. Nothing daunted their
cheerful disposition, and during the few days they fell to
my charge I was surprised to find them pitching my tent,
cleaning my boots, and performing a number of small
kindnesses which, in the estimation of the typical old sepoy
officer of Bengal [a European officer of a sepoy regiment],
would have so degraded his pets as to have disqualified them
for service.

While the bridge was thrown over the canal, some heavy
guns were brought to bear upon the enemy's position on

Field Force, Captain Clement Walker Heneage, 8th Hussars, who had
charged with the Light Brigade at Balaclava, and was to win the V.C.
Probably Lieutenant Robert M. Bonner Maurice, 95th Foot.

[1] 18 June 1858.

[2] 2nd Lieutenant Harry James Grant Gordon, Madras Engineers,
doing duty with the Madras Sappers and Miners.

the ridge, but with no good effect. Some of our elephants
and artillerymen were killed, and stocks of forage near the
canal set on fire. More infantry and guns could be seen
ascending the height: this drew the 86th, 95th, and
Bombay 10th and 25th Regiments across the canal, where
they attacked both flanks of the enemy's infantry. The
86th, rushing up the ridge, drove the enemy out of his
battery, and captured three of Scindiah's English made
cannon, leaving these to be turned on the enemy by the
10th and 95th. The County Downs continued to pursue the
enemy towards the city. Another eminence held by the
enemy was cleared by gallant leading of Roome[1] with his
men of the 10th. Five more pieces of artillery were taken
and the gunners hunted down the slopes to Gwalior.

The force was now fairly before Scindiah's capital and
its appearance was very imposing. In the background stood
the fort, a huge igneous rock with abrupt overhanging
cliffs, aided by every artificial means to defy assault. It was,
moreover, crowned by a parapet bristling with artillery,
constantly firing.

In front was the city, consisting of an old and a new portion. The former lies at the eastern base of the rock and
was built before the Christian era. Trees and gardens
surrounded it in great profusion, while palaces and monumental buildings dotted the foliage. On the left of the old
city stood the new, a growth of which the germ sprang
from the ancient Maharatta camp, and now had grown into
a large and flourishing capital, furnished with barracks,
magazines, and handsome public buildings. This modern
portion of Gwalior, still called the camp or luskhar, was the
object of our immediate advance, for though it was believed
that General Rose had not intended attacking it until the
next day, his impetuous attack and signal success had
driven matters too far to admit delay.

A rapid movement to the plain (while our camp remained well guarded in the amphitheatre before men-

---

[1] Lieutenant Frederick Roome, 10th Bombay Native Infantry.

tioned), now took place. Hordes of the enemy could be seen
in hurried movement, firing furiously. Little time was lost
in forming columns and crossing the plain to our adversaries: shrapnel was thrown at them in plentiful showers;
the 95th and 10th Bombay Infantry rushed along the
streets, joined by the 3rd Bombay Cavalry, and drove all
before them; the grand army was in full flight – cavalry
leading – in the direction of the British residency, a building
situated seven or eight miles distant, on the Agra road.

While pursuing through the streets, into which an ill
judged zeal had led the Bombay Cavalry, one of its officers,
Lieutenant Mills,[1] received a mortal wound.

Again the fugitives, in attempting to carry with them a
quantity of ammunition and guns, were intercepted.
Brigadier Smith overtook them with the mounted portion
of his force, captured several guns, inflicted all the punishment he was able, only desisting when darkness rendered
further pursuit impossible.

The fort was reported by some officials of the Maharajah
to be evacuated, nevertheless firing continued. Lieutenants
Rose and Waller[2] were placed in charge of the gateway and
Colonel Robertson occupied the cities. The night passed
quietly, but at daybreak the fort guns again opened on the
Luskhar. Rose and Waller, with some men of their regiments and some of the Maharajah's police, ascended the
winding steep to the outer gate at the foot of which were a
few shallow steps, but the outer gate, which is called
Hatipul, being closed, obstructed their entrance. This being
opened by force, the gallant Rose sped in, passing six other
gates, unclosed, but on reaching the archway of the last, he
and his party were opposed by a gun and a body of fanatics
who had sworn to die in defence of the fortress. Dashing
over the gun he closed with the desperate body of defenders

[1] 1st Bombay Lancers. Cornet William Mills of this regiment is shown
in East India Registers as 'killed in action, Gwalior, 19/6/58'.

[2] Lieutenants Wellington Rose and William Francis Frederick Waller,
25th Bombay Native Infantry.

and fell mortally wounded by the side of eight of his men.
The fortress was taken, but at the cost of one much beloved
in the force. Rose was one of the officers who escaped from
Gwalior at the time its Contingent mutinied. His companion in the gateway, Waller, received the Cross of Valour.

The entrance to the fortress was through a winding
passage between heavy masonry walls, watched by the
muzzles of traversing guns, and closed by seven gates. On
the rock, at a height of three hundred feet, were large
tanks of water and ample shelter for a garrison, but the
memory of conical hill north west of Jhansi was probably
too fresh in the minds of many of Tantia's followers to
suggest the occupation of a site so favourable for invest-
ment. It is clear from the experience of this campaign that
the mutineers never willingly occupied a position where
their retreat was in danger of being cut off, and further,
their chiefs invariably escaped at the first symptom of reverse.

The troops under General Napier which had occupied
Morar, having had a short respite, started the morning after
the capture of Gwalior, in pursuit, but while passing the
fort a detour was necessary as the fanatics, at that hour
being in possession, annoyed the passing column with
round shot, and when it had accomplished twenty-seven
miles at sunset, the enemy was reported to be yet some
miles distant.

A bivouack was ordered at the village of Samowli until
daybreak when the column again advanced, and overtook
the enemy at Jowra-Alipore. Here, near the village, they
had succeeded in bringing a large park of artillery: on
either side were stationed masses of infantry, and cavalry
hovered on their flanks.

General Napier disposed his force in two lines: in front,
Lightfoot's guns, supported by sixty Dragoons and two
hundred and fifty Contingent sabres; in reserve, fifty
Bombay Cavalry[1] under Lieutenant Dick, and a squadron
of Meade's Horse.

[1] 3rd Bombay Light Cavalry.

The enemy, as usual, fired first. Our Horse Artillery galloped to a small eminence, opened on the enemy's right flank, when he turned and fled precipitately. The gunners and 3rd Contingent Cavalry dashed into the enemy's park and took it almost without resistance. The fugitives sought the cover of villages for shelter, while the cavalry accounted for as many possible. Two or three hundred were said to have fallen, but without infantry it was impossible to clear the villages. Private Nowell of the Dragoons won the Victoria Cross.

On the morning of the 26th, General Napier returned to Morar with his trophies – one elephant, twenty-five brass and one iron gun. Most of the former were British cannon, taken from the Maharajah's arsenal. Tantia and the Rao Sahib[1] again escaped.

Preparations similar to those of Calpee were again in progress for the distribution of the force, the operations of which were virtually at an end. Before separating, however, a formal reinstatement of the Maharajah Scindiah was directed. This took place at sunrise on the 28th of June, when Sir Hugh Rose and the Divisional Staff, together with all officers off duty, escorted him to his palace in Phool Bagh. The city was all astir; the streets, so recently the scene of war and bloodshed were thronged by a hundred and fifty thousand of Scindiah's subjects who, gaily clad in bright colours, and apparently rejoiced at the issue of events, rendered the scene both pleasing and impressive.

After the usual ceremonies of the Durbar, the Maharajah desired to express his gratitude by distributing a medal to all who had been engaged. The proposal found favour with Sir Hugh Rose and Sir Robert Hamilton, and few or no dissentients existed then among the officers of the force, but, like the prize money for the campaign, it was never heard of more and the proposal died with the echo of our guns.[2]

---

[1] A nephew of the Nana Sahib.
[2] This gift, which never materialised, was described by Sylvester as 'a star of most elegant design, the metal to be of frosted silver, the crest

Again permission was accorded me to join General Beatson, and taking advantage of Captain Abbott's return to the Nizam's territories, I left with his regiment on the 29th of June. This time I had no forebodings of recall, moreover, I had become so thoroughly exhausted of late that it was only by great effort I could perform any duty.

The rain now fell in torrents, the hot winds ceased, and the rapidity with which the parched, dusty soil changed into a carpet of emerald green was marvellous. The cooler atmosphere, better food, and sleep, were indeed luxuries we fully appreciated.

Simultaneously with our departure, the 2nd Brigade returned to Jhansi for the monsoon. General Napier assumed command at Morar and Sir Hugh Rose with two of his staff joined Abbott's escort to the Dekkan. We made long marches, losing no time by the way. Sir Hugh and two of his staff generally encamped some short distance from Abbott, and often extended his hospitality to us at dinner. At Goonah, through which we passed, Captain Mayne was busy organising two regiments of cavalry, but here Sir Hugh's camp was plundered of much private baggage and, amongst other prized articles, a presentation sword was taken. Every effort then, and subsequently, was made to recover the property, but in vain. The village of Goonah was surrounded and searched, fruitlessly.

On the 11th of July we had reached Puchore, and here Sir Hugh Rose left us by bullock train to assume command of the Poona Division of the army. The roads had become knee deep in black mud, but even this was compensated by cooler weather. It is impossible to conceive what we should have done to overtake rebels under such circumstances. Seven troop horses belonging to the Hyderabad regiments

---

of the Prince of Gwalior, a snake of gold to entwine the bar – the word "Gwalior", and figures 1858, to be engraven on a facet where the bars cross, and an orange ribbon to suspend it'. (*The Campaign in Malwa and Central India.*) Cornet Charles Forbes, 3rd Bombay Light Cavalry, stated in a diary that acceptance of the 'Gwalior Cross' was not permitted.

died in one day, and the mortality among the baggage animals was of course greater. On reaching Indore we could discover no trace of the past; the buildings had all been restored.

At Simrool rain fell in torrents which sadly impeded the march of Abbott's corps; I therefore hurried on alone, deeming the country tolerably safe. Nothing could exceed the beauty of the ghauts as I descended the wild wooded ravines, with torrents of water pouring down each gorge and rocky fissure. Deepening the gloom were huge clouds, so heavily laden with rain that they gladly rested on the highest peaks and summits. The glorious redundance of vegetation, and animal life amongst it, was indeed a happy change from the superheated, sterile, and parched ravines of the Jumna.

Attended by one native groom, I accomplished about twenty miles each day upon the road, where scarcely a year ago we had suffered so severely from cholera. Few persons would have considered my journey a pleasing one amid torrents of rain and terrible roads, but as I had become inured to the sun, I could very well march the entire day, and each night, by placing myself under care of the head of each village, I took no harm. Everywhere chuppatties [flat unleavened cakes], eggs and milk could be procured in abundance, and these required no more talent to cook than my syce [groom] was equal to. One thing, however, was very disagreeable: from the moment I arrived until my departure from any place, I was the cynosure of all eyes, and those who know India will recollect how, for long hours, a Hindoo villager will stand immovably with a fixed and stolid stare at anything novel, neither will he betray the slightest emotion of either surprise, pleasure, disgust, or annoyance. If I smiled I got no smile in return, if I laughed, the same impassive stare continued. The sight of an officer in uniform, I thought, could hardly be a novelty in their eyes, and at times the interest I attracted puzzled me exceedingly.

At length, at Adjuntah, the crowd that flocked to the

serai in which I had halted so thoroughly irritated me that I begged my horsekeeper to drive the people away, but he demurred, and said on no account, as it was purely a matter of respect, and conduced considerably to my safety as well as to the facility with which I procured fresh bullocks and provisions at every stage. An explanation followed: the faithful Ramah, who had accompanied me from Kirkee through the whole of my wanderings, was laden with valuables – no doubt looted from the enemy's dead – and fearing for these, as well as his life while travelling in this unprotected state, he had made a practice of telling the head men of each village that I was the great General who had led the force from the shores of Western India to the Jumna; that I in fact had conquered all the rebel hordes of Tantia and the Ranee, and he further requested me to recall how vigorously he had polished my sabre on arrival in each halting place, and this too, he assured me, had been done for the furtherance of the same desirable object, and the natives had invested that scimitar with supernatural powers. The idea was by no means bad, and I knew not whether to be most angry or amused. The natives of the Dekkan must undoubtedly have thought – if they ever think – that we treat our successful generals badly enough by sending them off, when done with, long journeys alone, in mud and rain, to feed on boiled eggs and indigestible chuppatties.

Adjuntah, famous for its celebrated temples, carved from the solid rock, has long been the residence of Major Gill, who under the direction of Government, copied the most interesting paintings from the interior of the caves: many of these, however, were destroyed by fire in the South Kensington Museum. Major Gill's residence was an old Hindoo temple which he had fitted as a dwelling. It was, moreover, the same in which the Duke of Wellington slept after the battle of Assaye,[1] and where he wrote his dispatches.

[1] Fought on 23 September 1803, when Wellington (then General Wellesley), with 4,500 European and Native troops, defeated Scindiah with over 30,000.

Major Gill is famous for hospitality, and hearing that a stranger had arrived in the serai, he at once invited me to his house and received me with as much kindness and attention as though I had been the veritable conqueror of Central India. His residence, embosomed in choice trees, and covered with every variety of flowering creeper and rose, looked into a yawning ravine which at that season echoed with the roar of a torrent, and on either side was a dense dwarf jungle, from which Major Gill had shot many a leopard and tiger. His collection of pictures and photographs of dead game were full of interest, and he begged me to tarry, but I was now close to Jaulnah, long since vacated by the hospitable 6th Madras Cavalry, and as General Beatson had chosen it to organise his two regiments, I hastened onwards, reaching it at noon on the 29th of July.

I well recollect how impatiently I cantered the last mile, with the cantonment in sight; how pleasant it appeared to me as its church and buildings dotted the luxuriant fields and gardens for then, above all times in the year, vegetation was most abundant; neither can I recall a more desirable Indian station than Jaulnah.

Riding to the cavalry lines, I found them full of natives just such as we had been killing. Scarcely one in a score was dressed in uniform, but the remainder in every imaginable variety of dress. These then were Beatson's troopers. I followed one, whom I requested to point out the General's residence. My only suit – an undress cavalry uniform – had long been strengthened by reinforcements of leather, and though hardly calculated to make a favourable impression, it was the best I had for the occasion. His bungalow was besieged by applicants for enlistment, strings of horses hung about what had once been a garden, but now, tramped by men and horses, looked much like those I had left behind in Gwalior.

Seated at a table covered with pistols, small arms, and a few papers, were the General and his Brigade

Major,[1] surrounded by a bevy of the cutthroat looking desperadoes such as I had encountered outside. Some of these were seated on the floor, others standing. The former were the native officers who rose and saluted me. The General, who was clad in a green baize tunic and red baize overalls tucked into jack boots, welcomed me cordially and introduced me to his braves. A bed in the adjoining room and the table at which he sat was all the furniture in the establishment and he assured me this was his habitual complement. The remaining necessaries of life were always kept in his holsters ready for any emergency. Ordering his saddle to be brought, he emptied them on the table while the Dekkan nobles (as he characterised his native officers) looked on without a smile. I cannot recall all the items which were produced: a hoof pick, piece of soap, a tin cup, a powder horn, wads and bullets, a loaf of bread, some tea, and a towel occur to me. I was both tired and hungry, having ridden thirty-six miles since daybreak but politeness compelled me to appear interested in this puerile display. I silently hoped it might be long ere I was invited to dine with my new chief; I had perforcedly lived too much of the Spartan life of late to desire its adoption for a mere idea.

The holsters repacked, I contemplated a speedy retreat to hunt up some of his European staff which I fervently hoped did not practice similar vagaries, but I was not so easily released, and my jaded horse stood waiting in the sun. I must first come and try a little pistol practice in the verandah; in vain I protested I would not engage his valuable time, but he would take no refusal, and cramming several revolvers and a brace of 'over and under' pistols into a cashmere shawl which was girded about his waist, we adjourned to the verandah. Here, at one end, was hoisted a three

---

[1] Probably Captain Edmund George Wood (6th Madras Light Cavalry) who had succeeded Beatson's first Brigade-Major, Major John Hackett (H.M.'s 44th Foot), the latter having resigned the appointment on 5 May.

dozen beer case inscribed by a chalk circle. The general and
Brigade Major shot wide, while the wily Asiatics cried
'shabbash shabbashee bahadur'! And now came my turn. I
requested a bottle might be substituted for the circle, and
drawing my revolver, by a happy chance I smashed it to
atoms amid cries of applause. The General looked astonished
and walked within doors, evidently understanding the
secret of his friend Sir Hugh Rose's victories. It is needless
to add that, having made a great success by accident, nothing
would have induced me to hazard a second shot.

Returning my revolver to my belt with an air of having
done nothing more than usual, I received permission to
depart, and gladly enough sped away to the officers of the
1st Regiment. Thank Heavens! they were not Spartans, but
good soldiers as I afterwards found them, and yet took the
enjoyments of life when they had the opportunity.[1] Colonel
Becher, better known in Bengal as 'Charley Becher',[2] was
the type of an irregular cavalry officer: a good rider, a good
soldier, and a good fellow. He commanded my regiment.
Major Wilson,[3] late of the Adjutant General's department

[1] Sylvester's account of his arrival does not quite conform to that given
in his *Diary*. He there describes how, on entering the lines at 2 p.m.
he 'soon found out the acting Adjutant & Colonel, two most gentlemanly
and pleasant fellows, the latter a very handsome fellow'. These would
be Lieutenant Charles Henry Clay, 13th Bombay Native Infantry, and
Brevet Lieutenant-Colonel Charles Grant Becher.
After this meeting he had tiffin (luncheon) and it was not until later,
in the evening, after dining in the Mess of the 2nd Regiment, that he
called on General Beatson. The shooting incident does not seem to have
occurred until 12 August.

[2] Brevet Lieutenant-Colonel Charles Grant Becher (born in Calcutta,
1811), started his military career as a Cornet in the 5th Bengal Light
Cavalry. He also served with the 1st and 4th Light Cavalry, the 8th
Irregular Cavalry, and the newly-raised 5th Bengal European Light
Cavalry in 1858. He had served in several campaigns, including
Gwalior, 1843, and the 1st Sikh War, 1845–6, when he was present at
Sobraon. As will be seen later, he did not live long after Sylvester
joined him. As inferred by Sylvester, he commanded the 1st Regiment,
Beatson's Horse.

[3] Captain Thomas Fourness Wilson (13th Bengal Native Infantry),
in command of the 2nd Regiment, Beatson's Horse. He served in the

in Bengal, commanded the 2nd corps, and so far as I could discern, General Beatson had been most fortunate in his European officers, but he had already become exceedingly unpopular; some had resigned and others were about to do so. This was discouraging, but knowing that our corps would soon leave on service, we all agreed to do our best to stay, and as this was my first service with irregular cavalry, I found much to do, and much in the system of organisation to surprise me.

It appeared that Government had directed General Beatson to raise two mounted corps for service, and authorised him to advance desirable and reliable men a small sum of money wherewith to equip themselves with horse, lance, and saddlery, Government provided sword and carbine. These sums so advanced were to be recouped by instalments retrenched from their monthly pay which, to the trooper, was about three pounds or thirty rupees. He then became a free lance, obeyed all commands, keeping himself, equipment and horse effective at his own expense.[1] General Beatson placed a very liberal interpretation on the permission to advance, and often lent as much as thirty-five or forty pounds to each trooper, and this, in the aggregate, amounted to a very considerable sum.

To the native officers advances for eight, ten, and even more equipments were made, and they found men, gear and horses, drawing pay for the whole and making what profit might accrue. Unprincipled men, after drawing forty pounds, would bring to the ranks a horse and equipment which had cost him ten pounds less, and thus the regiment suffered, but the service was popular. Much of the immediate profit made was spent in nauches [entertainments, with dancing] and debauchery. The sweepings and idlers of the Nizam's capital [were enlisted], some of course who had

---

Punjab, 1848–9, and during the Indian Mutiny was at the battle of Chinhut as D.A.A.G. to Sir Henry Lawrence, and was with General Windham at Cawnpore, December 1857, in the same capacity. Died 1886.
[1] The 'Silladar System'.

been accustomed to arms, others were strangers both to arms and the saddle, and amongst the enlisted we found two of the disaffected troopers of the 1st Hyderabad Cavalry who had mutinied in the presence of General Woodburn's column the previous year – a sure sign they preferred serving our Government after trying their own.

Every effort was being made to make this discouraging raw material effective, and teach the men the rudiments of drill and discipline. General Beatson's system was very peculiar; sometimes he suddenly marched upon a peaceful village, surrounded and stormed it with dismounted troopers, greatly astonishing the inhabitants who, in such troubled times, imagined their turn had arrived for slaughter. At others he raised an alarm of fire in cantonments, and turning us all out at midnight, would call the roll and punish the missing.[1]

About the time I joined the 1st Regiment, it had been completed in men and horses. The former had, however, no uniform save jack boots, and it may be readily therefore guessed how exactly they resembled Tantia's horsemen: nevertheless, General Beatson officially reported to Lord Clyde, then Commander in Chief, that this corps was 'now ready to cut its way to Hindoostan', and I had barely time to provide myself with the necessaries for another start. In less than a month after my arrival we proceeded on active service: orders were to be furnished us on our route.

[1] Any such system of training, designed to simulate as much as possible actual service conditions, would cause a raising of eyebrows in those days. At a much later date, it was only in the face of great opposition, that General Sir James Hope Grant (the great cavalry commander of the Indian Mutiny), on taking over command at Aldershot in 1870, was able to resuscitate the Autumn Manoeuvres, first instigated by the Prince Consort in emulation of the Prussian system, where troops worked against each other as opposing forces.

X

The Pursuit of Tantia Topee

B Y the time I left Jaulnah with Beatson's Horse[1] most of
the rebel strongholds, excepting Oudh, had been broken
up. The destruction wreaked on our cantonments during
the Mutiny was fast being effaced, torrents of rain had
cooled the atmosphere, given new life to the jaded and sun
stricken troops, and washed the gore from many a battle-
field. The fords of the Jumna were occupied by detachments
of our soldiery.

The fate of all the independent princes had been decided;
they had stood by us in our extremity, as the Bhopal Begum,
been distrusted, as Holkar, or thrown in their lot with the
rebels, like the Ranee, so that we had no fear of any other
great combination with Tantia and his colleagues. No other
course was open to them but to imitate the beasts of prey, and
hide in impenetrable jungle, even as they had followed
their example of bloodthirstyness in the Mutiny: consequently, Tantia and his demon horde commenced a
marauding and vagabond flight through the forest clad
tracts of Central India, always having the Dekkan in view
as a land of promise. There, their agents, with ample
means, were secretly advocating their cause and endeavour-
ing to prepare for their advent. There, every large city and
wavering regiment in our pay was sorely tempted, but it
required no sagacity to discern the game had been played
out.

Meanwhile, Government, with ample reinforcements of
British troops and increased facilities of transport, dispatched

[1] 4 September 1858. Three days later they were entertained by
Major Gill at Adjuntah, and were photographed in 'every possible style'.
(*Diary*.)

flying columns in every direction so as to give the rebels no rest. In proportion as their treasure dwindled, their influence diminished and Tantia's sun began to set. No longer able to pay his way, he and his myrmidons swept the country like a locust cloud and left the same sad effects behind. Many of the petty chieftains must have been sorely perplexed; to refuse the rebels aid was to be grievously plundered, to aid them was to incur the displeasure of Government. One after the other, Tantia managed to visit the independent states, and by fair means or foul, temporarily replenished his treasury, often possessed himself of guns, but seldom with recruits.

Tantia's tactics again resembled those of the beasts whose domain he invaded, and in whose lairs he slept. He never attacked nor fought until hunted down, yet was ever ready for a treacherous descent to plunder our baggage or to attack unarmed followers.

In the pursuit, Divisions, Brigades, Regiments, and Detachments of troops, regular and irregular, mounted and foot, commanded by officers of every rank and description, were engaged. The larger the force and heavier the impedimenta, the smaller the chance of success. Those alone without wheeled carriage could follow the track when Tantia discarded his guns. Oftentimes he was without tents or provisions; these he plundered as he required. His horses, when footsore and exhausted, he left as food for vultures, replacing them on the first opportunity, not infrequently by attacking our followers. His cavalry could hover round ours like shadows and always distance them if chased, yet still every new leader who took the field hoped that his would be the good fortune to bring home Tantia's head on his saddle bow. In addition to the ordinary excitement of war, it was a lottery open to many, and a handsome money reward.

Many an officer, whose patrons had languished in despair of finding an excuse to shower on him the honours of the Bath, sped to the pursuit with the decoration in his pocket.

He had but to write a dispatch and be forthwith gazetted to
the most honorable order, and nowadays these honors command a money price in the directorships of companies
limited! Prodigious marches were accomplished, and once
on scent, officers and men threw aside tents and baggage
and threaded wild jungle tracts, forty miles a day. Tantia
did fifty, or sneaked into his pursuers' rear. Not always the
rebels alone had to be kept in view; those wishing to
preserve independent command were compelled to steer
clear of other forces commanded by officers senior to themselves. The energy thrown into the pursuit was immense:
down stony hill sides, in the depths of rocky valleys, and on
the banks of muddy streams, skeletons of horses, mules,
camels and bullocks testified that it was more than flesh and
blood could bear. Force after force and column after column
pulled up, dead beaten.

Now and again, some of our troops, more fortunate than
the rest, killed a few of the enemy who, disgusted with their
ill fate, died fighting. Their information of our movements
appeared always of the best, but the villagers in independent
states were invariably retentive to us; the sympathy of the
people was with the rebels and the exaggerated statements
of their success, disseminated by Tantia's followers, obtained
credence. Whole tracts of country were deserted at our
approach, and finding none to sell forage and grain, we
helped ourselves, and then were stigmatised one degree
worse than the enemy.

As Tantia's power waned, the genuine sepoy deserted to
Hindoostan; Velliatees, Bheels,[1] Bundeelas and robbers
supplied his place. They were better for his purpose, accustomed to arms and predatory life from childhood. They
were excellent marksmen and accustomed to jungle warfare; attired in russet or olive green, they threaded paths
which few save Indian officers could attempt. Some were
mounted on camels and ponies, and doubtless like ourselves

---

[1] Bheels: an aboriginal tribe to be found in the Western Ghauts on
the north-west border of Hyderabad.

were often sorely pressed and needy; many were shoeless
and dependent on rags for protection against the rocks and
thickets. At night they sought sequestered and densely
wooded ravines lest their cooking fires might betray them,
and but for the treachery of one of his race, it is doubtful
if the genius of flight would have ever been caught. Much
more probably, in the garb of a devotee or villager, he
would have joined his friend the Nana in the fastnesses of
the Himalayas.

Once in his career he made a bold attempt to enter the
Dekkan, and actually crossed the Nerbudda. Here he found
three lines of defence through which he could not break;
he turned, entered the Taptee valley, and recrossed the
Nerbudda into Rajpootana, and though reinforced by
cavalry under Ferozshah,[1] he suffered several defeats in
succession from troops under Michel, De Salis, Parke and
Becher.

Instead of cutting our way to Hindoostan as General
Beatson imagined his regiment would be called upon to do
while he remained at Jaulnah, drawing large pay and
squabbling with his officers, we received orders to join Sir
John Michel's[2] Mhow Field Force, organising to pursue
Tantia Topee and his followers.

We pushed on with all haste to Mhow, but torrents of
rain, swollen rivers, and almost impassable roads were a sad
hindrance, and without more covering than the white
calico in which natives usually clothe themselves, the
appearance of our men was, as may be conceived, miserable
in the extreme. They were a sorry contrast to the 14th
Dragoons with whom I traversed this route a year before,
but the comparatively easy duties with an irregular corps,
the greater freedom and ability to march by day instead of
night was a change I thoroughly appreciated. How sick had

---

[1] Son of Mirza Nazim and cousin of Akbar Shah, King of Delhi.

[2] Sir John Michel (1804–86). Joined 57th Foot in 1823. Kaffir Wars,
1846–7 and 1852–3. Chief of Staff, Turkish Contingent, Crimean War.
Commanded a Division in China, 1860. Field Marshal, 1885.

I become of the constant nocturnal marching, every night's silence and the first hour's sleep broken by that same harsh unwelcome trumpet's blast, succeeded by the shouts of men, pitiful moaning of camels, crashing of tent pegs and neighing of horses; the bustle of men hurrying to and fro to find their ranks, the clanging of scabbards, and cries to 'fall in'! Over all, too, reigned an unearthly light, thrown by the fitful glare of burning forage.

With my present regiment we mustered but four European Officers.[1] We were little hampered by paper work and the daily march over, time was our own. Having twice traversed the road to Mhow, all was familiar to me, but at Simrool our Colonel rode to Indore and received instructions from Sir Robert Hamilton which diverted us to Bhilsa, and while wending our way thither, we were directed to obey the instructions of Brigadier Parke,[2] but it scarcely wanted a critic's eye to pronounce us already unfit for service. The terrible state of the roads had dragged off horse shoes faster than our farriers could tack them on. The animals, far too young, were in great part back and girth galled, and the men's clothing was in tatters.

On the 25th of October we were not far distant from Saugor, and about midnight, a dispatch from Brigadier Parke reached us, directing the regiment to patrol between Bagrode and Ratghur – the fort which Sir Hugh Rose had dismantled some months before. The country around us was everywhere thick with trees and shrubs, game too was in abundance, which, together with wild pea fowl, amply supplied our mess. Plentiful shade covered our tents, and the men, except in rain, never used even the blanket stretched across a pole after the fashion of the *tent d'abri* which was all they carried to shelter them from rain and

---

[1] Colonel Becher, Captain Henry Thurburn (1826–97, Second-in-Command), Clay (Adjutant) and Sylvester. Thurburn was an officer from the 42nd Madras Native Infantry, and is frequently mentioned in Sylvester's *Diary*.

[2] Lieutenant-Colonel William Parke (1822–97), 72nd Highlanders. Served in the Crimea.

cold, so that we resembled, when halting, a vast gipsy encampment, and now that the monsoon was ceasing, we often
had bright days, not very much too hot, except perhaps at
noontime.

I think that not one of the four of us believed we had
much fighting power in our command, nevertheless, considering the miserable material from whence the troopers
were recruited, they were apparently well behaved and
willing, and the kind of life was much after my own
desire.

We were one day's journey from Bagrode when Parke's
dispatch arrived, and intended going there on the morrow;
accordingly, a small party of our troopers had gone on about
4 p.m. to collect supplies for our camp, and we retired to
rest as usual, to be awakened almost immediately by a great
commotion in the lines, and the trumpets sounding 'Boot and
Saddle'. The forage party had returned hastily: Tantia, the
Rao Sahib, and ten thousand men were already in possession. Striking our camp and piling it under care of a few
troopers, we started for Bagrode, sending ten miles to our
rear, asking reinforcements from Parke's force.

It was bright moonlight and about midnight we reached
a pass in the hills which debouched on Bagrode. Halting at
its highest part, there in the plain below, the cooking fires
of the enemy were distinctly visible about two miles distant.
We consulted as to the possibility of riding a stampede
through their camp, which I believe would have stricken
them with terror, and caused them to abandon their
baggage and spoil. No confidence, however, could be felt in
a band of raw mercenaries such as ours, all untried as they
were. It was decided therefore on sending two men – if
volunteers could be found – disguised, into the enemy's
camp, in order to ascertain its position and strength. Two
responded to the call, and having, in dress, simulated them
to villagers, we awaited their report. It was piercing cold
and I had ample time, while standing to my horse all night,
to realise that, if there were many pleasant advantages in

serving with irregular horse, it was also disagreeable to want confidence in the face of the enemy.

It was close upon daylight and our spies had not returned. We were in a densely wooded pass, almost at the mercy of a few infantry if the men had played us false, therefore it was determined to retrace our steps to open ground, and encamp at Gwarispore. Here our baggage joined us, and discovering a better though more circuitous route, we reached Bagrode, disappointed of any reinforcements from Brigadier Parke, but as I have previously remarked, all those in command of flying columns wished to have the merit of capturing Tantia, and reluctantly spared reinforcements to rival commanders.

On reaching Bagrode we found the headless trunks of our two men,[1] but Tantia, with his force, had flown. The head man of Bagrode at first stoutly denied having had an interview with Tantia, but afterwards admitted having furnished him with supplies, after which he left as suddenly as he came, but we were not always to be thus disappointed and I must trace the rebel progress after their discomfitted departure from Jowra-Alipore, until I renewed acquaintance with them.

Nothing daunted by the loss of his park to Sir Robert Napier, he resorted to a fresh field for its renewal, and as our Government permits so much artillery to lie scattered about India, in the keeping of independent chiefs, he had not far to search. The Rajah of Jalraputtan, on hearing of his approach, fled for solace to his seraglio, and afterwards to a British force at Soosneer for safety while his soldiery, previously in heart and now in body, joined the standard of Tantia, thereby recruiting his numbers to about ten thousand men who were fairly armed and dressed, nor did they want for guns or treasure, having helped themselves to nearly forty pieces of cannon from the fort and city, and

---

[1] These two brave volunteers, who must have known the fate which awaited them in the event of discovery, were Davy Singh (1st Troop) and Ram Singh (4th Troop).

then marched leisurely to Rajghur with, it is supposed, the intention of marching on Bhopal, the capital of one of our staunchest friends, the Begum.

Captain Hutchinson,[1] however, as political agent, procured intelligence of a proposed movement on Rajghur, and was the means of our joining the column under Colonel Lockhart[2] at Soosneer, with that of General Michel from Mhow. This column, marching from four in the morning until the same hour in the afternoon, arrived in time to see the rebels in the act of pitching camp on an eminence near the threatened city. The forced march had so tired General Michel's infantry, consisting of part of the 72nd Highlanders,[3] 4th, 19th and 22nd Bombay Regiments, that they were yet three miles behind, and even the mounted branch of his force were too fatigued to act, and was therefore retired to the infantry to recruit. It is due to the 19th Bombay Infantry to mention that they volunteered to proceed, fatigued as they were, alone.

Both forces appeared to agree to postpone the engagement for a day and both threw out cavalry pickets and videttes; the rebels, out of bravado, placed two to our one. The cavalry at General Michel's disposal comprised three weak squadrons of H.M.'s 17th Lancers and two of the 3rd Bombay Light Cavalry, and while the latter were encamping, the attention of a trooper was called to the somewhat suspicious movements of a prowling figure, dressed as an old woman. Making a closer investigation, he discovered it to be a rebel spy who was accordingly shot.

Tantia had lost nothing of his old caution, and in the event of a reverse, sent off his treasure to Mucksoodnuggar. At 3 a.m. in silence, the next morning, General Michel endeavoured to steal a march on the rebels, but they had

---

[1] Captain Alexander Ross Elliott Hutchinson (13th Bengal Native Infantry) served in the Punjab, 1848. Present at Goojerat.

[2] Lieutenant-Colonel Archibald Inglis Lockhart, 92nd Highlanders.

[3] Later 1st Bn Seaforth Highlanders and now amalgamated with the 78th and 79th Highlanders as The Queen's Own Highlanders (Seaforth and Camerons).

gone. Nearing Rajghur, the Rajah approached the Major
General on horseback, with an affection of friendship, and
on being required to show a road by which the force could
pass the town and river, indicated a stony and almost impracticable footpath, with the object, as it presently appeared, of gaining time for the rebels. An ample road, and easy
ford was shortly discovered by the aide-de-camp, and the
cavalry under Sir William Gordon[1] crossed, pushed forward
a reconnaissance, and almost immediately discovered some
of the enemy's horsemen in the jungle on the Bioura road.
The reconnaissance was continued, to ascertain Tantia's
position. Meanwhile, the artillery and infantry breakfasted.[2]

The rebel cavalry was observed to be in line on a hill
covered by brushwood and low jungle, and doubtless being
well informed of General Michel's strength, or rather
weakness, advanced sixty troopers under two officers, but
the General, desirous to keep them from investigating his
small numbers, advanced a troop of the 3rd Cavalry in
skirmishing order under a cornet.[3] Prompted by the ardour
of inexperience, he continued to follow the retiring horsemen until he came in sight of one of the enemy's cannon,
when, collecting a handful of his men, he dashed at the gun,
took it, then, in company with an officer of the 17th
Lancers[4] tempered with the same zeal, he emerged suddenly
on an open plateau in the face of two hundred of the enemy's
infantry, two guns, and about sixty horse. A volley of
musketry and a charge from forty horsemen obliged the
cornet and his band to ride for their lives, the cornet with
some difficulty keeping in advance of a long spear carried by

[1] Captain Sir William Gordon, 17th Lancers, described by Sir
Evelyn Wood as the most finished horseman he had known in the army.
Within three months of joining as a Cornet from Earlston, Kirkcud-
bright, he won the Subalterns' Cup. Charged with the Light Brigade
at Balaclava.

[2] 15 September 1858.

[3] This probably refers to a Cornet Albert Purcell Currie.

[4] Lieutenant Evelyn Wood, who records the incident in *From Midshipman to Field Marshal*, but without naming the Cornet.

one of the pursuers. Luckily, the sight of the pennons of the Lancers, who had been steadily coming up, relieved him from his critical position.

So thick was the brushwood and undulating and stony the ground hereabouts that our reconnaissance had actually passed the rebel force to the right. The Lancers now went left wheel, the artillery came up, and a harmless cannonade ensued, though the enemy, possessing three guns and a thirteen-inch mortar, had the best of the range over General Michel's four light field pieces. One shot carried away the top of a dhooly in which was being carried the breakfast of the officers of the 19th Regiment.

Not only had the dense brushwood been the cause of the cavalry missing, in their reconnaissance, the main body of the enemy, but in addition, another party of his foot-men were discovered as our infantry arrived from their breakfast, and by them driven in to the river. Unable to escape, they dived beneath the surface, but finding it diffi-cult to respire in the new element, rose again and were shot.

The main body now commenced a rapid retreat on Bioura, sorely pressed by General Michel's cavalry only, for the infantry were unable to keep pace, and being much distressed by the midday sun, fell out in great numbers. Seven guns were abandoned to the pursuers in one nullah, and at five in the afternoon it was of necessity stayed. The whole park of twenty-seven guns had been captured and many of the enemy killed. The Lancers and Bombay Cavalry halted beneath the shade of some trees, and Lieutenant Shaw[1] of the latter regiment, who had received a sunstroke, died there.

A day's halt was necessary, and the 4th Bombay Rifles took the captured guns to Indore. During the halt, Captain Mayne joined with his newly-raised regiment. Tantia, exasperated at the loss of his guns, marched through the

[1] Lieutenant George Malcolm Shaw, 3rd Bombay Light Cavalry. Aged twenty-two years when he died.

forest tract of Mucksoodnuggur to Seronge — where he
blew his Adjutant General from a gun.

General Michel and the Mhow force pursued through
Nursinghur almost to Bairseah, but the monsoon descended
with such force that they were compelled to halt. It was of
course as bad for one as the other, and on one occasion but
five miles separated the enemy from a pursuing force, yet
neither could move. Who but those who have experienced a
life under canvas can form an idea of the misery of being
weatherbound, and pitched in a badly drained position? A
testy Quarter Master, if very precise in his lines and dis-
tances between tents, thinks it but a duty to locate one
across an inequality of ground which, during a heavy
tropical storm, becomes a rivulet, and then one peg after
another releases its hold, and if this happens at night, down
comes the heavy wet tent, from which it is difficult to
escape, wet to the skin, and one's bedding drenched.
Oftentimes, when with the Dragoons, we had to entrench
the plot on which each horse stood, to prevent his bed and
forage being washed away. Servants become paralysed and
useless in such times, cooking fires are extinguished, and as
you peer outside into the dungeon dark sky, from whence
the torrents fall, hissing and splashing, there is not a ray of
comfort in existence.

With returning sunshine, the Mhow force followed
Tantia towards Easaughur and endeavoured to operate
against him with Brigadier Smith's brigade, but Tantia
arrived first, beat Scindiah's wretched troops under the
Shah Subah, took two guns which they abandoned in the
town, after sacking it. Brigadier Smith, on arriving, saw
Tantia's rear guard leaving, the main body having gone to
Mungrowlee, and some few cavalry to Ranode.

General Michel who that morning left Seronge, oppor-
tunely arrived at Mungrowlee and was just pitching camp
as the rebels came marching in. Their advance was seen by
a mounted picket which galloped in. The Mhow force lost
no time in moving out to a small hill on the north, and

though seen by Tantia, he appeared not unwilling to risk an engagement, and huddled his masses into the best shape possible during the limited time allowed.

Le Marchand[1] opened his guns and threw shot into Tantia's most advanced mass, which caused it to give way, when suddenly cries of alarm were heard in rear of our lines. Sir William Gordon, with fifty Lancers, galloped back and discovered a party of Velliatees displaying great bravery against six unarmed bearers carrying a wounded Highlander: him they had killed and some of the bearers had been wounded. The sight of the lance pennons caused the Velliatees to disappear into the heavy jungle, but their heads were still visible among the foliage. To advance in order was impossible, but the words 'Open out and pursue at a gallop' were scarcely given before his fifty followers, regardless of bush and briar, were among a nest of these treacherous backwoodsmen and accounted for upwards of eighty, their gallant leader scoring three of these.

During the advance, at the outset, the rebels were observed to abandon a wounded man who was being carried on a native bedstead. The wretched man, who had been a subedar [captain] in a Bengal Infantry Regiment, after watching the advance of our troops, opened the breast of his tunic, bound a handkerchief across his eyes, and requested to be shot.

During the action front and rear, three hundred had been killed, some prisoners and six guns taken; the remainder fled across the Betwa to Tal-Behut.

The rebels now having entered Bundlekunde, it was determined to follow them with three columns, the right or infantry column under Colonel Lockhart, the centre under Colonel De Salis,[2] and the left an infantry column with two guns and some native cavalry attached, under Brigadier Smith.

The centre column, on gaining the Betwa river, was

[1] Lieutenant Charles Smith Lemarchand (or Le Marchand), Bengal Artillery.
[2] Lieutenant-Colonel Rodolph de Salis (1811–80), 8th Hussars. Charged with the Light Brigade at Balaclava.

compelled to construct a ford. The rebels had somehow crossed as it existed. It was the intention of General Michel, who with his staff accompanied this column, to advance due east after crossing the river, but Captain Mayne, who had preceded, to ascertain the nature of the roads and freedom from rebels, was fired on by Bundeelas in a difficult and jungle clad pass leading to Jaclone. This intelligence induced the Major General, by forced marches south, to join the column under Colonel Lockhart at Narut, and from thence the force would have moved in a direction north-west towards Lullutpore, but at one o'clock on the morning following his arrival, intelligence was received to the effect that the rebels were moving across his front, to loot the friendly state of Tehree, and that on the previous evening they had halted at Sindwaho, fifteen miles north of Narut.

Consequent of this report, another change was made in the route, and at daybreak, the enemy's pickets were again sighted, under a group of trees not far from Sindwaho. Leaping into their saddles, these horsemen galloped off with the intelligence of General Michel's arrival. Meanwhile, our force was advanced until the village came in sight, and there, in a well chosen position, was Tantia's entire force.

Preparing to attack, our four guns were maintained in a centre position while Colonel de Salis advanced with the cavalry to the right, in order to feel the enemy's left and cut off their retreat from Tehree. At this moment the enemy opened a rapid and well directed artillery fire, causing many casualties among a squadron of the 3rd Bombay Cavalry. Several shots were especially directed upon them. One fell beneath the left troop leader's horse, and the following shot killed three horses immediately behind him. Tantia's cavalry hovered round ours, and his infantry advanced towards our guns.

Orders were given for the cavalry to charge, which they did, led by Sir William Gordon, the infantry previously firing a volley. In this successful affair, 8th Hussars, 17th, and Bombay Lancers were engaged, and it was computed upwards of five hundred of the enemy were slain, and six guns captured, together with the palanquin belonging to the Nawab of Banda. Inside this vehicle were fresh blood stains, unluckily not those of the Nawab who gave himself up with an entire skin shortly afterwards. Amongst the spoils were several women, and one so attractive that either her beauty or blandishments won the heart of a native soldier who requested permission to wed her.

Soon after the decisive charge had taken place, the 3rd Bombay Cavalry, while in support of two guns on the left, near a field of high jowarree [millet], observed a body of the rebels emerging, and soon afterwards were fired upon so heavily that several horses were wounded. The officer commanding retired them from too close proximity, and then the rebels, composed of Velliattees and sepoys of the 36th Bengal Infantry,[1] formed into a rude square or gole. Evelyn Wood of the 17th Lancers,[2] doing duty with the 3rd Cavalry, attacked these men singly, commencing with the corner man, a Velliattee. Strange to say, the others stood at the charge with musket and bayonet, unwilling to move from a fancied security in that position. The Velliattee, having escaped the first blow aimed at him, drew a two-handed sword with which he endeavoured to slay his antagonist, but missing his aim, fell beneath Wood's charger, a favourable subject for dispatch, but gaining his legs with amazing quickness, he returned to the combat, when a young trooper[3] rode to the rescue, and on him the

[1] The 36th Bengal Native Infantry mutinied at Jullundur, 7 June 1857.

[2] Field-Marshall Sir Evelyn Wood (1838–1919). Entered the Royal Navy as a Midshipman and served in the Crimea. Transferred to the army in 1855 with a Cornetcy in the 13th Light Dragoons. Transferred to the 17th Lancers as a Lieutenant, 1856. Served in Ashanti, 1873–4; Zulu War, 1879; 1st Boer War, 1880–1; Egypt, 1882; Sudan 1884–5. Field Marshal, 1903. At the time Sylvester wrote his narrative, Wood was probably commanding the 90th Perthshire Light Infantry (later 2nd Bn The Cameronians).

[3] Dhokul Singh, who was promoted to Corporal, and eventually to Risaldar-Major and A. D. C. to the Commander-in-Chief, Bombay, and to the Duke of Connaught. In *From Midshipman to Field Marshal,*

Velliatee turned his attention, but in delivering his blow too hastily, the trooper escaped with a mere graze on the back, and the tulwar's force was expended in severing the crupper of the trooper's saddle, and spine of his horse; this however placed him at the mercy of a well delivered cut which clove his skull.

Three of the group now threw down their arms and shouted loud for pardon; the next, however, showed fight, and was engaged accordingly by Lieutenant Wood, at whom he rushed with clubbed musket. The bayonet, however, being fixed, caught in the rebel's drapery and exposed him to a well delivered point which ran completely through him. This exciting combat occupied the few moments necessary to bring up the remainder of the 3rd Cavalry, who finished the work so well begun.

Tantia's men fought well at Sindwaho,[1] as they did on many occasions. The cavalry of our force were in the saddle from 2 a.m. until 5 p.m. and gladly embraced the opportunity to halt and encamp, but they had protected Tehree.

After this engagement, the Mhow Force marched upon Lullutpore, and while encamped at some distance, Tantia's forage guard, unaware of its dangerous proximity, entered the village. The cavalry at once sprang into their saddles and scoured the country, capturing some carts and animals laden with ammunition, but the rebels were hard pressed and driven to a desperate move. They marched from north of Lullutpore to Kurai, passing within four miles of General Michel's force, between it and the Betwa, and at one time

---

Evelyn Wood describes the Velliattee as being a fine broad-shouldered man, over six feet in height, armed with musket, sword, and shield. The remainder were a small Velliattee (wearing a doublet of flexible mail and an iron skull-piece with flexible curtains), and ten or eleven sepoys of the Bengal Native Infantry, in coatees, cummerbunds, and langotis (short tight drawers). Apart from Dhokul Singh (for his action awarded the Order of Merit, 3rd Class), The Light Cavalry do not seem to have given Wood good support. In 1881, Dhokul Singh was promoted in the Order of Merit to 2nd Class, and for his gallantry during the retreat from Maiwand (27 July 1880) to 1st Class.

[1] Fought on 19 October 1858.

the two forces were in close proximity. This constant marching necessarily involved great wear and tear, and many of our infantry were ragged and shoeless; nevertheless, they were willing and cheerful, and from Lullutpore proceeded to Multowa, and thence to Khimlassa where the enemy had just left. Leaving Khimlassa, they proceeded to Kurai and while debouching from the town to the plain, saw Tantia's army in full march southward. General Michel's staff concluded that the part of the enemy seen was his front, but it subsequently turned out to be composed of tired footmen and others mounted on ponies, who, being unable to keep pace, had lagged.

General Michel now ordered his left shoulder to be brought up and the enemy appeared inclined to stand; a nearer inspection of our solid ranks, however, struck terror, and they fled. Three bodies of cavalry were loosed at once, under the command of Sir William Gordon, Captain Mayne, and Colonel Curtis.[1] The two former were most successful: Mayne's Horse and the 3rd Cavalry under Oldfield[2] killed about a hundred and fifty, over six miles of ground. The entire loss inflicted was estimated at three hundred and fifty, by which the rebels were much discomfitted and broken up.[3]

There can be no doubt that the force under Sir John Michel deserves the credit of destroying Tantia's power as a commander and degrading him to the position of a hunted bandit. The repeated blows and constant unrest the arch rebel received from the Mhow Force completely disheartened him, and after the action of Sindwaho, those of his force who were driven north never joined again; some took service with Maun Singh;[4] others followed in wake of

---

[1] Lieutenant-Colonel William Frederick Curtis, 1st Bombay Lancers.
[2] Captain Francis John Oldfield, 3rd Bombay Light Cavalry.
[3] 25 October 1858.
[4] Maun Singh, Rajah of Narwar, a vassal of Scindiah, by whom, previous to the Mutiny, he had been outlawed, but he was powerful and had been left more or less unmolested.

Tantia, and crossing the Nerbudda, dispersed in the Putch-murree hills; others hung about the valleys of the Taptee and Nerbudda, while some few got far enough to amuse the Jaulnah Field Force, with which was Beatson's 2nd Regiment. Tantia and the treasure marched to Bagrode.

XI

Tantia Topee, Will-o'-the-Wisp

BEATSON'S Horse had seen his (Tantia's) camp fires while waiting in the wooded gorge, and next day picketted their horses not far distant from the smouldering ashes.[1] Accepting the vakeel's [an authorised representative] assurance that not a ghost of an enemy remained, the second in command[2] and myself resolved to ascend a hill close to our camp, which afforded a good view for many miles, and scarcely had we reached the summit when we descried Tantia's camp about six miles distant, and midway was a large body of cavalry, which, with an opera glass, I identified correctly as belonging to it though pronounced to belong to one of our own forces by my companion.

We descended the hill as fast as our legs could carry us, which, being seen from our camp, threw it into great commotion, the cause of our haste being correctly surmised. Colonel Becher and the Adjutant, Lieutenant Clay, had already fallen in the regiment and we dashed off in line across country. It was by no means the first time I had done this, with other cavalry, but in my life I had never witnessed such a scene. The pace was frightful and six men out of eight had lost all control over their horses. Many had purposely from fear, or from bad riding, left their saddles while their now freed horses added to the excitement of the rest. All order was lost and to make matters worse, Colonel Becher, who had been carried in a palanquin on account of sickness many days previously, was compelled to fall to the

[1] Sylvester here returns to narrating events in which he himself took part.

[2] Captain Thurburn.

G

rear, and indeed, as I shall have to relate, died thoroughly exhausted not long afterwards.

Just as we came up with the cavalry, a deep dry nullah crossed our path, and into this fell more of our troopers, headlong, together with our second in command. Again more riderless horses were galloping amongst us. Fortunately, our Adjutant, Clay, a bold and intrepid pigsticker, was to the front, and by dint of much shouting at the handful of men who had kept pace, we dashed amongst the mounted rebels in some sort of line. They drew up into close order as though intending to receive our charge, but not liking the pace, broke and fled. Our men followed right well and the Adjutant and myself set to work with our hog spears[1] in earnest while the troopers, with their sabres, almost brought to my mind General Beatson's vision of 'cutting our way to Hindoostan'![2]

We came upon some of the enemy mounted on camels, and in pursuit of these the Adjutant and myself unluckily separated, and being five or six miles from camp, in scrub jungle, I was obliged to abandon further pursuit, moreover, one of those who had followed me best lost his bridle arm which was completely severed by a tulwar cut. Twisting a piece of turban tightly round, he begged that I would not let it trouble me until I reached camp. We collected all the stray cattle and turned homewards, discovering some of our dismounted men busily plundering the dead. It was useless to complain; there are always men in irregular horse who do it. Clay returned soon afterwards, having been shot through the helmet and spear handle, but otherwise was unhurt.

It will give some idea of the wooded nature of the country in which we were operating when I relate that a private of the 8th Hussars, while strolling out of camp bounds, could not find his way back, and after many hours of wandering,

---

[1] Made by Bodraj of Aurungabad. (*Recollections of the Campaign in Malwa and Central India.*)

[2] This first charge of Beatson's Horse took place on 26 October 1858.

arrived in our camp at Bagrode, and we subsequently learnt that the cavalry we had engaged were on their way to our camp, also mistaking it for their own which [they] had just left.

That night we remained watchful, thinking it very possible that Tantia might meditate revenge. Our little affair was considered very successful; we had killed between forty and fifty of the enemy and our Colonel made favourable mention of the Adjutant and myself to General Michel who shortly afterwards rewarded the former with an appointment in the Erinpoora Force which he now commands.

A reply was received from Brigadier Parke in answer to our modest request for two guns; he could not spare them as he feared Tantia would make a desperate rush for Bhopal, and as a matter of fact he was on his way there when we disturbed him, but only to alter his route for he was again marching parallel with us. Colonel Becher resolved, therefore, that as we were not sufficiently strong to attack on account of Brigadier Parke's refusal, we would reach Bhopal with all haste. At Gwarispore we saved the Government bungalow from destruction by having outmarched Tantia who encamped at Gysut, four miles distant, but so closely did we resemble rebel cavalry in our absence of uniform, and clothing of rags, that the kansamah [cook] had already departed from the bungalow and hid in an adjacent ravine, with all his crockery and cooking pots.

The proximity of the enemy caused great excitement in the regiment and great fear amongst our followers. We had endless alarms, especially at night, when the men on picket often fired furiously to keep their courage from shrinking. On reaching Bhilsa we ourselves had to patrol through the night which was intensely dark, and our men could not be persuaded the rebels were not hidden in the gloom: in the excitement left by their maiden fight, recollected images were as vivid as actual impressions. We found Bhilsa well worth a visit; its Topes are the subject of a

work by Major Cunningham,[1] its tobacco is famous, and the
longest piece of ordnance in India was lying in the village –
useless of course. It had lain there many years and probably
does so now.

On the 30th of October, at Kurree, we were but a few
miles from General Michel who was interviewed by our
commandant. Parke had already reached Bhopal, and
Tantia, frustrated and almost surrounded at Ambapanee,
now had but one route for escape, and this was across a ford
of the Nerbudda, guarded by Lieutenant Kerr, V. C.[2]
Tantia was equal to the occasion; he divided his forces, and
by a ruse drew Kerr across, and once having cleared the
ford, made a masterly march over the river towards
Baitool where we had a large treasury. Once over the
Nerbudda, it was feared Tantia had gone for the Dekkan,
and our Colonel, strengthened by a troop of 17th Lancers,
two Horse Artillery guns, and a squadron of 3rd Bombay
Cavalry, was directed to follow, but one day's halt at
Bhopal was necessary to get our regimental gear into
repair; besides, the visit was a pleasant change to us all
after so many weeks in the trackless forests of Bundlekunde. It was therefore with pleasant satisfaction we saw
the gilded minarets of Her Highness the Begum's palace
glittering in the morning sunshine amidst the plentiful
groves of trees which ornament her capital; she moreover
was famous for her cordial welcome to all British officers,
and energetic support to their government, nor had anyone
been so steadfastly our friend during the recent trials as
Her Highness.[3]

[1] Major Sir Alexander Cunningham (1814–93), Bengal Engineers.
Obtained a cadetship through Sir Walter Scott. Was present at Chillianwallah and Goojerat. Wrote *The Bhilsa Topes or Buddhist Monuments of
Central India (1854)*, Topes being monuments erected over sacred relics
of Buddha or on scenes of his acts.

[2] Lieutenant William Alexander Kerr, 24th Bombay Native Infantry,
Adjutant of the South Mahratta Horse, who won the V.C. at Kolapore,
10 July 1857.

[3] Nawab Sikandar Begum of Bhopal. (1816–68).

Our tents were pitched in one of her gardens of orange, citron, jasmin, and rose bushes, and just without were many buildings, pillared and domed, each chronicling some mythological event. Supplies for us and our cattle were in such abundance that even they appeared to be sensible of having emerged into more friendly territory. Our appetites, too, sharpened by weeks of indifferent food, were not forgotten. A train of servants approached, bearing on trays a feast that would have graced the halls of Lucullus; there were stews, curries, pilaus, sweetmeats and fruits of endless variety, accompanied with a message of welcome, enquiries for our health, and an invitation to the palace at the hour of 3.[1] What a contrast to our reception by Holkar and Scindiah! Here everything was frankly and cheerfully done, while at Indore and Gwalior, rightly or wrongly, it was impossible I could divest myself of the idea that treachery and covert deceit filled the atmosphere.

At 3, as appointed, down came the state elephants, with gorgeous trappings and howdahs, to convey us to the royal presence. With them was a large cavalcade of her soldiery, and these were doubled by all our native officers, gorgeously bedizened in tinsel of silver and gold on many coloured garments, for strange to say, each one managed to produce a gala dress from amongst his scanty baggage. As we threaded our way through the streets of the beautiful city, abounding in buildings and groups I longed to stay and sketch, the inhabitants gave us looks of welcome.

At length, on reaching the palace courtyard, we passed the household troops dressed in British uniform. It became them so quaintly, and together with British drill, rendered them so exceedingly comic that we had some difficulty in preserving a becoming gravity of countenance as the line presented arms. The scene reminded me of the Sultan's

[1] It is evident from Sylvester's *Diary* that this visit to the Begum took place on 16 October and therefore ten days before the first wild charge of Beatsons' Horse.

museum of stuffed soldiers at Constantinople. I almost expected to see the iron rod between their feet, which screwed them to the ground, but who knows, we too, in the howdah, may have been a ludicrously pompous quartette, dressed in scarlet helmets and white horsehair plumes which tilted ignominiously by the fore and aft pitching of the mammoth's body as he knelt to deposit us at the entrance, the first motion involving a clutch at the handrail to prevent being shot out in the rear, and the second threatened to plunge us headlong amongst the lay figures. A moment more, and a final stroke at our beards, we followed our conductors through a series of dark passages and low staircases, lit by the glare of torches, to the presence of royalty. Those unaccustomed to oriental palaces, the smell of burning cocoa nut oil and blackened ceilings would hardly fail to impress unfavourably, but it must be recollected that the object of architects in England is to admit light, but in Asia, to exclude it, for what so precious as cool shade in the tropics?

Having traversed the sooty passages, we emerged on a flat roof covering one of the palace towers. It was cushioned and carpetted in scarlet, and shaded by an awning. Here we were received by Her Highness' chief engineer and superintendent of public works, who conducted us into her presence. She received us with much cordiality, unveiled and attended by one lady companion only. One after another, some forty of 'Beatson's nobles' made their obeisance and were seated, after which the Begum, in a few intelligent sentences thanked us for the part we had contributed in saving her city.

I had now time to survey the state room: it was long, low and narrow, its floor covered by Persian carpets, its ceiling with a cloth of gay damask. Running down the centre of the room was a long English dining room table, laden with ornaments and curiosities of French and English manufacture: stuffed birds, artificial flowers, stereoscopic views, musical boxes (several of which were all set going at once),

singing birds, and a host of gay trivialities reminding one of
a fancy bazaar. A few badly executed prints and quaint en-
gravings adorned the walls, but the prospect from her
window was magnificent, commanding as it did three or four
miles of lake, on one side beautifully shaded by a wooded
hill, at the base of which, tufts of feathery bamboos dipped
in the water. On the opposite shore, the mangrove, bulrush,
lotus and water lily literally teemed with wild fowl. Far
beyond all were grey forest hills through which Tantia, un-
tired, was wending his way to Baitool.

Our native officers were thoroughly amused by the
collection on the table, but many of them were startled at
the public appearance of an unveiled follower of the prophet,
while we admired the independence of the Begum, who,
strong in her own honest principles, refused to be bound by
benighted prejudices. Her only child, a daughter, was at
that period just wedded to the most athletic officer in Her
Highness's army, and the motive urged for the choice
amused us.[1] The same friendly spirit towards the British
appears to have been transmitted to the child, who now
reigns in her mother's stead, and shortly before I left India,
she was invested in Bombay with the Grand Order of the
Star of India.

Showers of rose water were thrown over us, and coffee
with betel and pan [betel leaf possibly with spices, etc.]
handed round before we took our leave, with her assurance
that everything in her city and territory was at our service,
and as the engineer who spoke English fluently pressed us
to accompany him on a small steamer anchored beneath the
palace, we readily availed ourselves of the offer and were
well repaid by the scenery as we sped lightly over the water,
almost startled by the cries of 'ease her', 'back her', 'stop her'.
The engineer had been educated after a prevalent English
fashion in India, and a conceit not uncommon resulted.
I asked if he ever attempted to explain the propelling

[1] The Begum's daughter, Nawab Shah Jehan (1838–1901) married,
first, Bakshi Bahi Muhammad Khan, who died in 1867.

power of the little craft to the inhabitants, to which, with a
scornful air, he replied, 'Why should I teach the brute
creation?'

On returning from our cruise, a second invitation bade us
return after sunset, in order to see the palace lit up. To be
invited by such an ally was to be commanded and we went
accordingly, passing through her lighted streets and
gardens which were as though the fairies had been enslaved
to drive the firefly host among the giant leaves and scented
flowers. The palace, with its countless coloured lights on
every point and pinnacle, must have seemed another milky
way to those in higher worlds than ours.

We rallied our Colonel by the way home, on the court
paid him by our eastern queen. It cheered him, all drooping
as he was from work and watching far beyond his strength,
for he had waited weary years, fondly hoping for the time
when he should shine in that bright, peculiar host of heroes,
dubbed with mystic letters alphabetical, and, now the prize
was in his grasp, and spirit willing, his strength was sapped
and Azrael's [the Muslim's Angel of Death] dart hung
poised over him.

Not with us alone, but with many who were galled by
incessant work, the effect of a holiday was beneficial, and
that same night we again set out in pursuit, but this time
strengthened by two guns, a weak troop of the 17th Lancers, and two Horse Artillery guns. This was a sop to
Cerberus, for Colonel Becher, though an Indian Officer, was
senior to Parke and others in the field with a brigade, and
none were more competent to handle mounted troops. In
vain he asked his rights and pleaded seniority.

In two days we had crossed the river and were on the
rebel track. They were fourteen miles in advance, at the
village of Mooltye, proclaiming themselves but the advanced
guard of the Peishwa's force, which, glutted with victory,
was now returning to the Dekkan. This was fairly believed
despite the animated skeletons they bestrode, the naked
hoofs and crippled feet; despite their ragged clothes which

hung in tatters on the wayside bushes; and how they ex-
plained the cruel necessity which abandoned their wounded
to the hovering carrion birds, I cannot say.

At this time we had spies in their camp who told us that,
though dispirited and distressed for beasts of burden, yet
they were resolved on going to Poona. These spies were
curiously rewarded by being permitted to seize three times
as many rupees from a heap as they could fairly gather up
in each clutch, and these, owing to the puny hand of the
Asiatic, were strangely few when counted, yet there was an
appearance of reckless magnificence in the mode of pay-
ment which pleased them.

On arriving at Budnoor,[1] the cantonment of Baitool, we
were exceedingly welcome. The political agent, MacGeorge,
and his tiny party had fortified the jail with gabions
[wicker work filled with earth] and all was ready for a
siege, in place of which they entertained us sumptuously.
Being prevented in their descent on Baitool, and probably
informed of our reinforcement, Tantia forced a march of
twenty-three miles and that same night the Banda Nawab,
who understands the English language and character, wrote
a letter which he forwarded by the hands of an old and
faithful servant, and in this he begged to know if his life
would be spared on surrender. He stated that his wife and
children were with him and begged a reply couched in the
English character (in case of its falling into Tantia's hands)
might be sent to a village twenty-five miles distant. His
request was complied with, but no promise given. He was
at liberty to gather what comfort he might from a copy of
Lord Canning's proclamation enclosed, and as I have
already related, he gave himself up to General Michel in
consequence.

Tantia now made for the Taptee valley which is but
sparsely populated and yielded but a bare subsistence to his
followers. He plundered all he desired, burnt the villages,
and mutilated those friendly to the British, or any in our

---

[1] 10 November 1858.

employ. Our column attempted to follow, and though perhaps alone we might have succeeded, yet with the addition of European troops it became impossible. Nothing in the shape of food could be purchased; we were driven to cut the standing corn, while the soldiers chased and killed the village pigs notwithstanding our endeavours to dissuade them from meat so unclean, and to add to our difficulties, when at Goodgaum in the valley of the Poorna, we were again reinforced by a troop of the 8th Hussars and a squadron of 3rd Bombay Cavalry. Lieutenant Goldsworthy[1] was appointed staff officer.

Anything more charming than the wild wooded beauty of the valleys which we were now traversing cannot be conceived; the mornings too were positively cold and bracing, and those of us not subject to fever were in rude health. Herds of large game existed hereabouts — spotted deer, hog, antelope, bison, tigers, and bears — but news of Tantia failed us utterly. Our spies declared that he had gone to Burhanpoor, and we, starving, had no choice but to make for the fertile valley of Berar. On the 17th of October[2] we descended a thousand feet and entered a warmer climate. Next day we halted in the Nizam's territories, at Ellichpoor.

So sudden and determined a descent by the rebels towards the Dekkan brought a number of local forces into the field: Brigadier Hill[3] moved out the Nizam's troops to Dhool ghaut, General Beatson a force from Jaulnah, Sir Hugh Rose advanced to Ahmednugger, Colonel Tapp to Adjuntag, General Michel had arrived at Hoosingabad, and another force under Colonel Benson[4] was on this side the Nerbudda, in our rear. Nor should General Whitlock be forgotten: at this date he was still *going round*, marching and countermarching on the banks of the Dussaun river,

---

[1] Lieutenant Walter Tuckfield Goldworthy, 8th Hussars.

[2] Should be 17 November 1858. (*Diary.*)

[3] Brigadier William Hill, the first commander of the entire Hyderabad Contingent, which, until 1856, had consisted of the Northern and Southern Divisions.

[4] Lieutenant-Colonel Henry Roxby Benson, 17th Lancers.

and no length of road was so intimately known to all in his force as that about Saugor, and while a local celebrity called Dus Put was keeping him amused, he had not by any means abandoned hope of distinction by catching Tantia, and now that Tantia had actually come near unto General Whitlock, Dus Put's lair was allowed to remain in peace, and the General consulted with Mr Freeling,[1] the political agent, as to the precise amount and quality of salt to be used on Tantia's caudal member.

The rebels were almost surrounded, but though they divided under different leaders, the main body was not far distant from Asseerghur, and watched an opportunity to dash through our cordon into Candeish. Without precise information, Colonel Becher was deterred from moving rapidly in any direction, but crossing the Poorna to Edulabad, he was ordered to place his force at the disposal of yet another aspirant, Colonel Somerset.[2] Fortunately, before the day closed this order was cancelled, and to our great delight and astonishment, we were placed under command of Sir Hugh Rose, now advanced to Seerpore.

On the 2nd of November[3] I visited the graves of Major Follett and the Dragoons who died of cholera during our first advance into Central India, and at night a dispatch, from Captain Davis[4] of the police cleared up our doubts respecting the rebel position. They had turned their faces once more towards Hindoostan, and save some five hundred who separated to the Puchmurree hills, had recrossed the Nerbudda: not all at once, however, did they recross. Colonel Becher's force, now broken up in small parties, at Bampoor, Keygoon, Geysoor, Charwah, Hurda, Rye, and

---

[1] This may be Mr George Hamilton Freeling, Magistrate and Deputy Commissioner, Humerpoor.

[2] Lieutenant-Colonel Charles Henry Somerset, 72nd Highlanders.

[3] 2 December. On that day Sylvester was at Burhampore, where Follett was buried. (*Diary*.)

[4] The letter from Captain Davis was received during dinner on 2 December. (*Diary*.) This may have been Captain William Davis, 31st Bengal Native Infantry. He had been present at Maharajpore, Chillianwallah and Goojerat.

Peeplode, constantly came upon traces of them: now it was a horse tied to a tree, its owner probably secreted near; sometimes one of the traitors, who, convinced that his gods had forsaken him, surrendered; at others we found worn out horses or ponies and hereabouts we discovered a trooper of the 1st Bombay Lancers who had mutinied at Neemuch. While broken up in these small detachments, we suffered much from hunger, having no means to cook, and I was often compelled to eat parched grain, and considered a chuppattie a luxury.

On the 15th of November,[1] while out patrolling with thirty of our troopers and eighty Lancers under Captain Macartney,[2] we discovered the track, through high grass and thick jungle, by which three hundred and fifty badly mounted men and eight camels had crossed our line. The inhabitants who saw them described their plight as wretched in the extreme, and we were quite convinced of the impossibility of staying their flight in such ground, except by the merest accident.

The orders we received at this period of the chase were most contradictory and harassing: mile upon mile and march upon march, until I began to fancy there was to be no end. Once more we recrossed the Nerbudda and ate our Christmas dinner at Nemour, on its banks.

Tantia had not crossed without molestation. Major Sutherland,[3] who was on the Agra trunk road, heard of the exploit, and with two hundred Highlanders mounted on camels, and two hundred of the Bombay Rifle Corps, went forth to meet him, and came in view of some of his horsemen in flight.[4] Following their direction, he arrived in sight of Tantia's force on a distant hill, but it would not stay to fight. All that could be overtaken were cut up, and the main body fled to Oodepoor, closely followed by Colonel

[1] 14 December. (*Diary*.)

[2] Captain John Macartney, 17th Lancers.

[3] Major Robert Macleod Sutherland, 92nd Highlanders.

[4] The 200 Highlanders consisted of 150 of the 92nd and fifty of the 71st. It was on 24 November 1858, that they sighted Tantia's men.

Parke who caught and punished them severely. In this affair a squadron of the 8th Hussars under Major Clowes, and a troop of the 2nd Bombay Cavalry led by Captain Smith,[1] did good service, and Kerr at length brought the Maharatta Horse into action.

From Oodepoor the enemy passed through the jungles of Banswarra, and it was supposed, intended making a descent on the city of Indore. To prevent this, Colonel Benson, with his cavalry column, made one of the best marches on record. Starting from his encampment, as already indicated, some twelve miles north of the Nerbudda, he crossed the whole of his force, in boats, and reached Mhow, a distance of fifty miles in twenty-six hours. Beatson's Horse, though close to Goona on the Agra trunk road, was for a time out of the race.

Here I think the devil should have his due: Tantia, though hunted from the Jumna to the Dekkan and back again, without base, commissariat, arsenal, or ray of hope in the future, beset on every side, no carriage for his sick and wounded, no spot where even for a day he could rest in safety, often compelled to fight, and reported as disorganised, his forces dwindling, and a reward on his head, still struggled on bravely, giving the greybeards of our service a lesson in marching which had never entered their philosophy.

Leaving Mhow, Colonel Benson and his column marched on Rutlam, detaching a small body of Lancers under Major Learmonth,[2] one stage distant. These, however, rejoined at the expiration of three days, having seen nothing but wandering Bheels who did our people more harm by their thieving propensities than we inflicted on them.

At Rutlam, yet another aspiring officer started, in command of a Cavalry brigade. This was Colonel Somerset. He had with him, in the position of Major of Brigade, an

[1] Major George Gooch Clowes, 8th Hussars (who had been wounded and taken prisoner at Balaclava) and Captain George Smith, 2nd Bombay Light Cavalry.
[2] Major Alexander Learmonth, 17th Lancers.

officer of indomitable energy and great daring, one too who has since both deserved and received great rewards. This officer, Lieutenant Evelyn Wood, moved with his Brigadier on Pertabghur, and thus far they were accompanied by Colonel Benson's brigade. Here an order from Major General Michel directed them to proceed to Ashta with a hundred and fifty Highlanders mounted on camels, and two Horse Artillery guns. At Ashta, Colonel Somerset found the troops in readiness to form his brigade destined to act against Ferozshah, who, with a large body of cavalry, was said to have crossed the Ganges on his way to effect a junction with Tantia, at this time cowering in the Banswarra jungles.

En route to Ashta, Colonel Somerset and his Brigade Major shared the hospitalities of the Nawab of Jowra, through whose capital they passed. He was a sporting character with advanced opinions, and while he treated his guests to English fare which even included champagne and beer, they were much diverted by his splendid stable of Arabs, and zoological collection, for he had tigers, came-leopards, lynxes, bears, cheetahs, and other rare denizens of the jungle, both indigenous and exotic. The Brigade Major astonished his dusky entertainer by vaulting from the first storey balcony to the bare back of the giraffe, and here, astride, without more than a piece of rope on the creature's neck, by which to keep his seat, he withstood all attempts to dislodge him, notwithstanding the great speed and awkward gyrations of the giraffe. Great was the merriment, but at length the awkward and clumsy bounds induced a sickness and vertigo against which four years in the navy had not steeled the imprudent rider, and down he came, receiving a violent blow on the head from the creature's knee, another from its foot on his face, and it was feared by the spectators the freak would have a fatal termination, but after three hours' insensibility, the Brigade Major was himself again.

While Colonel Somerset was reaching Ashta, Colonel Benson pressed onwards after Tantia, and came upon the

wake of his force near Mundeesoor, and ran him hard,
nearly due east of Zeerapoor. He caught and engaged him,
killed a few of his men, and captured seven elephants with
five thousand rupees worth of silver. At Chuppra, Colonel
Somerset's and Colonel Becher's forces met. On the following
day General Michel with part of his troops arrived,[1] and
depriving Colonel Becher of all but his regiment of Beatson's
Horse, he transferred it to Colonel Somerset's command,
and having inspected the animated skeletons on which our
men were mounted, sent us to Kotah.

At this period, a squadron of the 17th Lancers under
Captain White,[2] and two hundred infantry of the 19th
Bombay Regiment, left Indore and marched on Deg.
Tantia, with Colonel Benson in hot pursuit, had just passed
through that place, and Colonel Somerset also was closely
following for he had given up opposition to Ferozshah.
Hearing that his force was insignificant, and meeting
Captain White's detachment at Soosneer, [he] attached it to
his command and reached Zeerapoor one day after Colonel
Benson's capture of elephants. The troops, after their sharp
run, stood in need of rest and were halting.

Here, notwithstanding the strong opposition, intelligence
was received that Ferozshah had effected a junction with
Tantia, and Colonel Somerset, taking with him two of
Benson's Horse Artillery guns, hastened onward sixteen
miles the same evening, halting an hour and a half to feed
his horses. He continued his way at half past 11 until half
past 6 the following evening, when the town of Satul was
reached. The enemy was still ten miles ahead! Again
halting but four hours and a half as a positive necessity, he
marched through the dark, over the worst description of
road and arrived before daylight at the reported rebel
position.

As day broke, a spy brought news of the presence of the

---

[1] 11 January 1859. (*Diary.*)

[2] Captain Robert White, 17th Lancers. Severely wounded at Balaclava.

rebels: Colonel Somerset at once started for the spot. Some
camp followers were located beneath a group of trees but
the fighting men had gone. A cloud of dust indicated their
direction. Our cavalry and infantry advanced at a trot for a
distance of seven miles, and debouching from a village,
came upon three thousand of their cavalry, drawn up in
line. They advanced on our guns at a walk. Their leader,
mounted on a grey horse, greatly excited, endeavoured to
animate his men; unfortunately, the first shot from our
guns knocked him over. Some of his followers dismounted
and carried him away; the remainder, now sensible of the
small force opposing them, endeavoured to turn its
left.

Excepting the escort with the guns, there were barely
fifty of the 17th Lancers under Captain White, who, to
make the most of them, formed 'rank entire' and advanced.
The sight of the two ridiculously disproportioned lines was
one of exceeding beauty and thrilling interest, nor was the
issue certain, with the odds so great against the Lancers,
but at this critical juncture the Highlanders – who had been
unable to keep pace – hove in sight and placed our guns
beyond all danger. The Lancers, having gone two hundred
yards, brought their lances to the engage, galloped, and
with a yell swept down upon the rebel cavalry who,
dreading the crash, hesitated, slackened their pace, halted,
opened out, and fled. Some fell speared at once, the remainder were pursued seven miles, leaving a track well strewn
with their carcases. Those who escaped by reason of the
fleetness of their horses, went crashing through the jungles
like demon hunters.

The Lancers now returned to Barode, from whence they
set out, and encamped or rather bivouacked, for the baggage
and commissariat, which had been completely distanced,
did not arrive until eight days afterwards. All were alike
badly off, none had tents, few bedding: the soldiers were
without tea, arrack, bread, or any of the supplies which the
Indian commissariat scarcely ever fails to supply, even

under the most disadvantageous circumstances, whether on the barren sands of Persia or devastated tracks of Hindoostan, but in this case the shortcoming was unavoidable and this the soldiery knew, and cheerfully subsisted on flour and such additions as the villages supplied. To add to their discomfort, the nights were exceedingly cold and it rained heavily for three days and nights successively. In the evening of the affair the three companies of the 9th Infantry[1] arrived greatly exhausted.

Barode was searched, and not fruitlessly: munitions of war were found stored for the rebels; chiefly they consisted of one hundred and seventy seers of leaden bullets, two hundred seers of gunpowder, a hundred mallets and some thousands of tent pegs and lamps. Besides these, an elephant and some prisoners were captured.

After separating from Colonels Somerset and Benson at Chuppra, General Michel with part of his force marched for Kotah in Rajpootana. Beatson's Horse, by a parallel route, made for the same city, and we reached it on the 22nd of January. Tantia, whose race was nearly run, appeared to be also making in that direction, and at this stage of the pursuit it was discovered that his route was by no means so erratic as commonly supposed, and though so hotly pursued by many columns, he seldom deviated from a prearranged line of country, and on that line supplies and grain were stored for his force. Could we have gained this intelligence, we might have entrapped him, but the supplies were consumed and the arch-rebel flown before any particulars reached us.

At Barode, during the search, a letter written by an official at Jalraputtan was recovered. It directed supplies to be stored for Tantia. Great were the efforts made by the Vakeel to regain the guilty paper: a thousand rupees were offered the Brigade Major, and these fair means failing, they foully robbed his tent of all save the bed on which he slept. All kinds of little treasures, including his four medals,

---

[1] This should be 19th Infantry (Bombay).

were cleverly abstracted, but the letter had been for safety deposited in the field treasure chest, and they failed to obtain it.[1]

[1] Evelyn Wood records this incident in *From Midshipman to Field Marshal.*

XII

The End of Tantia Topee

THE country between the Agra trunk road and Kotah was for the most part exceedingly wild, and this season was green and pleasant. Large tracts were covered with thorn and babool [thorned mimosa] jungle, and around the villages were splendid banyan and tamarind trees. At almost every halting place the large tanks or lakes literally swarmed with wild duck and teal, and when disturbed, they wheeled overhead in clouds. Along the swampy margins of these sheets of water snipe were equally plentiful, and started from the mud in wisps at every footstep. In the fields and trees, peafowl were in countless numbers, hares too, and painted partridges, were equally abundant: so far as flesh and fowl were concerned, we lacked nothing. Frequently on the line of march, sounders of wild hog could be seen at early morning, returning from a foray on the village corn, and on one occasion a herd ran violently through our regiment, much to the horror of Mussleman troopers, and our amusement.

General Michel's force was already encamped before Kotah when we arrived for a stay of some days, to recruit our horses, many of whom were so reduced in strength as to be unable to drag their legs up muddy river banks, and at every such place we left a few to die. The felt of our native saddles had so worked into the wounds on the spine that the men hesitated to remove them. We were in truth fit subjects for prosecution by that society whose noble aim is to prevent unnecessary torture, and nowhere on the face of the earth is its operation more needed than in India.

Could they, poor suffering brutes, have spoken, they would have joined us in the prospect of rest at a place so

full of interest as Kotah. The enemy had stood an eight day
siege here, months before,[1] and after amusing General
Roberts and his force, escaped through his lines. Kotah lies
on the right bank of the Chumbul river which, opposite the
city, is wide and deep, and though the country near is not
strikingly attractive, being often covered with huge sand-
stone slabs cropping up amidst stunted bushes, yet surrounding the city ramparts are magnificent gardens and
park-like enclosures of trees, trees too which grow gigantic
and in great variety of beauty. The cypress, pepul, mango,
tamarind, jack, and many others cast welcome tropical shade
over an undergrowth of orange, pomelo, citron, pomegranate, bamboo, jasmine, rose, guava, plantain and rose bushes.
There was yet a far greater variety than I can call to
memory, all artificially watered from the abundance in the
Chumbul.

On the east side were two lakes: the larger swarmed with
wild fowl, and the sacred bird of the Egyptians fed in
numbers. From the centre of the smaller sprang the surface
of a rock which had been appropriately chosen as the site
of a summer palace. This, brightly reflected in all its minute
detail on the clear water below, was a very type of beauty,
and suggestive of pleasant retirement from cares of state.

At the southern extremity of the city the palace was a
prominent object, abounding as it did with cupolas, domes,
tapering minarets and towering kiosks, all covered with the
profusely rich sculpture of oriental architecture. Splendidly
pillared and domed monumental buildings commemmorated
a long line of chieftains, progenitors of the chief then
reigning, who, amongst his subjects, had earned a celebrity
for prowess in arms, but to believe this it was necessary
not to see him. The armorial bearings of the family, judging
from their repetition on public buildings, consisted of two
elephants in deadly combat.

During the afternoon of our arrival I rode to the city,
which was walled, and the bastions bore traces of recent

[1] 22–30 March 1858.

repair, but no other vestige of the siege remained. The
streets, though narrow, were picturesque and the houses
well built. I had just time to think the men looked tolerably
friendly and the women very fair and pretty, when I was
compelled to withdraw to a side street, to make way for the
Rajah, then proceeding in state to visit General Michel.

First in procession came a body of matchlockmen in
native clothing: many had their long whiskers twisted over
their ears, and pieces of gay colored material passed beneath
their chins, and knotted over their turbans; all appeared to
be suffering from dislocated jawbones. Their fuses, in coils
attached to the matchlocks, were lighted. Next came a body
of well fed greasy looking cavalry on bloated horses, all the
more so in my eyes, accustomed to our emaciated troopers.
Standing martingales and cruel bits caused most of the
passing horses to walk on their hind legs only. Many of their
riders were terrible with the sword, for some wore two,
others three, besides carbines and pistols. Occasionally it
was the correct thing for one of these warriors to leave his
ranks, dart forward at a gallop, impale an imaginary enemy,
and drop quietly into his place again. In dress, uniform or
uniformity was unknown; Judson's list of simple dyes was
surpassed in variety of colour.

Next came the regular infantry, dressed as British
Grenadiers, marching with a pompous, stilted air, resembling marionettes rather than men. The commandant had
distinguished himself from the rank and file by cutting his
tunic from the selvage of the scarlet cloth, taking care to
preserve the word 'superfine' which, in gilt letters, ran
down his back; the last however was missing because he
was wanting in stature. All were armed with old flintlock
muskets which had probably done duty under Clive and
Wellington.

After the infantry followed the chantry priests, immediately surrounding the Rajah. It appeared their duty to
watch narrowly any flitting emotion of pain or pleasure on
the satiated features of their master. The uncouth noises

and facial twitchings, I noticed, provoked exclamations of sympathy and exhortation which doubtless soothed his dyspeptic qualms. Now came the Rajah, preceeded by his gaily caparisoned charger which, with pink mane and tail, and sides quivering with fat, was led by two attendants. The great man himself, half reclining on a species of sedan chair, was carried on the shoulders of a number of men and shaded by a state umbrella. In figure he was portly, in countenance unprepossessing, and altogether unlike a man who had won prowess with the sword.

Following were more matchlockmen with their jaws bound on, more marionettes, and last of all, two small brass cannon without limbers. The gunners were mounted. One carried the sponge staff jauntily across his shoulders, the other a lighted portfire.

Tired of the barbarous cavalcade, I returned to camp through the gardens, and here, in a quiet corner, found a beautiful graveyard overhung with foliage, its walls and tombs green with mosses, lichen and liverworts. Here sleep Major Burton,[1] his two sons, and a daughter who were murdered during the rebellion after a brave defence of themselves for hours on their housetop. Alongside were the graves of Hancock, two medical officers, and six or seven soldiers who fell during the siege. A mile distant were the remains of the once handsome residence of the Burtons, well situated on the river side, commanding a distant view of the city and miles of the meandering Chumbul.

Many an honest tribute from the avenging hands of our British soldiery was pencilled on the white interior walls of the room in which the bloodstain of the Burtons was still fresh: verses too, written with the charred timbers, bade their spirits rest in peace. A native gardener boy described the harrowing scene with sembled feeling, but unfortun-

[1] Major Charles Æneas Burton, born in Dinapore, 6 February 1812. Served in 8th, 40th, 28th and 73rd Bengal Native Infantry and 1st Bengal Light Cavalry. In Gwalior Campaign, 1843. He was Political Agent when murdered in Kotah on 15 October 1857, when the Kotah Contingent mutinied.

ately for him I had long ceased to believe in any feeling other than the deepest hatred from the Asiatic towards the European, and twenty long years of residence has further unveiled the cunning treachery deep rooted in the natives of India.

On returning to camp, I found that Brigadier Parke had sent in a confirmatory report that the main body of rebels had gone north, and it was doubtful whether their leader, Tantia, had not crossed over to Nepaul in disguise. In consequence of this intelligence, General Michel prepared to march on Jeypoor. The return visit to the Rajah had however to be made on the morrow and all officers off duty were directed to attend. Accordingly, about 4 o'clock in the afternoon, we set out for the city, accompanied by an escort of Lancers, and traversed a mile of narrow streets to the palace entrance. Here, dismounting we entered a large square courtyard where, on a raised and canopied dias, sat the Rajah, his son and courtiers. A native interpreter was in attendance and after the customary interchange of compliments, a nautch took place, of which we shortly very thoroughly tired, and is usual on such occasions, the beauties of the place were not exhibited. Then followed our investiture, one by one, of a garland of overpoweringly fragrant jasmine, while the Rajah sat complacently nursing a pet sword in his lap and chewing betel and pan.

Anything more ludicrous could hardly be imagined than the appearance of stout sunburnt officers in full dress, over which hung to the waist a garland of white jasmine. The general was first adorned. I had seen Paul Bedford as Grisi in *Norma* and my memory brought to mind the wreath of carrots and turnips alternating. Need I add, the parallel was complete?

Still wearing our garlands, we threaded a labyrinth of narrow, dirty passages and staircases, to gain the roof of the palace, from which a glorious view of the river, city, gardens, lakes and surrounding country was visible. Descending slowly, the Rajah leading with slow and stately steps, we viewed the interior of his palace. It was beautifully and tastefully furnished. Many of the walls were of elaborately sculptured marble, and one room was devoted to oriental paintings, but the treat of the day was to be witnessed from a balcony overlooking the elephant pens. A combat between two male elephants was ordered for our edification.

Immediately beneath us was a splendid specimen, with its huge tusks bound with iron rings to prevent their injury. Its hind legs were firmly secured to the wall of the building by massive chains, and together by cables, so that he was restrained from breaking across a stout broad mound of masonry, chest high, over which, in a state of great excitement, he watched for his antagonist to appear.

After a few moments' suspense, his antagonist appeared in the courtyard, with uplifted trunk and trumpeting furiously. Each dashed at the other across the mound, the object of which, as well as the tethers, was at once apparent, but even with these precautions the shock was terrific as the leviathan skulls met, while the noise of the huge tusks grating the one against the other was rather sickening and resembled that of giant oak boughs riding in heavy wind.

The elephant beneath our balcony needed no encouragement, but spearmen in waiting occasionally goaded the other into greater fury. Occasionally he was driven off to secure another charge, and then, with uplifted trunk and tail, the crash was renewed. If the attacking beast missed his aim, by clever fence on the other's part, his head was forced down on the mound and the attacked endeavoured to drag his opponent over. The barbarity was altogether on a scale too large to please us, and taking leave, we returned by torchlight to camp.

In the morning, General Michel had gone, and we had yet a few more days to halt and recruit, but the opportunity to fish in the Chumbul was not to be lost. Clay and I, provided with bait and tackle, took a ferry boat and dropped

down the river opposite the city[1] and here the steps of the
numerous ghauts [landing stages] leading to the water's
brim were covered with women, girls and children of all
ages, busied bathing and washing their gay coloured clothing. The scene was as pretty and the faces prettier than
anything analagous on the Grand Canal of Venice.

Anchoring under lea of a temple, we cast in our baits
which were instantly seized by huge Mahseer, far too
heavy for our tackle; nevertheless, we had no sooner
helped one over the boat's edge than another was ready.
The fish seemed positively too apathetic to resist their fate.
Every now and then a broad and ponderous tortoise, of
which there were numbers, swallowed our baits and bit
away our hooks. We were in a fair way of covering the
bottom of our boat with heavy fish, when our rods refused
more duty and I landed and bought bamboos instead. The
sport, however, attracted the notice of the Brahmins in the
temple above us, and shortly afterwards a note from the
Rajah begged us to desist as the fish were *sacred* and daily
fed by the priests. This of course we knew not before, and
regretting the end of such excellent sport, we returned to
camp, sorry to have inflicted a blow on Hindoo prejudice.

Next morning, at sunrise, we set out to wage war against
the wild hog, against which no objection could be urged.
One of the officials – a jemedar – promised to show us good
ground, but as he was not to his appointment, we started
alone, Clay and myself. Passing the site of the old Kotah
Residency, we reached the open country which was covered
by acacia shrubs, babool and scrub jungle. Here we beat the
bushes and found wild pig in numbers, but after making
futile attempts to keep them in sight and ride them, our
guide appeared and took us some distance, where the
country was more open. Here we found a herd of over
twenty, and dashing at the biggest, we shortly succeeded in

[1] 30 January 1859. Three days later, on 2 February, although he was
presumably unaware of it at the time, Sylvester became a Fellow of the
Geological Society of London.

spearing him. While we stood contemplating how to get our spoil to camp, another boar, still larger, passed in sight, and setting out alone in pursuit, I overtook and three times speared him, but on the last occasion my bamboo broke in half and left me at his mercy. Foaming at the mouth, and with a noise now eminently disagreeable, he charged and overthrew both myself and horse, while in his rage he rolled over us. My horse at once regained his feet and in vain I attempted to spring upon the saddle, but snorting with fear he dragged back at the rein I held while the boar for a moment meditated another attack, and then, to my great relief, trotted off with my half spear protruding from his back. My horse, a grey, and myself, were covered with blood and foam, nor was it until some time had elapsed I could quiet him and ascertain that, beyond a few gashes he had received from the boar's tusks, we had escaped unhurt.

I returned to my companion, and with the assistance of a native, we dragged his pig to the nearest village, hoping to get paid assistance to carry it to camp. Here we met with nothing but abuse, and while riding through the streets were assailed with threats and stones and were compelled to make an ignominious retreat. The Rajah professed his regret at our treatment and promised that his hunters should recover my spear and the hog's head as a trophy, but I never heard of either.

And now our few days' permitted rest were at an end; the morrow was to see us on our way again, and knowing this, the Rajah got up another little surprise for our amusement. At midday a hurried message from him stated that a tiger had just killed a bullock by the river side, and that he awaited our company to proceed to the spot. We were soon at the palace with our rifles, where our entertainer joined us in his pleasure boat with a numerous and gaily-dressed suite. These gentlemen were armed with elaborate matchlocks, he himself with an English rifle. In a second boat was his band. Aided by the current we soon accomplished eight

miles on the river which runs through a deep channel of old
red sandstone. The banks were bold and rocky and occasional boulders of the same formation lay in the bed of the
stream, their summits above the water level, and here on
these projections, basking in the sun, were numbers of
alligators and tortoises of great dimensions. The Rajah and
his staff declared that oftentimes British officers had been
known to catch these tortoises for edible purposes. We
hoped not.

On our way we saw several beasts of prey on the river
bank, amongst them a half grown tiger which we did not
molest. By and by we reached the mouth of a ravine which
ran down to the river and were told to be prepared. Immediately, a line of shikarees [hunters], firing blank charges
from matchlocks, swept from the distant end of the ravine
towards us, the reports of their firearms echoing in a
hundred rocky caverns – but there appeared no tiger. He
was stated to have broken back through the line of beaters.
We were subsequently informed that all sporting Europeans visiting Kotah were invited to kill *that* tiger. It was a
pardonable deception. We enjoyed the scenery and fired at
alligators on our return, while the band, in executing
English music, might well have accounted for the dis-
appearance of animals for whose savage breasts *music* had
charms.

On the 5th of February, being directed to cooperate with
Smith's brigade, we started in the direction of Indurghur.
At each halting place villagers reported the rebels to be
breaking up in despair, the largest number together being
about 1,500 men, and these had gone to the desert around
Bikaneer. We scoured the hill country around Boondee, but
met with none save friends. Several of our forces were in the
district of Tonk. We foregathered with Smith's brigade and
a force commanded by Colonel de Salis. Our Adjutant, tired
of the pursuit, left us for Deeolee, and our Colonel was sick
and dying, insomuch that we carried him on our route.
Nevertheless, the will-o'-the-wisp compelled us to continue

in what seemed now the almost hopeless task of catching him.

At length, towards the end of February, when the hot weather began fairly to set in, we received instructions to halt and suspend hostilities as Ferozshah and the Rao Sahib, with their followers, had made overtures of surrender to Brigadier Parke, and that 300 men had already been pardoned by General Michel. These were for the most part deluded cultivators of Oudh, and to all had been furnished a free pass and money to reach their homes. They were allowed to retain their ponies and camels which were in a deplorable condition.

The part which had made for the desert, though for a while safe from us, were threatened with starvation and went rapidly south to the Aravelli range of hills, but in consequence of the stout resistance offered by a few men of the Mhairwar battalion, they were driven from the first pass in the range, to another called Chutterbooge. Here too they were caught by a force under Colonel Holmes, which inflicted some loss on them, and Brigadier Honnor[1] killed others in a night attack. Colonel Somerset, pursuing south, pressed them so hard by a determined march of 122 miles with scarce a halt, that the fugitives fell exhausted by the way and preferred death to further struggle.

A feat quite worth recording was performed by a native officer of the 2nd Bombay Cavalry during this rapid advance. A party of five troopers, under Moideen Khan, was detached on the right flank to gain intelligence, and while thus engaged in the walled village of Khonkrowlee, Tantia's force arrived at the gates. The Subedar had just time to close them and attempt an escape at a second outlet, when again he found himself and party face to face with the rebel sowars, but dashing at a third gate, the six men got fairly

---

[1] Colonel John Holmes (1808–78). Major–General, 1862. Brigadier Sir Robert William Honner. Served nearly twenty years as a subaltern. Punjab campaign, 1848–9. Brigadier in Persia, 1857. Commanded Nusseerabad Brigade during the Mutiny.

out, and rode for their lives, pursued by 150 rebel horse.
For five miles the troopers held together and the pursuing
party had dwindled considerably though a great number
still followed, but the pace had told on one of the troopers'
horses and it was evident that in a few moments more the
rider must be cut up. The Subedar was equal to the
occasion; he halted, and fronted his little band, prepared to
accept the fortune of war. In a moment more the dastardly
pursuers turned, and Moideen Khan brought his men 72
miles to camp next day. He received the Order for Valour.

No means were neglected to introduce the Royal Proclamation of pardon amongst the fugitives, but it was not
adapted to their nature and they treated it with centempt,
and so, on the occasions we and other forces suspended
hostilities for a few days, they seized the opportunity and
(save the 300 I have spoken of as in no way guilty of murder
or mutiny) broke through our line, crossed the Agra trunk
road to the densely wooded districts of Nursinghur. On this
place all the forces rushed forthwith, and in addition, General
Showers brought troops from Agra to Hanotee.

It would be tedious to others were I to recount the
marching and counter marching which continued as ener-
getically as ever through the month of March, but the hot
season having then thoroughly established itself, some of
the larger force was broken up as being no longer required
to extinguish the now despicable ashes of the rebellion,
yet so long as a leader so able, influential, and determined as
Tantia, was at large, it was obvious that Government could
by no means afford to abandon active pursuit and General
Napier came down to Seronge, in the heart of the wild
territory which Tantia and the remainder of those still
abroad could not escape from.

From Seronge, in concert with General Michel, commanding Mhow Division, all orders emanated. A cordon of
troops was posted through Bundlekunde to prevent the
rebels going south, and Beatson's Horse was directed to
keep that portion between Bairseah and Shumshabad, but

so dense was the forest around us that it was wellnigh impossible for horsemen to act, and our march was made in single file.

About the 1st of April, the Rao and his followers crossed de Salis' line of baggage, killed a bandmaster, wounded a sepoy, and carried off some camels, but his force took their revenge. Existence while in these uncultivated and sparsely populated districts was difficult to maintain so far as food was concerned, and to an invalid, life was almost impossible; consequently Colonel Becher, now at the point of death, was carried to Indore where he died at the Residency on the day after his arrival.[1] He died as he had wished to do, in harness.

The very large tract of wild territory to which it appeared our future operations were to be limited, belonged to the Maharajah Scindiah who for some reason proclaimed a certain vassal and landholder, by name Maun Singh, an outlaw. During Tantia's wanderings, he and his ragged host paid a predatory visit to the village where Maun Singh resided and ruled. Maun Singh went forth, after the Oriental custom, to meet the arch rebel as he approached the confines of his district, thinking no doubt a little obeisance might moderate Tantia's exactions, which among others were that Maun Singh should join forces with him and wage a crusade against the British, but Maun Singh, never a great enemy of ours, was far too astute to embrace a cause so positively hopeless, and declining the proposition, was made prisoner.

Escape, so long as life lasted, was easy enough at times when Tantia was pressed to extremity, and thus, on a favorable occasion, Maun Singh regained his freedom, with malice rankling in his bosom towards Tantia. About the middle of April, while Maun Singh was in treaty with

---

[1] 'He died the day after reaching the Residency, very easily, & from what we gathered was unconscious, his end was so near poor fellow, we shall never see his like again, he died April 2nd & was buried with military honors in Indore.' (*Diary.*)

Quarter Master General Bolton and probably desirous to show his willingness to serve our Government, Tantia, unluckily for him, with *two* followers only, sought shelter in the territory of his former captive. Here then was at once an opportunity to pay off old scores with Tantia and regain at a bound favor with the British. There can be no question that the resolve to betray Tantia, even for so great gain, was not formed without hesitation; caste ties are stronger than those of freemasonry and curiously enough, the day before Maun Singh had made his resolve, Tantia had left his hiding place. Nevertheless, Maun Singh wrote to Major Meade,[1] requesting that a native officer and 50 sepoys might be sent for his disposal. These[2] he placed in ambush near a hut in a dry watercourse, and dispatched a servant to recall Tantia, on pretence of making an important communication. For once the wily Mahratta was deceived and returned to the place appointed, and here, under various pretexts, was detained until nightfall, and slept, as also did his attendants.

At a preconcerted signal, the sepoys crept from their ambush and Maun Singh softly took away Tantia's sword. The few moments preceeding their arrival were fraught with terrible suspense, but all had been well arranged: they rushed into the hut and in an instant Tantia and his servants were prisoners of the British. One zealous sepoy seized Tantia by the beard and angered him furiously until released by order of the native officer.

A waking glance showed Tantia what had befallen him and turning to Maun Singh he asked, 'What kind of friendship is this?' 'I never knew before that you were my friend' retorted his betrayer; and thus fell the Nana's great aide-de-camp who once led thousands to the field. He was carried to Sipree in a palanquin and betrayed no fear until set down accidentally at the foot of a gin which had been used for mounting guns. Doubtless his imagination

---

[1] Major Richard John Meade, then Gwalior Political Agent.

[2] 9th Bombay Native Infantry, under a Jemadar (Lieutenant).

conceived it to be the gallows in readiness. It was not so, but he manifested great fear until told that a chance of proving his innocence before a Court Martial would be allowed him. He was placed under a European guard, and when tried, made no defence. He declared that in all that he had done he had but obeyed his master the Nana who, to the hour of his death, he stoutly maintained had never ordered the massacre of women and children.

Among the witnesses at Tantia's trial was a villager of Maun Singh's, and when thus describing himself, Tantia interrupted by asking the witness how, if a villager, it came to pass that he was present at the Betwa. The witness was silent.

The court sentenced Tantia to be hanged, the Governor General approved by telegraph, and the execution took place at Sipree.[1] It is more than probable that the igno-minious fate of their leader deprived the others still at large of all hope. At all events, nothing more than bands of marauders were left for our capture.

[1] 18 April 1859.

XIII

Peshawur

For yet another year, through the hot weather and following monsoon of 1859, did we continue in the fastnesses of Bundlekunde, making long raids in all weathers. Once, on the 14th of July, we succeeded in cutting up about thirty, and on another occasion, three. We varied the sport, when at leisure, by stalking tiger, bear, or deer, of which there were plenty, but fever and dysentery were rife amongst us, induced by bad drinking water, and the only other European officer of the regiment left for England.[1] It may therefore be imagined that, with pleasure not less than surprise, I discovered while reading one of the Bombay journals, that Lord Elphinstone, mindful of my former desire to go to Africa, had now recommended that Lieutenant

[1] This was Captain Thurburn, who had fallen out with Clay who left the regiment on 22 February 1859. On the same day, Clay's appointment as Adjutant was taken by an officer named by Sylvester as Pearce or Pearse, 10th B. (Bengal) N. I., who was possibly Lieutenant Thomas William West Pierce, 10th Bo. (Bombay) N. I. He relinquished the appointment next day. On 25 March, Colonel Becher left the regiment and on the next day Lieutenant James Becher Tudor (5th Bengal Native Infantry) arrived as Adjutant, and on 19 May, Captain Edmund George Wood (6th Madras Light Cavalry) was appointed to command the regiment. Tudor resigned the Adjutancy on 1 June and was succeeded by Lieutenant John Lewin Sheppard (4th Bombay Rifles) who, in his turn, resigned on 7 July, the day after Tudor actually left the scene. On 29 July, Thurburn, who was ill, left for home, and about 26 September, Lieutenant Hervey Morris Stanley Clarke (15th Madras Native Infantry) arrived. (*Diary*.)

On 8 July, Sylvester entered in his *Diary*: 'We are but two left and not over friendly either.' The other officer must have been Wood, Thurburn having by that time gone away, sick.

As may be imagined, all these changes amongst the officers of Beatson's Horse (by this time anything but a 'band of brothers') had a deleterious effect upon the morale and discipline of the regiment.

H

Kenelly of the Indian Navy, and I, should set out at once from Zanzibar with the object of following up Burton and Speke's discoveries. We had but to wait Lord Stanley's sanction as Secretary of State for India, when we should be at liberty to proceed.

My mind was so full of the project, and desire so strong to start, that mentally I often consigned the present guerilla warfare to perdition, but another year dawned and Beatson's Horse were still at the old work, but had undergone two changes in their Commandant. The second, Lieutenant (now Colonel) Evelyn Wood[1] was to be the last. While, however, the regiment remained intact, he laboured hard to make it efficient, and was enthusiastic in pursuit of marauders.

At this time, January, 1860, a force was in preparation for China. Two irregular regiments were required. We volunteered, but Lord Clyde very properly chose Probyn's and Fane's corps: Speke too had desired to return alone to East Africa, and I perforce remained in the jungles.

On the 11th of May we were ordered to march into Goona for the purpose of being disbanded: I can scarcely say that I was sorry. We were not alone subjected to the process: it appeared that Government, in its extremity,

[1] Evelyn Wood (referred to by Sylvester, in his *Diary*, as 'Wood junior') assumed command on 1 December, 1859, in place of Captain E. G. Wood. The officers then consisted of Evelyn Wood, Clarke (Adjutant) and Sylvester who, in his *Diary* described 'Wood junior' as being a 'jolly fellow with lots of common sense, hard working, seen much service & very agreeable as a companion but with a total disregard of dress'. For his part, Wood later considered Sylvester to be a man of unusual ability who had carried off all the prizes in all subjects at school and had made a considerable amount of money from wealthy Indians in Bombay, but disliked his profession and would have made a good cavalry officer.

When Wood joined, Sylvester and Clarke were not on speaking terms, and he found it necessary, in order to make them talk in Mess, to place the bread in such a position on the table as would force them to ask each other for it. These efforts at reconciliation were retarded when Clarke (who was shortsighted) shot off Sylvester's helmet and peppered him in the neck, having mistaken his fawn-coloured puggaree for a hare.

permitted any enterprising officer to raise a body of horse, consequently, so many raw levies had been sanctioned that now Lord Clyde had time to turn his attention to re-organisation, he was bewildered with a host of cavalry named after Smith, Brown, and Tomkyns. It was of course bad policy to send adrift so many men who had served us in our need, but it appeared, however, to be a necessity, and those whose services were no longer required received a gratuity of fourteen shillings, and cursing our ingratitude, went their way, but as there can never be another mutiny in their fighting days, perhaps it matters little.

On the 17th of the month we reached Goona, and Captain Mayne, after completing a sufficient number from Beatson's two regiments, the Mynpoorie Levy, and other bodies of Horse to form two corps, disbanded the rest. These two corps are now the Central India Horse. I was appointed to the 2nd Regiment, one of the subalterns of which, Lieutenant Jennings,[1] was a son of the Reverend Mr Jennings who, with his daughter, suffered the worst of fates from the mutineers at Delhi, and it was always the wish of young Jennings to do what he could, with his own hand, to avenge their massacre. On the 7th of June, a party of rebels were said to be in the neighbourhood of Raghaghur. The officer commanding the Sikh troop,[2] accompanied by Jennings, went out in search and came up with them in a dry water course, on one bank of which the rebels were strongly posted among trees and undergrowth. It was by no means a fair country for horsemen to act against infantry, but Jennings, embracing the opportunity he had often prayed for, dashed at his enemy and had already killed two when he fell from his horse, shot through the chest. The Sikhs did what they could under the

[1] Lieutenant William Henry John Jennings (2nd Bengal European Light Cavalry), serving with Mayne's Horse.

[2] Lieutenant Edward Ridley Colborne Bradford (6th Madras Light Cavalry) serving with Mayne's Horse. Later K. C. S. I. Chief Commissioner, Metropolitan Police, 1890–1903. Lost his arm after being mauled by a tiger, 1863.

disadvantageous circumstances and recovered his body and sword, not however before the former had been sadly mutilated. Twenty-five of the enemy were killed, and many of their grisly heads were brought in by the Sikhs at their saddle bows. Poor Jennings' body was borne in upon a native bedstead and buried next morning at Goona.

The affair in which Jennings fell was the last encounter of which I have any recollection, though De Kantzow,[1] whose knowledge of native character is consumate, induced some few to come in under the amnesty. We built ourselves sheds of date palms and thatched them with the very plentiful coarse grass which grows around Goona, and though the regiments were out in turn, rebel hunting, yet all bade fair for rest and shelter in the forthcoming rains, but even with this prospect in view the service was unpopular and one by one the officers left. Wood resigned in consequence of a severe reprimand from the Governor General's agent in Central India, Sir Richmond Shakespeare,[2] who considered that his conduct towards the Rajah of Nursinghur had been harsh and cruel, but Wood's disposition, in common with that of thorough soldiers, brooked nothing short of complete allegiance on the part of native rulers towards the Government, and his determination to leave a force working under the orders of Sir Richmond Shakespeare was thoroughly concurred in.

I resolved to be no exception to the general exodus, and

[1] Lieutenant Charles Adolphus De Kantzow who distinguished himself by his brave conduct during the mutiny of his regiment, the 9th Bengal Native Infantry, at Minpoorie. He was appointed to the command of 3rd Mayne's Horse, but he could not get on with Captain H. O. Mayne, and their differences resulted in both of them having to leave the regiment, the name of which was changed to the Central India Horse. This was most unfortunate as both were fine officers.

[2] Brevet-Colonel Sir Richmond Campbell Shakespear (no final 'e'), (1812–61). Supported De Kantzow in his quarrel with Mayne. He became a 2nd Lieutenant in the Bengal Artillery in 1821, and saw service in the Afghan Wars, 1838–9 and 1842, Gwalior, 1844, and in the 2nd Sikh War. At the time of which Sylvester writes, he was Political Commissioner of Baroda District.

as others (who had not endured a tenth part of the labour
and exposure I had continuously undergone for upwards of
three years) scrupled nothing in asking for brevets and
honors, I did not hesitate to ask Sir Hugh Rose, who had
succeeded to the supreme command in India, to permit me
to join the Sikh cavalry at Pekin. This favor he readily
accorded,[1] but the delays of Government are proverbial,
and many a day passed restlessly and discontented until I
obtained permission to leave. Once free, I tore off to Agra
and down the trunk road, with the mails, to Calcutta, a
journey of nine days, during which I rested one night,[2] but
only on applying for my sea passage was informed that the
Sikh cavalry and other troops had re-embarked for India.
How I anathematised those who had delayed me,[3] but it
was evident that I was regarded by every official as an
interloper. To belong to the Army of Bombay and serve in
their crack cavalry corps was certainly irritating, and it is
surprising that, even to this day, this feeling pervades the
different Presidencies, and is fostered by the deplorable
system of local armies.

I soon tired of the so-called City of Palaces, which I
should more properly characterise as a city of offensive
smells, and palatial only in contrast with the squalor and

[1] He was posted to Probyn's Horse, at that time, officially, the 1st
Sikh Irregular Cavalry. In 1861 the designation was changed to the
11th Bengal Cavalry.

[2] He arrived on 11 December 1860, the journey having cost him 270
rupees. (*Diary*.)

[3] On his arrival he reported to the Adjutant-General, Lieutenant-
Colonel (later General) Septimus Harding Becher (1817–1908) and on
hearing of the departure of Probyn's Horse from China, his disappointment appears to have been softened by the thought, expressed in his
Diary, that he was 'very glad for it had saved me the misery of much
sea sickness and perhaps consequent illness as happened to me in
Persia. I cannot but say I am disappointed not seeing the campaign &
very sorry to have lost the loot of Peking, however when [sic] cannot
always be lucky'. It is to be regretted, however, that he was not able to
leave behind him what would doubtless have been a meticulous
description of a land and people then unknown to all but a handful of
Europeans.

wretchedness of the native portion of the city, and extravagant mode of living amongst Europeans. It was, however,
a great change from the jungles about Seronge.

A few days after arrival, I went to Barrackpore, and
there, doing duty with the European depot, awaited the
Sikh cavalry. The welcome a stranger receives in Indian
stations was never better exemplified in my twenty years'
experience than that which greeted me at Barrackpore.

On the 24th of January, the first ship arrived in the
river[1] and within a few days seven other ships landed men
and horses on the open ground before Fort William. The
British bell tents, which had sufficed for a winter in North
China, were a sorry protection against an Indian sun: it
was in fact actually more tolerable to sit outside in the
breeze than beneath them. For the heavy dew which fell at
night, close to the river side, they were efficient.

The men of the regiment, Sikhs, Affghans, and countrymen of the far north, so handsome in physique compared
with those in lower Bengal and its bygone army, were
almost as great a curiosity in Calcutta as they would have
been in London. They were, moreover, laden with spoil:
handsome silks, plain and profusely embroidered; gold,
silver and jade ornaments; china; works in ivory curiosities,
and strangely droll dogs. Every man had a bronzed, hearty
expression and a frank honesty of face which besides his
stalwart figure, proclaimed at once how much he differed
from the native of Hindoostan. Their uniform, a loose dark

---

[1] Sylvester went on board ship and met Probyn, 'a fine looking
fellow but not so striking as I had anticipated'. He later added that
Probyn 'had entirely changed the uniform from silver to gold and blue,
the cut of everything was altered also and the whole *very* expensive
indeed he seems a most recklessly extravagant fellow and seems to
expect the same of all his officers'. (*Diary*.)

The military career of Colonel (later Sir) Dighton Macnaghten
Probyn (1833–1924) started when he became a Cornet in the 3rd
Bengal European Cavalry in 1849. He was at the siege of Delhi as a
Captain, and gained the V. C. at Agra. Promoted to General in 1888.
Comptroller of the Household of Queen Alexandra, and extra Equerry
to King George V.

blue serge blouse, bound round the waist with a scarlet shawl, set off their ample stature. Breeches, boots and a turban of ample size and flowering drapery, completed a dress at once handsome, soldierly, and workmanlike.

To say the regiment was the feature of the season is hardly to describe the popularity it earned at sight, independently of the fact of good service done and prejudice broken through by leaving the country and fighting battles for the infidels across the black water. Early and late our lines were crowded with sightseers, and the European community were desirous to buy vases, silks, or other spoil from the men and camp followers, or perhaps curious to see something of camp life. As toilettes were of necessity performed outside, I discovered, after the first morning, that it was necessary to be up betimes or remain beneath my blanket.

During the evening, the maidan [esplanade or parade ground] was thronged with European spectators in carriages, and on horseback, and crowds of natives, driving or on foot, to see the men at their games with sword or lance. It was both strange and humanising once more to see a well dressed civilian crowd, with ladies to boot, but I am not sure that I was not a little bored with the amenities, so thoroughly had I been broken to the rough life of troops on service, nor was I sorry, after the horses had regained their condition after shipboard, to leave the banks of the Ganges and its pleasant evening parties on board the budgerows [large Ganges boats, much used by Europeans]. The life led to disquieting thoughts and longing for Old England, especially when encamped alongside huge Indiamen and steamers fresh from home.

During the first ten days in February, the whole regiment, troop by troop, men, horses, and baggage, were sent by rail to Raneegunge, and on the 11th I left, with the head quarters, crossed the Howra ferry by steamer, and reached Raneegunge. Here several men and camp followers were attacked by cholera, which clung to us for some distance up the Grand Trunk Road, which we now steadily

followed. At Benares[1] we learnt our destination was
Sealkote in the Punjaub, and though it involved many
months' marching through the hottest period of the year,
yet we were all well satisfied. The homes of many of the
troopers were thereabouts, and it was good policy to permit
them to proceed on leave, well laden with plunder from the
Imperial Palace of Pekin, and so far as it concerned me, the
prospect of visiting Cashmere and Himalayas filled me with
delight, and I knew, moreover, that when all the world is
at peace, India generally has a little frontier campaign on
hand. Consequently, the prospect of more field service was
fairer here than elsewhere.

The fame of the regiment preceeded it, and as we passed
the large towns and military stations on our way, large
crowds came out to see the *Chin-ke-risala* [regiment from
China]. Leading the way was a curiosity in the way of the
mounted Tartar trooper, complete in his paraphenalia of
war. Tartar ponies, dogs and carts were positive testimony
to unbelieving natives that, though our Government, three
years previously, had recalled the China Expedition to
punish their misconduct, yet nevertheless, the matter had
but lain in abeyance, and a fit season, had been found to
punish the celestials also.

Anything more monotonous than the country on either
side the Grand Trunk Road it is impossible to conceive:
rice fields as far as the eye could reach over a plain scarcely
relieved by a tree of any size, wretched mud built villages,
and fragile, half starved, dark skinned inhabitants; the road
itself, perfectly straight and bridged, but much worn and
fetlock deep in dust.

In those days, another short piece of road, between
Allahabad and Cawnpore was connected by rail, and this
Government permitted us to use. At the latter place we
visited the places which mark a red page in Indian history.
The well was a wretched looking spot amongst broken
ground and shallow ravines of the same nature as those, so

[1] Reached on 10 March 1861. (*Diary.*)

much larger, at Calpee. Near Wheeler's[1] entrenchment new barracks had sprung up, and an obelisk marked the covered well into which he had thrown his dead. A more unprepossessing cantonment than Cawnpore I had never seen.

We reached Delhi[2] about the middle of May and encamped outside the Lahore gate of the city. It was the year in which a widespread famine occurred, and for upwards of two hundred miles we had marched through the stricken districts. Supplies were both scarce and expensive. Our lines were daily crowded round with bands of starving men, women and children who eagerly seized on the grains of corn as they fell from the nose bags of our horses. Their gaunt and skeleton figures testified but too truly to their starving condition. Government certainly administered relief, but it was not so complete as in the famine of last year. Our men gave freely from their plenty and fed and clothed any who were willing to serve as camp followers, but almost to a man they stole what they could and deserted as soon as their strength had been restored.

The thieves around Delhi appeared to be as numerous and adept in that propensity as the Rajpoots near Kotah. I invariably slept in fear of losing all I carried with me. Though our lines were guarded by sentries, yet on dark nights a dark skinned native, well greased all over, walking on all fours, so nearly resembled one of the numerous dogs which prowl the country everywhere in India by night, that the thief so disguised had little difficulty in gaining our tents, through the canvas of which they cut a passage

[1] Major-General Sir Hugh Massy Wheeler, K.C.B. (1789–1857), Bengal Army. Defended Wheeler's Entrenchment at Cawnpore, 6–26 June 1857, when he surrendered on terms to the Nana Sahib, and together with his wife and practically all the survivors of the siege, was brutally murdered. He had served in the 1st Afghan War, 1839–40; Army of the Sutlej, 1845; 1st Sikh War, and in the 2nd Sikh War, 1848–9.

[2] When near Allyghur, shortly before arriving in Delhi, Sylvester was joined by his dog 'Wickles' which he had left behind, presumably at Goonah.

H2

and plundered all they could lay hands upon, even the watch or revolver from beneath one's pillow. Used to so much noise by night in cavalry lines, the sleeper is not easily awakened, and any attempt to seize the greasy thief, even should opportunity offer, is generally a failure and may result in smart gashes from his knife across the wrists.

We visited every spot about the city, memorable in the siege, but the heat in tents was 116°, daily dust storms constant, and the atmosphere always thick and yellow from impalpable dust, even though the Himalayas, which I felt so desirous to see, though not below the horizon, were yet unseen. Anything beyond two miles was lost in muddy haze.

After crossing the Sutlej, though the entire country was parched with drought, yet the population was no longer suffering from famine. Loodianah and Umritsur were both interesting cities, moreover, the great temple of the Sikh religion was in the latter place, as also the abode of the Goroo or high priest of the disciples of Nanuk and Govind, so that we halted there to enable our Sikhs to get absolution for having crossed the sea. A great deal of their prize, and a little penitence, made this easy. Their temple must outvie Solomon's of old. It stands on a rock in the midst of a sheet of water: it is well built and the entire exterior, roof, walls, pillars, domes, kiosks, and doors, covered with gold. The reflection on the water adds to its gorgeous reality.

As we marched north, skins grew fairer, physique better, and the people were altogether more manly and independent. One fact, however, was noticeable: in every town, city, or village, we met men disbanded from Government service, either idling for want of employ, or going to their homes. It was said that 60,000 men of those who had been enlisted owing to the Mutiny, were now disbanded. Luckily for us, no more mischief was brewing.

At the beginning of June we reached our destination, Sealkote, thankful once more to get beneath a roof, but even with closed doors we could scarcely keep the temperature below 100°.

My first impressions of the Punjaub were disappointment; the eye wearies of an interminable expanse without tree or hillock, a strange contrast to Central India. The five rivers, with their flat, arid banks and shifting sandy beds were vastly tame after the Chumbul and the Nerbudda, and though so close to the Himalayas, the haze shut them out. There appeared to be an entire absence of large game which was ever a source of amusement in Central India. My last regiment, in Goona, had killed upwards of thirty bears and twenty tigers since I had left it, but here there were greater luxuries – excellent houses, better food, and proximity to the mountain ranges offered great facility to escape the hottest weather. I was not in a mood to quarrel with anything in the shape of rest and shade, moreover, the station possessed many advantages in barracks, churches, hospitals, stores, houses, and a prospect of cold weather. We were hospitably welcomed by the 7th Hussars and 71st Highlanders, with whom, under far different circumstances, I had parted at Gwalior.

A few days after our arrival, heavy rain temporarily cooled the air and cleared the atmosphere of its tawny thickness, and going without, to enjoy the change, the Himalayas burst suddenly on my astonished gaze. Had I approached them gradually or seen them through a less clear sky than immediately after rain, or even gone out expecting to see them, perhaps I might have been less surprised at their exceeding beauty and grandeur, and though from Sealkote the lowest range may be distant, as the crow flies, forty miles, yet it appeared within an easy five. Range followed range until the highest, dazzling white with snow, formed the most delicate tracery against the bright blue sky – but not formally did one range crown another, but each was broken into valley and rugged spine, while every tint, from virgin white to purple gloom, resulted from the shadows, and now I understood the exceeding love of the Punjaubee for his country, and the preference shown it by Europeans.

It was years before I grew tired of that splendid mountain chain, for when all around was barren, parched and thirsting, imagination sought those purple glens and saw their cool streams running through moss, and fern, and lichen, and to know the fir, the oak and mistletoe grows there, and that groves of rhododendrons painted the wild banks, and that a few hours life in these altitudes would bring relief to one's saddened and jaded feelings, was in itself a companionable idea, full of consolation in exile.

The weather continued furiously hot until the middle of September, and as usually happens after famine, a wave of cholera appeared and spent its fury in Lahore, about sixty miles distant. Here, in a short time, it carried off 534 out of a garrison of 2,162, or above 22 in every 100. It followed the Grand Trunk Road to Peshawur without appearing to travel along branches, and Sealkote and other places so situated escaped without a single case.

The cool weather had barely set in before we were under orders to march on Peshawur, and set out for that place at three in the morning on the 5th of October, though why the small hours should have been chosen I cannot say, excepting that it was part of the system of Clive and others of venerated memory, and none of those present with my regiment had undergone a course of modern marching under Tantia's tuition. We passed the pretty station of Jhelum on that river, crossed the battlefields of Goozerat and Chillianwalla,[1] and skirted, the greater part of our way, the splendid mountain range which separates Cashmere from the Punjaub.

From Rawalpindee, a large and favorite cantonment, Mount Murree, the great sanitarium of the Punjaub was visible, and further on, at Attock, we crossed the Indus. Here a group of barren rocks springs from the plain, and the river, at a rapid pace, rushes through a rocky gorge and

---

[1] Two battles of the Punjab Campaign, fought on 21 February and 13 January 1849, respectively. On both occasions the British were commanded by Lord Gough.

is spanned by a bridge of boats, the scenery from which
bears contrast with the Iron Gates on the Danube. On one
of the rocks rising from the left side the stream, the formidable fortress of Attock stands, and on the opposite bank,
beneath the ridge, is the wretched looking village of
Kyrabad. The rocks, barren as they are, abound in Ovis
Ammon, of which we shot several.

Before debouching into the Peshawur valley we passed
through the military cantonment of Nowshera on the Swat
river. The cold here in early morning was intense. Twenty
miles distant from Peshawur we entered the valley, which
is for the most part irrigated, and its greener and more
cultivated appearance contrasted pleasantly with the general
barren aspect of the Punjaub. Once in the valley, hills
surrounded us on all sides, the highest being about 5,000
feet.

The cantonment, some few miles distant from the mouth
of the Khyber pass, differed from anything I had seen
previously. The houses and buildings were almost wholly
built of sun dried mud bricks, of the same colour as the
soil – a very dirty brown. The roofs, flat, also of sun baked
mud, but smoking chimneys were to me the greatest
novelty. For nearly ten years I had been in superheated
atmospheres and the luxury of wanting a fire to sit beside
was both great and strange. Every house had its garden,
either large or small, with a little rill of muddy water for
irrigation. Peas, cauliflowers, cabbages, lettuce, strawberries
and other fruits and vegetables at this season grew as in
England, while the walnut, apple and willow flourished by
the water side. Peaches were cultivated in extensive groves,
many acres in extent, and were of excellent flavour and
large size: grapes were equally abundant, but these were
brought in immense quantities from Jellalabad and other
places in Affghan territory, and cheap enough to be within
the reach of all.

About the middle of November we burnt fires indoors
throughout the day and sat around them at night after

Mess. It was common to see little naked urchins shivering in the sun and playing with thin sheets of ice which formed over the watercourses. Once, but only once, did I see it snow for a short while, but it never lies on the ground in the valley. Our regimental overcoats, made of sheep skins, cured with the wool on, were grateful wear morning and evening, and the stirrups were painfully cold while on parade near the Khyber, for the lowest hill ranges are covered by snow in winter, and the Sufed Koh, near Jellalabad, is crowned with snow always.

Strange to say that with so much enjoyable cold weather, Peshawur is I believe the most deadly climate in all India to Europeans, neither do natives of other parts of India suffer much less when garrisoned in the valley. This insanitation of the place is unfortunate as it is incumbent on us, now that we have pushed our frontier across the Indus, to maintain a very large force there. At the time of our arrival, the 21st Hussars,[1] four batteries of Artillery, the 7th Royal Fusiliers, Sutherland Highlanders,[2] two regiments of Native Cavalry, 1st, 4th, and Ferozepore Regiments of Native Infantry were under the command of Major General Sir Sydney Cotton.[3]

The cantonment is seven or eight miles distant from the lowest range of hills through which runs the Khyber: a strip of this, some miles wide, is known as the 'neutral ground' and besides being against our orders to venture upon it, it is in the highest degree dangerous to be anywhere near it unless well mounted, for the prowling and lawless Khookhee Kheyl tribe are always ready for murder or for capture to exact a ransom.

[1] Raised as 3rd Bengal European Cavalry in 1858, and became the 21st Hussars in 1861 and later 21st Lancers. Now amalgamated with 17th Lancers as 17th/21st Lancers.

[2] 93rd, later 2nd Bn The Argyll and Sutherland Highlanders.

[3] Sir Sydney John Cotton (1792–1874). Entered the army as a cornet in the 22nd Light Dragoons, 1810. Served in the Madras, Bengal, and Bombay Presidencies for many years. Put down disaffection in Peshawur during the Mutiny.

The hill tribes were a very constant annoyance to us on dark winter nights when they frequently prowled around cantonment, and notwithstanding some eight miles of pickets and guards, always loaded with ball, they succeeded in entering the horse lines, and despite the sentries there on duty, would place stockings on the feet of horses and walk them noiselessly through cantonment and away to the hills. Occasionally the raid was upon an officer's stable: a crowbar sufficed in their hands to make a sufficient exit through the soft sundried bricks wherewith to take a valuable horse, and even though discovered by the sentries, it was impossible to do more than fire at random in the dark. Once during my stay in Peshawur the despicable cowards crept behind a sentry on guard, and stabbing him through the back, carried away a number of arms from the guard house. Again, the treacherous and revengeful Shere Ali,[1] afterwards murderer of Lord Mayo, was the trusted guardian, on her morning rides, of the Commissioner's eldest daughter. I recollect them often at the mud walls we built for our troopers to jump over at drill, where many congregated to see our ordeal practised on recruits.

Notwithstanding the cruel treachery with which the Wuzerees and Afreedees invariably behaved towards Europeans in their power, yet soon after our arrival three soldiers of the 93rd Highlanders deserted with their arms and uniforms, and marched into the Khyber with a view of taking service with the Shah of Persia, whose kingdom they were convinced lay immediately on the other side. They had in fact located it on the site of Jellalabad, and anxious to rival the success of Avitabili[2] and Van

---

[1] Shere Ali (1842?–72) was a Khyberi. A mounted orderly of the Commissioner of Peshawur before 1862. In the Umbeylah Campaign, 1863. Convicted of the murder of a tribal enemy he was condemned to death, but was sent to the Andaman Islands. He murdered the Governor-General, the Earl of Mayo, when he was on a visit to the penal settlement at Port Blair, 8 February 1872, for which crime he was hanged.

[2] Paolo di Bartolomeo Avitabile, born 1791 and died some time after 1845. He was a Neapolitan in the artillery of King Joseph Bonaparte

Courtlandt[1] among the Sikhs, determined that neither the want of money, provisions, nor knowledge of the language beyond broad Scotch, should stay their ambition. Fortunately they commenced to indent for provisions on a village which was tolerably friendly to our rule, and here, after one had been stoned to death and the others injured, they were captured by villagers and brought to camp almost starving.

A great deal of grain and other produce came through the passes, for sale in the camp and city, and all tribes save those in disgrace were encouraged to trade on the condition that arms were not worn in our camp. Grapes, apples, walnuts, ice, turquoises, Cabul coats, shawls, socks, swords, chain armour, horses, and blankets were among the produce of the towns in Affghanistan, and less plentiful articles from Persia and Russia were offered for sale. Almost every officer, during the cruel hot nights in summer, slept upon a thick skin of Russian leather as being cooler than any woven fabric, while the fragrant odour so familiar to us in England, possessed the virtue of keeping away in a limited extent the atmosphere of mosquitoes and sand flies.

Besides our force in occupation of Peshawur, a chain of forts, nearer the foot of the hills Nuchnee Abazai and Shubkudh were garrisoned by us and at the latter place was a squadron of my regiment. For a while there was no active service, but to belong to a force under Sir Sydney Cotton was to be constantly on parade. He was a martinet of the old school, lived in his uniform, and kept all under his command very constantly in theirs. To be seen in public dressed in plain clothes involved instant arrest. He never passed over the smallest dereliction of duty. He was exceedingly unfortunate in serving so many years in India

and Murat. Served Ranjit Singh in the Punjab and assisted General Pollock in Afghanistan, 1842.

[1] General Henry Charles Van Cortlandt (1815–88). Employed in the service of the Maharajah Ranjit Singh. Cooperated with the British in several campaigns and served at Ferozeshah and Sobraon. Raised Hariana Field Force during the Indian Mutiny. Commissioner of Mooltan. Retired 1868.

without seeing active service more than a single expedition against one of the hill tribes, and this it was said he mismanaged,[1] but few could handle large bodies of troops on parade equally well with Sir Sydney Cotton, and here at Peshawur the number of troops was large, and wild open country in the valley, ample. Often in the cold weather the divisional exercises lasted the entire day, ending at dusk with a march past, at which time the ladies of the station assembled behind the flag staff, and the regimental bands were an agreeable change after the smell of so much villainous powder.

There were a large number of married British ladies in the cantonment, but its sickly climate was prohibitory to those who had not taken the final plunge. In two years experience, four arrived; of these, two died, one succeeded, and the remaining one left the place.

During the entire cold season in which we marched on Peshawur, we found ample excitement though at times I should have been glad of another week after Tantia. When off duty, for the most part I was fully occupied in the construction of a race course and training horses for races which were to come off on the arrival of the Commander in Chief, Sir Hugh Rose.

Horse racing and steeple chasing were as much in favour as earthquakes were in fashion, for in the commencement of 1862 scarcely a week passed without one. That which will ever linger on my memory happened during morning service on Good Friday. Of the two churches we had all assembled in the largest, which was a very handsome and capacious building. The whole of the Protestants of the 21st Hussars, Sutherland Highlanders, and Artillery, were assembled with their arms. The custom of carrying arms to church does not obtain in other stations but is always necessary in Peshawur, so near the frontier tribes. These men, with their officers, civilians, and European officers of other corps, must have, including many women and children,

---

[1] 1st Euzofzai Expedition, 1858.

made our congregation fifteen hundred or upwards. As the officiating clergyman was about to commence the communion service, an unusually severe earthquake almost threw us off our balance, and was at the same time accompanied by a loud rumbling noise. I cannot tell where the panic commenced but in the twinkling of an eye every creature save myself and Colonel Probyn dashed at the open doors while some of the Highlanders charged the windows with their rifles and a wild cry rang through the building, such as one might expect to hear from a crew about to be engulfed. The doorways, though large, high, and open for the sake of ventilation and coolness, were unequal to the crush. Dragoons, artillerymen, Highlanders, women and children, were all struggling together, and strange to say, the tremulous motion had all ceased, nor had the church fallen, or any part of it. It was said the clergyman cleared the altar rail at a bound; this however was not so, but his exit at the back was marvellously rapid.

I am unable to account for our not having caught the infection, but from the first I knew that it was an earthquake and saw the futility of moving. No sooner had the congregation reached the open air than each began to accuse the other of having unnecessarily bolted and loudest amongst those condemning the extraordinary exodus was the Brigadier who, though corpulent, was said to have leapt the churchyard enclosure before coming to a halt. After a while, pale and ashamed, all reassembled and the service was concluded.[1]

The church tower did, I believe, receive some slight damage, but the houses, being of one storey only and built of mud, sustained none. The mud roofs, after long, continuous rain (which was common enough during the

---

[1] This occurrence seems to have brought some unpopularity to Sylvester as is evident from an entry in his diary: 'My article on the panic during the Earthquake on Good Friday is getting me slightly notorious as a writer, half the Officers didn't like the disgraceful flight of themselves and men brought prominently before the public.'

cold months) became soft and porous and permitted copious leakage during the terrible heat which commenced about the end of June. It was not uncommon to have an hour's rain, after which, diminished evaporation in a saturated atmosphere of a 100° rendered the climate oppressive in the extreme, and not the least disagreeable part of the Peshawur hot season were the myriads of tiny sand flies which, favored in their devoted attentions by the stillness of the nights, placed sleep beyond possibility, and being so much smaller than mosquitoes, the curtains arrayed against these latter pests were useless.

The long Mall or chief road through cantonment, some miles in length in the cold season and guarded by mounted troopers at short intervals, was entirely deserted in the hot months. Sir Sydney Cotton and Staff migrated to the mountains of Murree, the example was contagious, and all who were at liberty followed his example and fled the pestilential valley.

The long, hot days, shut up in a dark room beneath the punkah [a large fan suspended from the ceiling and moved by means of a cord], or passed in rooms underground, after the camp life I had become accustomed to, were dreary enough, and having charge of the 21st Hussars, and staff duties in addition to my own, I was unable to see Cashmere as I desired, thus I was punished by not falling sick as others did, and to mend matters, cholera, which had on two occasions affected the troops, returned a third time in its most virulent form. Its ravages amongst the population in the city were frightful. Natives submit to it with less complaint than Europeans; with them it is God's pleasure, and our sanitary precautions appear almost impious in their sight.

During the whole of July and September the plague was amongst us, though every precaution was taken to guard against it. Sir Hugh Rose adopted the very proper measure of ordering all officers on leave back to their afflicted corps. Nothing was neglected to cheer the drooping spirits of the soldiery: bands played more frequently in the barrack yards, their food was liberal, and good drains were spotlessly cleaned, barracks fumigated, cannon fired to windward of habitations, officers wore fearless countenances, but all was useless. The thrice fired volleys resounded from Protestant and Catholic burial grounds night and morning.

Even in the great heat the affected regiments moved into camp, and tried by easy marches at the foot of the hills to leave it behind, but it kept them company. The 93rd Highlanders suffered most: six officers were seized almost simultaneously. Four of these, Colonel Macdonald, Major Middleton, Dr Hope, and Ensign Drysdale succumbed.[1] The men of the 21st Hussars suffered in less proportion, but the two regiments, about 1,800 strong, were so sickly, and a large proportion of men so reduced in strength by repeated attacks of fever, that Government sent them to the Huzara hill country to recover.

A circumstance occurred at this time which conclusively shows how little is known of the nature of this Eastern scourge by those who profess to comprehend its laws. Dr Hathaway,[2] who stood high in favor with Sir John (now Lord) Lawrence,[3] was appointed sanitary inspector of Bengal, and after having minutely examined our horse lines and abodes of the men, observed to Colonel Probyn and myself that should cholera perchance invade Peshawur, our regiment would be decimated. This appalling and prophetic warning, made some months previous to King Cholera's actual arrival, was not by any means borne out by experience; four cases occurred amongst us, and all recovered. If Pettenkofer[4] and others would confess that our knowledge

---

[1] The deaths among the 93rd and their families were sixty men, thirteen women and twelve children. Adding the four officers to these, the total was eighty-nine. The three regimental officers were Brevet Lieutenant-Colonel William Donald Macdonald, Major William Gustavus, Alexander Middleton, and Ensign James St. Clair Drysdale.

[2] Surgeon Charles Hathaway (1817–1903), Bengal Medical Establishment. Private Secretary to Lord Lawrence, 1864–9.

[3] Sir John Lawrence, Viceroy of India, 1864–9.

[4] Max Joseph von Pettenkofer (1818–1901), a German chemist and hygienist.

is not greater than the hairdresser's who wished to imply
that it was in 'the hair of the hatmosphere and not in the
'air of the 'ead', the truth would be apparent.

Anything more depressed to the spirits in the long, hot
days of Peshawur than these epidemics of cholera cannot be
conceived. It was not exhilarating, while attending the
funeral of a friend, to walk or stand on planks covering
ready excavated graves, but these were a necessity in order
that burial might immediately follow death.

About the middle of October the early mornings became
suddenly chilly, and the advent of cold weather is always
known by long lines of wild geese which are seen flying
over the station. The grateful feeling and renewed health
and spirits consequent, are more than worth all the previous
suffering. Unfortunately, however, at this time the peculiar
remittent fever of the valley is more rife than at any other:
few constitutions, native or European are proof against it,
and I suffered with the rest. It was no uncommon circumstance, during October, for a regiment to have an in-
sufficiency of men able to mount its Line Guards, all the
rest being sick in hospital. It was the same with our
servants; all were down with fever. I have no pleasant
reminiscences of my attack; the pains in the head, eyes, and
bones generally were exquisite and reminded me of what
a Frenchman said of gout: 'put your ankle in a vice and
screw it up until you can bear it no longer; that is rheuma-
tism: one turn more and you have gout'. We might say the
one turn more characterised the racking pains of Peshawur
fever.

XIV

Furlough in Cashmere

OUR Commandant, Colonel Probyn, had once been a distinguished member of the Punjab Irregular Force, a force which is entirely independent of the Commander in Chief, but is mainly subservient to the orders of the Lieutenant Governor of the Punjaub. This force for nearly thirty years has protected our north-west frontier and is located in a long line of stations from Hoti Murdan to Scinde. Not only is it celebrated for its deeds in arms, but it is a fact that there exists a clannish and exclusive feeling amongst the European officers, and this is lasting, even if one of their number transfers his allegiance to the supreme military authority, and thus, initiated by our Commandant, a pleasant interchange of civilities took place between our regiment and the officers occupying Hoti Murdan and Kohat, the two posts in their line nearest to Peshawur, and to this intimacy I owed the opportunity of visiting Kohat.

It was always a pleasure to pass a few days there, though a rough ride of forty-five miles across the Kotul or pass was necessary to gain the outside of the mountain chain which encircled Peshawur. The pass is without the line of British territory, and tribute is paid annually to the tribe which holds it, that we may not be molested in transit. Very often, however, in consequence of frays between the neighbouring tribes, the road is unsafe. It is a wild and craggy defile, in places covered with low jungle, and the greater part of the way, sheet rock or loose stones and boulders make the riding difficult. Here and there, at the narrow parts of the defile, small watch towers are perched on overhanging rocks. From one of these a couple of matchlock reports greeted us[1] and tiny puffs of smoke curled from a loophole. I suppose these were indications of friendship though we certainly did not delay to cultivate the first overtures, but clattered through the rocky gorge, perhaps at a pace which was scarcely decent. Just then it was unpleasant to reflect that a Pathan is entirely faithless to his engagements, and the very sight of an infidel is sufficient to excite his fierce and bloodthirsty nature. Each man is said to count his murders with pride and mothers pray that their sons may be successful robbers. The open country is pleasanter riding, when among Affghans, though even there the villager who follows the plough does so with a matchlock at his back, and sword through his waistcloth, and every man one meets is armed.

Once in Kohat, so large a programme of amusement and good cheer had to be discussed that perils by the way held no place: cricket matches, hawking the Crested Obara, or a run with Paget's[2] hounds: at night, by torchlight, the weird dances of the native soldiery, to music which would make the bagpipes pale, sky races, steeple chases, and the gallop back into the valley of fevers was a coveted change, but prized beyond all were the sixty days privilege leave granted annually to military officers. This period in the valley of Cashmere had long been a bright spot in my dreams of the future, and, when again jaded by the hot weather of 1863, after ten years' service, I applied for permission to start, yet, though the performance of my duties had been arranged during my proposed absence, the only leave I had ever asked was refused unless I would declare myself sick. This alternative I declined, and General Garvock[3] overruled the petty spite on the part of the local

[1] An entry in the *Diary*, of 22 February 1863 (his birthday) records his being at Kohat for three days with 'a party of some fifteen Peshawurrees'.

[2] Captain William Henry Paget, commanding 5th Punjab Cavalry.

[3] Major-General John Garvock. Served in the Sikh campaign and in South Africa with Sir Harry Smith, 1848. Commanded a Division in Peshawur, 1863. Died 1878. An entry in Sylvester's *Diary* (15 June

head of our department[1] which would have thwarted me.

On the 26th of July I left the hot, moist climate of the Peshawur valley by mail cart, and travelling at a gallop through the night, reached Rawalpindee at daybreak, staying there through the heat of the next day. I set out again at night, by palanquin, with relays of bearers, for Murree which is, I believe, about six thousand feet above sea level. Long before daylight the delightfully cool and rarified atmosphere had sent me soundly to sleep, despite the jolting shuffle and monotonous song of the bearers. But what could equal the daylight of waking among cool, green mountain peaks enveloped in clouds, and an atmosphere fragrant with pine forests? Gone the blinding glare, the dust, clouds of sandflies; no more irritation from raw patches of prickly heat; gone the heavy, oppressive weight which made one's very soul grow weary, and in place thereof a sense of thank-ful joyousness that made me independent of the palanquin, and long once more to tread the cool ground and brush the rain drops from the brake and fern which grew by the winding roadside. Sometimes, while skirting some huge cliff, I overlooked the treeless plain of the Punjaub, all hidden in its hot, pestiferous haze, through which I had no curiosity to penetrate. I knew it but too well and felt its baneful influence after walking many yards.

Once in the station, good roads wind amongst the dwellings which are perched on steep acclivities, and amongst woods and patches of pines, admitting glorious views over distant ranges. At every turn some unexpected beauty was exhibited, and from some of the eminences the scenery was sublime.

At breakfast I crouched over a wood fire in sheer delight, and was glad to accept the loan of a pilot coat. The whole day was occupied in providing provisions for the trip.

1863) reads: 'given the refusal of my house to General Garvock either for sale at £500 or rent at £10 a month'. He later records having let the house to the General.

[1] Probably Surgeon-Major John Macintire, Bengal Establishment.

Appetite once more began to force its claim and the racking thirst was at an end. Rusks, flour, potatoes, tongues, tea, sugar, coffee, bullets, gunpowder, cooking utensils and liquors were necessary for the march, besides nine gallons of the excellent beer brewed at Murree.

On the 29th of July I marched out of the station accompanied by four servants and two mules carrying a small tent, clothes, guns and provisions. Every step of the first stage to Dewal brought relief to the mind and eye, and as the entire thirteen miles is an incline over a well made mule road, walking required little effort. It is cut, for the most part, along a mountain side, and the steep, rocky bank on my right was covered with wild strawberry, ferns, mosses, orchids, and running to a great height, was capped with firs. Oftentimes the track laid through the deep shade of belts of pines, and now and then debouched on little plots of more open ground.

At Dewal, an old fort on a grassy slope offers capital accommodation for a halt and the descent from Murree being so considerable, the sun became unpleasantly hot, rendering the shelter of a roof acceptable. Many tiny flat roofed dwellings were visible on opposite spurs and sloping hill sides, even little patches of cultivation were attempted.

Much refreshed by a few hours' rest, at 4 in the afternoon I again set out to walk a second stage, to Kohala ferry, ten miles further. The descent continued to the valley of the Jhelum river which I could hear roaring over its rocky bed long before I had accomplished half the distance. Here and there small groups of flat roofed dwellings were passed. The scenery was not in any degree similar to that of the morning journey and the heat increased with every step, and not forewarned against this, I was fairly exhausted, accomplishing the twenty-third mile with painful difficulty.

The territory to the Jhelum is British, and the road in places skilfully cut on the face of a precipitous cliff overhanging the gorge in which the Jhelum roars deep beneath.

It was dark when, trembling from fatigue in every muscle, I reached the river and passed the night on its bank. At this spot the water rushes through a narrow gorge, smoothly, but above and below it leaps from one huge fragment of rock to another, roaring and breaking into whiteish foam, and just below the ferry, sweeps round huge boulders, and circles under the opposite bank into a very forbidding eddy.

As I looked by moonlight on the great volume of rolling water, I cannot say I liked the prospect of crossing, but in these matters, if natives are permitted to act after their time honoured fashion, they are mainly to be trusted, therefore, next morning, with mules, servants and baggage stowed in a flat bottomed boat, very much higher up the stream than the spot on which we desired to land on the opposite bank, we were loosed, and like an arrow sped down with the current, but the ferrymen were equal to the occasion, and by prodigious efforts, shot us across, where others grappled the boat.

And now at once commenced an almost perpendicular ascent to the halting place of Dunnoh. Occasionally the road is varied by short descents, but for the most part it involves most cruel exertion, and as the Jhelum at Kohala is not much higher than the plains of the Punjab, the sun in the hot months is extremely powerful. Water is unattainable and shade scanty until some eight miles have been accomplished and the region of pines reached once more. In the grassy plain at Dunnoh lies buried an officer of the 21st Hussars who died of fatigue while making this march.[1] Green hill summits, crested with trees, surround a small shed built for travellers by the Maharajah whose territories begin, with execrable roads, at Kohala ferry. I slept at

[1] 'There is a head and foot stone raised on the spot and a railing round them with the inscription "Sacred to the Memory of Phillip Hammond Esq., Cornet, 21st Light Dragoons who died suddenly near this spot on the 23rd August when on his way to Cashmere deeply regretted by his brother officers, by whom this tablet is erected".' (*Diary.*) This was Cornet Philip Hamond, 3rd European Light Cavalry (later 21st Light Dragoons). Born in 1838, he died on 23 August, 1861.

Dunnoh and was severely bitten and hauled at by flat in-
finitesimal plagues, but the cuckoo called all day – a
welcome sound after ten years' absence. One such ten
miles as those on first entry of the Maharajah's territory
was a sufficient labour for the day.

Starting early on the morrow, I walked to Maiha.[1] The
first four miles are a steady incline to the river Uggur, the
country very wild and uninhabited. A few huts on the road
give shelter to the runners who carry the post letters.
Everywhere the country was covered by shrubs or trees: I
noticed the apple and pear growing wild and laden with
very sour fruit; grey and painted partridges were calling
in the bushes. The Uggur is a busy, sparkling little stream
wandering through the hills and at the point usually
crossed is a natural cavern, or rather, large grotto, its clefts
filled with a miniature forest of ferns, mosses and liverworts watered by icy jets from the rock.

From the river to Maiha it was steadily uphill and the
sight of the shed, miserable as it was, proved welcome. A
few flat roofed huts and a group of fine cypress trees form
the village from which I procured milk, and pears of stony
hardness. Dwellings were dotted about on distant hillsides
and some of the flat steps were cultivated. Grass grew in
great abundance, and was much appreciated by the baggage
mules. The high range which had to be crossed on the
following day was buried in cloud, wreathed among the
pines of the forest covering it. During the afternoon,
watery clouds rolled about the hills, followed by vivid
lightning, peals of thunder, and torrents of rain. Mules and
servants huddled into the shed and shivered with cold until
bedtime, when, but for myriads of fleas, I should have
slept soundly.

In the morning the rain had subsided and I set out for
Chukar. Everything was delightfully fresh, the trees,
bushes and wild flowers brilliant in colour after the downpour. The ascent of the range cost me two hours of difficult

[1] 31 July 1863.

walking. In many parts the track was undistinguishable; in others, through the slopes of the pine forest, it was over my ancles in viscid yellow mud. Occasionally it skirted high sloping acclivities, often wound round the narrow edge of precipices overhanging cloud filled valleys below, and here the passage of mules was made hazardous from projecting crags which, abutting on the road, threw mule and baggage into the abyss below. This accident befel one of mine while ascending the range, but catching in a jutting tree, both he and his load were saved, with much difficulty.

It was bitterly cold on the summit. Drifting cloud prevented my seeing more than the giant trunks around me, but during the steep four mile descent to a stream in a valley below, flitting glances through the vapour permitted a view of stupendous hills covered with forest, and beautiful open valleys broken by shining streamlets. So steep was the descent and so soaked with mud and water that I frequently lost my footing, and at times I despaired of the mules.

Chukar is a pretty village, situated on a conical eminence, so that one house towers above another. Numbers of poplars grow luxuriantly, high mountains encircle it, and after the heavy rain of the night previous, watery cascades ran down their fissured sides. Some of these had a beautiful effect, leaping from one rocky fragment to another and sparkling amongst the trees and underwood shadowing their descent. Showers fell throughout the day and as the little upper roomed house could not be closed, clouds entered the room and made it so bitterly cold that I was fain to spread my bedding and retire between my blankets greater part of the day and I can easily conceive very violent colds or even worse illness may be contracted by the sudden transit from the burning plains of the Punjaub to these mountain tops. The cold here was a few degrees too much for my lively companions of former nights.

Our waking was still *in nubibus* but as the route for the day, to Huttee, was for the most part an incline to the bed

of the Jhelum, I fancied a few hours' walking would carry
me below the region of clouds, and so it proved, for long
before reaching the halting place, the sun shone unpleasantly
hot, and through the rarified atmosphere, burnt considerably. The path was stony and every inch of ten miles, a
great part of which ran along steep mountain declivities,
the slopes of which were overspread with light and elegant
foliage relieved by jutting fragments of rock, clothed with
moss and half hid by tufts of flowers and tangled wild vine
and rose bushes. Here too, by the foot track, I found
(among the ferns), violets, and lilies of the valley. The last
three miles of road overhung the Jhelum, the bed of which
is full of boulders, and its great incline caused the waters to
rush past with a noise and rapidity which made me shudder
to see. The heavy rains of the previous days had swollen,
muddied, and lashed them to an angry foam.

At Huttee,[1] close to the bungalow, a small tributary of
sparkling water mingled with the muddy stream. I fished at
its confluence and caught a small Mahseer of three pounds
weight, which supplied me a dinner. There is little else
besides milk procurable from the two or three houses which
lie in a basin of hills.

Next day's march was very severe and full sixteen miles to
Chukotee. Skirting the Jhelum almost the whole distance,
the rugged path tore all the shoes from my mules and in
those wilds no means existed for restoring them. The
halting place was so miserable a shed that I preferred my
tent, and though distant from the Jhelum, I could hear its
angry roar. The scenery here is less sublime, the landscape
more open. There were grassy slopes covered with blossom-
ing clover; below the halting place was a large valley
cultivated with rice. The greatest possible attention was
everywhere given to my wants and I was careful to see that
food and carriage really was paid for. It is a common trick
of Indian servants to charge their masters and cheat the

---

[1] 2 August.

suffering Cashmeerees by appropriating a huge portion of the cost.

Though the resting place here was far inferior to that at Huttee, yet the temperature and climate were perfect; the thermometer, at the hottest period of the day was 75° in the shade. Close to my tent ran a stream of sparkling icy water which would at that season have been worth a Jew's eye in Peshawur.

I was now approaching the far famed valley and the next stage, to Orei, was over a very undulating track, skirting dangerous precipices. In places perfect beds of English wild flowers blossomed by the road side and the hawthorn, hazel, blackberry and ivy grew amongst English weeds and grasses. Orei lies in a mountain bound valley through which the Jhelum runs its troubled way, and not far from the rest house a rope bridge spans the stream, so frail and high above its level that it looks a mere cobweb in the scale of scenery. Here I met two officers of the Highlanders[1] whose holiday was over and were making hasty marches to the plains.

Very few inhabitants are seen in the journey to Cashmere, and these, though fair and of good physique, have no fresh colour, are badly dressed, and wear an oppressed and melancholy countenance; with all English medicines are of great repute, quinine and fishooks being invariably asked for. One of the greatest pleasures enjoyed by travellers is the safety of their property, for this, in the wildest and loneliest tract, is perfectly secure. The penalty inflicted for thieving is loss of the right hand at the wrist, and I have heard it said that a bag of coin on the road side is safe provided none but Cashmeerees pass by.

More fleas at night and off again at daybreak, seventeen miles to Nowshera, the first four of little interest and

---

[1] His *Diary* records his having met three Highland officers on this occasion (4 August), these being Lieutenant Henry Brooke Wilson (71st), and Ensigns George Lyddon Morley and Augustus Henry Turner (79th).

steadily up hill, after which the character of the country entirely changes and a level grassy path runs through forest glades which in all respects are most thoroughly English, and it is easy to cheat oneself into the belief that lovely home scenery surrounds one. Large pines, mountain ash, hawthorn in blossom, chestnut, hazel, wild pear and apple shaded the way for miles. Tufts of mistletoe studded their branches and the pensile branches of the wild vine and honeysuckle hung in the thicket. Now and again, open patches of verdure, smooth as an English park, gleamed in the sunshine. Here wild stocks and balsams brightened the patches and walking was so easy that anything short of feelings of delight was impossible. Agreeable emotions added to the loveliness of the way.

The bungalow at Nowshera is situated close to the river bank, beside an orchard, and under its windows the waters of the Jhelum fret and foam over a broad, rough bed. Groups and rows of poplars are studded about the village near which are forest clad hills abounding in black bear. I caught a few fish called 'Punjabees' by the natives, but they were not of great size. More applications for medicines, fishhooks, bullets, gunpowder and steel pens. After my arrival[1] I was waited upon by an official of the Maharajah's, whose function it was to apprise the Cashmere authorities of my rank and advent, in order that I might be met, on entry, with a welcome and present of provisions.

At daybreak I started on the last march, to Baramoolla. It is about eight miles through a peaceful valley studded with villages amongst clusters of walnut, poplars, apple, cherry, pear and plum trees. The view is bounded on all sides by hills and gentle slopes which rise one behind the other, their summits (at the early hour I marched) enveloped in a soft aërial tint, more and more shadowy and indistinct as they receded into distance until lost in mountain ranges far remote. The river too, which is still followed, had left its rocky channel; its wild and rugged course is

[1] 5 August.

changed to one of calm beauty, harmonising with the meadows on its banks.

Baramoolla is an exceedingly picturesque village on the right bank, opposite to the comfortable upper storied bungalow provided for visitors to the valley. The bungalow is situated in an orchard, the trees of which were laden with fruit then almost ripe, a sight which amazed and delighted my Indian servants. Neither can I say that I was less pleased to have reached the valley and finished for awhile the toilsome marching. Eleven years of the plains and two hot seasons in Peshawur are poor training for athletic work. Here I engaged two large flat bottomed boats with awnings, and breakfasted, admiring the Swiss like village of pretty gabled houses while my baggage was stowed away, servants and kitchen in one boat, myself with bedding spread couch fashion on the broad flat floor of the other. These boats are about half the size of English canal barges, but infinitely lighter. The proprietors or manjees live on board and cook, sleep, steer and paddle at the rear end. In the large boats one does not see much of the male population; the women manage them, and were to my thinking the prettiest in Cashmere, their features, as a rule, regular, and their noses aquiline, mouths pretty and faultless, teeth pearly and white to a fault. In complexion they were less fair than the better class of townspeople but the warm healthy glow mantling the sunburnt cheek was far prettier than a fairer skin, and reminded me of rosy-cheeked russets. Their dress was exceedingly simple, one garment – a grey woollen blouse fastening low round the neck and reaching to the knees, girt or worn loose at the waist – sufficed. The legs and arms, from knee to elbow downwards, were bare. This costume is hardly suggestive of scrupulous cleanliness but it enabled them to be constantly in the water, either to land or tow their boats, or bathe. This they did by walking gradually into a deep spot and raising the blouse as gradually, until it rested on their heads. Nothing could be prettier than their hair, parted in the centre and drawn plain to the occiput where, in a number of small plaits, it was gathered together below the waist and woven into a large tassel with a species of mohair, this reaching to the lower edge of the skirt. On the crown of the head a little close fitting scarlet skull cap completed the costume. No more becoming dress could be devised for the rounded limbs and graceful figures of young or middle aged women, but for the faded and aged it was hideous.

XV

Furlough in Cashmere (2)

THUS afloat, in charge of an old crone and several attractive daughters, we started up stream for Sopur. Sometimes they paddled with broad spadelike oars, and when the bank admitted, they towed; the crone steered.

Beautiful meadows reposed on either bank, backed with distant lofty ranges of great beauty. Villages were passed occasionally where happy looking rustics and blue-eyed children were tending their cattle or lazing at their doors. Myriads of insects were sporting away a short existence over the streams and banks. My four servants, tired out and insensible to every charm but rest, were snoring a quartette in the boat behind. I laid on my back and read *Lalla Rookh*. Nothing but a professed cook was wanting to complete the sum of human happiness, far from the sound of trumpet or official call, reaping health and spirits in a country where sport and food were abundant, climate perfect, people obedient, and where as yet Jones, Brown and Robinson had not carried their knapsacks.

As night approached we anchored to the bank and the cooking fires were soon going. Fowls, ducks, milk and eggs were cheap and plentiful: these, with the little accessories brought from the plains, furnished a capital repast.

The second day on board, the boats took us across the magnificent Wullur lake. It is many a league across and for miles together its surface spread with the leaves and flowers of the lotus and singara. Heads of ponies and cattle could be seen on the distant banks, but cattle are forbidden food in the territories of Cashmere: its Sultan, a Hindoo, permits never a life to be sacrificed and regards with horror the faintest allusion to beef eating. It is almost impossible,

without having endured them, to conceive the clouds of
mosquitoes on the Wullur: there was an unceasing hum as
of bees swarming, and killing them during their attack was
down right hard muscular exertion. Protecting every inch
of bare skin, I kindled a fire of damp wood and sat in the
thick of the smoky column until I reached once more the
river, and at the halting place of Shadipore, left them behind. Fish here were in great plenty and with a fly I caught
sufficient for all on board.

Awakening on the morrow,[1] I found myself in sight of
the rows of poplars so numerous about Sirinuggar, the
Maharajah's capital: my fair crew had been towing since
three o'clock. There is nothing striking, but much that is
curious on entering the city up stream. The river is wide
and deep and its waters are civilised to smoothness, its banks
on either side four or five feet. About the water level, the
houses, wholly built of wood, grow thicker and thicker and
at length are continuous with the city, but for singularity,
irregularity and quaintness, they are unlike anything I have
ever seen. Four or five bridges cross the stream at intervals:
they too are wholly wood, including the piers, three or four
of which to each bridge are built in the bed of the river.
Tiny floating wooden houses are tethered to the bank on
either side and serve insanitary purposes for fouling the
water. Stone steps run from almost every house, beneath
the water level on which the women and children (many of
exceeding beauty and fairness of complexion) wash and
bathe, after which it appeared they took little heed to dry
their skins, and at the approach of curious Englishmen,
hastily threw on the single toga and ran laughing up the steps.

As the river appeared to be the boulevard and great high
way, it was crowded by every variety of small open boat,
from the barge like affair on which I rode, to the tiny canoe
carved from a single trunk. People of note, and the ruler,
owned gaily canopied craft but no such thing as a sail
exists in all the valley. Many of the houses were provided

[1] 9 August 1863.

with pretty looking balconies overhanging the stream. I do not recollect a single glazed window in the city, but many houses were provided with frames closed with white paper or white calico as substitutes. After eleven years among dark faces, or sickly hued white ones, it was indeed refreshing to be amongst rosy cheeks and blue eyes once again.

Near the upper part of the city, which lies pretty equally on either bank for about a mile and a half, the palace of the Maharajah is passed on the right. Amongst so many ill-constructed wooden dwellings, this, being of stone with some portion of its domed roof gilded, thrusts itself on the visitor's attention, but there is little about it worth notice as a building. Further up stream, green banks and sloping lawns are dotted at tolerably regular intervals by the picturesque wood chalets built for British visitors, which are plentifully shaded by willows, rows of poplars with luxuriant vines trailing up their stems, and magnificent chenar trees. Each house is two storied and in each storey there are two or three small rooms. The gable roof is covered by sheets of cloth, like bark from the silver birch, and plastered with a layer of earth on which wild flowers often grow and blossom luxuriantly, but though so many familiar plants and flowers and trees are seen in Cashmere and its mountains, I never once saw the daisy. During an absence in the East of twenty years, excepting on one occasion, I could not find the wild daisy. The exceptional occasion was on a well irrigated shady lawn at Mooltan, in the garden of General Van Courtlandt.[1]

Impatient to see all my leave permitted, I laid in a store of potatoes, flour and provisions for a trip in the mountains towards Tanskar. A single day passed in one of the residences on the right river bank enabled me to procure every necessary, including a suit of the delightfully soft, warm pushmeena, manufactured from the wool of Ladak. The cost, including a cap, was sixteen shillings; time of making –

[1] This is the General Henry Charles Van Cortlandt already referred to.

five hours. A party of ten or twelve tailors seated beneath a plane tree near my dwelling appeared equal to any emergency.

Baboo Mohes Chunder, the very civil and obliging agent of the Maharajah Runbheer Singh,[1] welcomes all European visitors on arrival with a boat load of edibles, and I received accordingly a sheep, some fowls, ducks, firewood, flour, tea, sugar, vegetables and other provisions. This custom, I believe, has fallen into abeyance in consequence of the great number of officers and even ladies who resort to the valley. The large game shooting and other attractions are not now what they were, and I am told the expense of everything has quadrupled. At the time of my visit I purchased a live sheep in the Wurdwan Valley for one rupee and this I believe was a fancy price. Ducks were fourteen to a rupee, fruit was nominal and might be had for the trouble of gathering.

On the 11th August, bidding adieu to a few officers of regiments in the Punjab I had foregathered with, I started for Islamabad by river, a distance of thirty-five miles. The pace up stream was slow but the climate and scenery left nothing wanting. On the right bank, orchards now teeming with ripe fruit were backed up by a steep and somewhat conical hill surmounted by a temple and called by the natives Tukt-i-Suliman. On the left bank of the stream the valley runs flat and uninteresting for ten or fifteen miles, terminating in low hill ranges. Straight up stream, in the direction of Islamabad, the snowy ranges were visible and indeed this was so in almost every side against the horizon, and herein lies one of the great beauties of the valley.

The journey to Islamabad occupied two days. It is a small village and the stream was too shallow to proceed further. Slept in the boat and at midnight was disturbed by a most violent thunder storm, common enough at this season. The

[1] Maharajah Runbheer Singh of Cashmere (1832?–85). Supplied a contingent of troops to serve with the British at Delhi during the Indian Mutiny.

lightning played along the water in flashes which dazzled me, and the thunder rolled sublime among the mountains. A few moments of such a downpour proved the permeability of the plaited rush awning of the boat and water to soak my bedding. Lighting a pine torch, I gathered it beneath a waterproof until the rain abated. The river was muddy at daybreak but the air had become so free from misty vapours that ranges, which yesterday were shadowy and indistinct, were now seen in every detail, with snow capped summits, and long lines of snow or ice marked the fissures and clefts far down into the valleys.

Bade farewell to the boats, and with four hundred pounds of rice and other impedimenta, all carried by coolies, set out for the higher ranges. Two days' walking carried me to the deep dense forests lying along the spurs beneath. Here and there I passed a few very primitive log cabins, generally built in open spots near a stream of water of surpassing purity, everywhere sparkling with light as it rippled over its pebbly bed or washed the knotted roots of giants of the forest, and near the cabin dipping pool, water cresses, water docks, and the ranunculus grew abundantly. As I approached the high ground beneath the ranges, I was often waistdeep in wild flowers and tall grass.

Proceeding onward, I entered the gloomy ravines, dark with pine, chestnut, oak, walnut, apple, plum, and a number of other familiar trees. The apples hung in clusters so thick as in the distance to appear like huge bunches of primroses. Yellow plums about the size of pigeons' eggs were equally plentiful and both fruits were excellent eating. Year after year there was none to gather this abundance, and black bear in great numbers fed upon it.

The loneliness of the ravines and pine forests, and their deep broad, sombre shadows, were most impressive, for though in winter time the twelve-tined Nungul calls for his mate, and the ibex and musk deer attract the hunter, yet in summer they have followed the snow line and during the live long day no sound is heard save the occasional scream of jungle fowl.

At length I arrived at the last group of huts, called Gowrun, at which food or milk could be procured, and henceforth on my way, prepared to be miserable so far as creature comforts were concerned; having moreover, none but human carriage to depend upon and to carry food for all my party, I left every superfluous article behind in the hut of a shikaree or hunter who accompanied me. Shoes were no longer of avail to climb the rough, stony mountain side, and adopting the straw plaited sandals of the mountaineer, I set out for the snow.

From Gowrun we followed the bed of a stream for some miles up a steep gorge. The water was seldom more than ancle deep and had its origin in the melting snow above. It was consequently very cold to the feet and the smooth pebbles rolled beneath our tread and caused the straw sandals to chafe uncomfortably. On either side the torrent, the gorge was thickly beset with lofty pines and closely tangled underwood, so that we could not leave its bed for the soft carpet of acicular leaves and fir apples which for ages had lain undisturbed, but after a while all other trees save pines were left behind, and even these grew stunted, while oppressed breathing told of rarified atmosphere and lofty regions. After each score of steps upwards I was compelled to pause for breath.

Sometimes passing clouds enveloped us, obscured everything, and heated as we were with the exertion, chilled us to the marrow. The nearer we reached the top of the pass, which is known as the Ikpatran, the steeper and more difficult became the ascent. Huge grey coloured rocks and boulders lay tumbled in all directions. At length we gained some patches of dirty looking snow. How the six coolies managed to clamber through such a march, with seventy pounds of rice and salt each, was to me amazing, and it was not surprising they should yet be some distance behind, which was inconvenient as the damp cloud had thickened into a steady downpour. The shikaree who accompanied me counselled shelter under a large natural cairn of stones, but the cold rendered this unbearable. My teeth chattered with cold and my blistered feet were extremely painful, and I have a shrewd idea I was not just then enjoying myself.

Still we pushed on through a narrow, stony pass, on which was a great deal of last year's snow, and on the higher ridges to our right and left, immediately above us was the snow line. Nothing could be more barren than the rocky gorge upon which we had arrived. A few gnarled bushes of juniper grew in places among the rocky debris, the road was tolerably level, and we pushed on through the rain to seek the shelter of two shepherds' huts which the shikaree promised should be found some few miles further, at a place called Lutterwan. The solitude was broken by the shrill, piercing cry of an animal which abode in the rocks and which the shikaree called a drin.

After proceeding a long distance onward, we failed to find the promised shelter and consequently crouched beneath a rock and by means of a flint, steel and gunpowder, kindled some dry branches of juniper until the coolies arrived. I now learnt that the best time for shooting on these high ranges is from the middle of May to the middle of June. The weather then is invariably fine but later is as invariably wet. The rain did not abate and was often mixed with snow throughout the night, but dry blankets and the English bell tent made life endurable. The cold, however, was intense, and my Hindoostanee servants felt it bitterly and complained of headache. At daybreak everything was still obscured by cloud, but I went out and succeeded in shooting a couple of drin. They were a species of marmot, about the size of a hare, skin foxy red, and feet black.

Towards noon the clouds cleared away and the valley of the Wurdwan in all its wild and savage grandeur burst on view. It is nearly forty miles in length, and was lying at the foot of the rocky defile on which I was encamped. The snowy Brahma mountain range bounded it on every side in

icy chain, and sloped in wooded spurs and ravines to the
grassy plains below. Beyond all, in the direction of Ladak,
and towering to the height of 23,000 feet, were the two
peaks of the Koon Noon, their pure white conical summits
of eternal snow faintly visible against the clear and delicate blue. Nothing in the shape of a habitation in all that
vast tract could be seen, though shepherds' cabins, so I
was told, exist at a place called Inshin. The only signs of life
were vast flocks of sheep grazing in the valley, and from
our altitude of 12,000 feet, each herd seeming as a compact
moving mass.

Next day I moved my camp and passed the missing
Lutterwan, which was a shepherds' station. Walking
amongst the crags just beneath the snow line, I found them
less devoid of interest than at first sight. A number of
elegant plants were scattered amongst them; the sun dew,
an occasional orchid, and abundance of wild rhubarb, the
stems of which were eaten raw, as a vegetable, by my
carriers whose capacity for carrying loads over these rugged
tracks was something marvellous. One pound of rice, a little
salt, and in money an equivalent of sixpence *per diem* was
the wage laid down by Government, but they often received
presents of mutton when a sheep was killed.

I tried hard for ibex, and though we saw a herd some
miles distant and stalked them for three days diligently, yet
the weather was fatal to sport. Perhaps two hours of early
morning promised nothing short of halcyon skies and
illimitable views; suddenly the bright clearness was lost,
and a cold, damp atmosphere ushered in a pitiless downpour, and then, with feet soaking wet from tramping in icy
water, to be huddled beneath a rock for shelter very considerably damped my ardour. One's tent offered but little
comfort in a temperature at freezing point, and it was most
difficult to get anything to eat beyond half raw mutton and
chuppatties.

After some further days of perseverance in stalking ibex
in the Traillee Nullah and Guzzerni, and with my bones

12

aching from constant cold and wettings, I was of necessity obliged to leave the region of cloud. During the last night, however, fresh snow fell and the cold was intense. I failed to sleep; the servants did not attempt it but shivered around a fire until morning. The ranges, in the fresh garb of white, looked lovely, especially those at the head of the Wurwan and about Kistawar. My face smarted in the keen air and fingers stiffened with cold on the rifle.

On the 22nd of August I descended once more to the pine forests and encamped at a shepherds' hut called Doopa-dollow. It rained heavily but the temperature reached 60°. I saw a red bear digging roots and had four shots at him, but he succeeded in walking off, bear's grease and all. Next day, at a few huts, I was enabled to get eggs, milk, and fowls. I was below the cloud, and the sun, though little powerful, was very cheering. I moved each day some few miles, generally encamping in lovely wooded basins under spreading walnut trees, the fruit of which was then ripe, and we ate great quantities. The Cashmeerees set little store by them, but occasionally obtained oil by expression. The sudden change to the warmer zone, and regions of beautiful forest, after the desolate yet sublime scenery of the Wurwan, was to me as Satan's first view of Paradise.

Daily after breakfast my servant and coolies beat the ravines while I and the shikaries posted ourselves in commanding positions at the narrow outlets near the summit. Here, for the most part the game broke out, sometimes huge deer (*bara singha*), often black bear which abounded and ate up at night any little patch of mukki [Indian corn] which the villagers endeavoured to keep from their ravages. These small plots of corn, planted on spaces reclaimed from the forest, needed watching by the aid of blazing pine torches throughout the night, otherwise they were devastated in a few hours.

On the 1st of September, as my leave was drawing to a close, I went to Verinag where there existed a summer house of the Maharajah's. It is built around an octagonal tank of water literally alive with fish, and filled by a spring of crystal water. There are a few village huts, but Verinag is close beneath almost perpendicular hills, and save fishing, there is little to interest anyone. Not far distant is Achbull which is well worth a visit and is fairly in the valley. Achbull is a lovely spot with many beautiful springs, and even yet in tolerable preservation. Tanks, fountains, ornamental waters, buildings and gardens exist which are remnants of the greatness and magnificence of the Mogul Emperors of Hindoostan. By them the beauties and charm of Cashmere were fully appreciated.

Marching through the meadows of the valley was now an easy matter, and I passed a few days by the grassy river banks, fishing. Near the village of Kurwya exists a sequestered stream, not unlike some parts of the Wye in North Wales. It was literally teeming with fish, and by means of little white tufts of cotton wool attached to artificial flies, I caught a species of trout in great numbers, by fishing in the rapids. They averaged from one and a half to two pounds each in weight, and oftentimes I had two of this weight on my line simultaneously.

Time pressed on; a few days in the capital and I should have to bid adieu the valley with all its loveliness. I followed the stream from Kurwyne to its junction with the Jhelum at Brijibara, here breakfasting with some old acquaintances of the Cameron Highlanders.[1] I took boat, dropped down stream during the night, and once more arrived at Sirinuggur. Here the shawl merchants, lapidaries, goldsmiths, papier machee manufacturers occupied a day. I quite believe that a person unacquainted with the value of shawls may pay a price in excess of that for which a similar article may be purchased in England, for the merchants of Cashmere are Shylocks at a bargain. The papier

---

[1] Captain George Thomas Scovell, Lieutenant Robert MacGowan Borthwick and Ensign Charles Robert Kennett Fergusson, and one other, not known to Sylvester. (*Diary.*) Scovell served in the Indian Mutiny.

machee work is quite unique and cannot be purchased except in Sirinuggur. It has not yet found its way to any shop
in Europe.

Within a short distance of the city, by boat, are the
famous gardens, Nishat Bagh, Shalimar, and Nussen Bagh: a
very delightful day may be passed in visiting them. I
dispatched my servants and cooking utensils to Shalimar,
where they prepared dinner, and left the city early in the
morning, and passing up a branch stream of very pure crystal
water in which groves of chenars were brilliantly reflected,
arrived at the foot of the Tukt-i-Suliman. Here a rude lock
gate guards the entrance into a lake of the same purity, in
which numbers of fish may be seen at great depth, and the
mountains which slope to its surface on every side are most
faithfully pictured upon it. The lotus grows here in great
perfection, and both flowers and leaves attain gigantic
proportions. The air was fragrant from their blossoms.

I passed the celebrated floating gardens, some of very
considerable size and tethered to the bank on to stakes. They
appear to be composed of a mass of luxuriant vegetation, the
roots of which are all matted and tangled so as to form a very
firm raft of great thickness. Vegetable debris serves as mould,
and everything appeared to grow upon them in rich profusion. Some of these islands supported trees and even light
built cottages covered by vines and other trailing plants.
Cucumbers, water melons, and plants of their order yielded
abundantly and pretty blue eyed girls paddled canoes,
hollowed from a single tree trunk and laden to the water's
edge with fruit and garden produce.

The Nishat Bagh is first reached: it is a lovely spot at the
foot of a mountain slope. The garden occupies a number of
large terraces extending some distance up the declivity and
upon the lowest is a summer palace or pavilion with a ter-
race on the water's edge, from which a handsome flight of
stairs leads to the boats. At the time of my visit repairs were
being made to this place which must, in the time it was
built by the Mogul Emperors, have been indeed an earthly

paradise. The centre of the building is a large domed space
of great height, and its floor a square sheet of water in the
midst of which several fountains play. Spacious verandahs
look upon this central space and open into charming little
rooms behind. These are covered with painting and most of
the ceilings are coloured in well known shawl patterns. The
roof without, and the many verandahs, are covered with
earth and planted with flowers.

The gardens are a tangled and neglected wilderness of
fruit and flowers. Many of the trees are of considerable age:
the apple, pear, plum, cherry, walnut, poplar, chenar grew
in wild confusion and yielded plentifully, but for want of
cultivation the fruit was smaller than the same kind here in
England. Some years ago, officers on leave to Cashmere
were permitted to take up their abode here and consequently these beautiful gardens were lost to the many as
places wherein to pass an enjoyable day.

Breakfasting here, I was paddled across some miles of
sleeping water, passing a village on shore in which is a
temple visited on certain days by crowds of Cashmeerees
who believe that a hair of Mahomed is treasured here.

Passing up a narrow canal from the lake, I reached
Shalimar. The approach is not so imposing as Nishat Bagh,
but the gardens are even more beautiful. There are many
small summer palaces rising from the centre of ornamental
water and surrounded by fountains. I counted upwards of a
hundred jets around one of these buildings, and the roof of
each was a parterre of flowers. Both buildings and
gardens had suffered more from time and decay than
Nishat.

I found dinner awaiting me, with an abundant dessert of
grapes and peaches, after which the day was too far spent to
see the remaining garden and I returned by moonlight to
Sirinuggur. I am of opinion that any description would fail
to convey an idea of moonlight on that lake.

On the 11th of September I dropped down stream to
Baramoolla, on my way back to duty and fell in with a

party of Italians[1] who were conveying silkworms' eggs to their country. One hundred and twenty Cashmeerees were engaged carrying the cases in which these products were packed. I never heard the result of this venture, but although provided with Government introductions, the Italians met with great opposition in gaining the quantity of eggs required.

I returned to Peshawur by the route I had come, and as the season had considerably advanced, I saw the forests in the many hues of autumn foliage, and over the higher ranges trod on fresh fallen snow. It was a little depressing to be leaving so perfect and bracing a climate, but we seldom wanted for occupation or excitement in my regiment: I little expected however to be soon in the field again.

[1] A party of three. (*Diary*.)

XVI

The Umbeylah Campaign, 1863

COLONEL Probyn who commanded my regiment was on
leave at Simla when I rejoined. Simla is the head
quarters of Government during the hot months in India.
His presence there placed us in possession of early intelligence of meditated hostilities on our northern frontier and
the matter had scarcely been rumoured before some of the
Punjaub regiments received their orders to march. Not
belonging to the Punjab Irregular Force, we feared our
services would not be required, but confident in his presence
at head quarters, and perhaps owing thereto, we were
directed to join a force then accumulating near Hoti Murdan.

A few lines will enable the reader to understand how it
happens that we have very frequently a little war on hand
beyond the Indus, and the one for which we started on the
3rd of October, 1863, was the twentieth expedition of its
kind. The extreme limits of our Indian empire, on the
north west border, are mountain districts, minor ranges of
the Hindoo Koosh. These ranges, which in rugged spur and
stony defile, touch the plains of Hindoostan, are inhabited
by tribes of men for the most part our equals in courage and
physique. Their fastnesses offer no attraction to us and indeed an advance beyond our present line would unquestionably be a most expensive and fatal policy. On the other hand,
for the purpose of rapine and plunder, frequent depre-
dations are committed by them in our territory. It is to
punish these outrages we occasionally send expeditions into
the hills, and on the whole these have sufficed to maintain
our frontier in peace.

A little more history, however, must be told in order to
show that the expedition of 1863 was not in the first instance

made against any of these border tribes, and it must always
be a matter of regret that our unwarrantable intrusion
into their fastnesses at Umbeylah led to the most formidable collision we have ever had with them.

Forty years ago, a Bareilly Syad [a Lord; descendant of Ali,
son-in-law of the Prophet], Ahmud Shah, obtained a wonderful ascendency over the whole of the Euzufzye clans in
the Peshawur valley. After an extraordinary career he fell
in battle with the Sikhs in 1830 at Balakat in Huzara, and
his surviving followers, all Hindoostanee fanatics, were
permitted by the Sikh conquerors to proceed to Mekka.
Arrived at Attock, they turned sharp up the right bank of
the Indus and established themselves at a place called
Sitana, nearly opposite Torbeyla, in the country of the
Othmanzye clan. Their incessant hostility and intrigues
against the British Government during the Mutiny in 1857
led to an expedition for the purpose of expelling them from
Sitana, in 1858. This expedition, under Sir Sydney Cotton,
was but half successfull[1]: the Hindoostanee fanatics fell back
from the Indus further inland. They removed to a place
called Mulkah, situated on one of the southern spurs of the
great Mahabun mountain, and the Othmanzye and Gudoon
tribes entered into an agreement with the British Government not to permit them to resettle in Sitana.

To Mulkah, some months before our expedition, repaired
the son of the late titular King of Swat, Syud Akbar, who
claimed an ancestral right in the Sitana lands. At his per-
suasion, some hundreds of the Hindoostanees returned to
Sitana and reinstated him, and themselves, at that place.
The Gudoon and Othmanzye tribes were called on by the
British government to fulfil their contract and to prevent
the re-occupation of Sitana, but they refused. A blockade
was therefore instituted on our part and all communications
between the British territory and the Gudoon and Othmanzye tribes stopped. The exasperation thus caused was fed

---

[1] An account of this is to be found in Sir Sydney Cotton's book, *Nine
Years on the North-West Frontier of India*, 1868.

by the Hindoostanee fanatics who were liberal in their offers of money to the tribes affected by the blockade, as well as to the adjoining tribes, on the condition of support and assistance. They were sufficiently successful to induce them to threaten Umb on the Indus, a place some miles above Sitana, and though not in our territory it is separated by the Indus river only, and owned by a feudatory of ours, the principal part of whose lands are in the Huzara.

The first precautionary measure on our part was the dispatch of H.M.'s 101st Royal Bengal Fusiliers[1] from Rawalpindee, and some of the Punjab Irregular force from Abbottabad. At this time, Mahommed Azim Khan withdrew with his troops from the frontier district which he governed, to make an attempt on the Cabool throne, and this doubtless gave the fanatics some confidence. They actually fired in bravado across the river at our troops, and taunted them by every means in their power.

Government at length decided on sending an expedition to Mulkah for the purpose of destroying it and to break up the band of fanatics. My regiment started after a few hours' notice. On reaching the Cabool river, we crossed, the horses and baggage by means of five small boats, a work of great labour which occupied us from daybreak until after midnight. At 5 a.m. next morning we marched on Hoti Murdan in Euzofzai. Euzofzai is an immense, flat, treeless plain extending to the southern slope of the Mahabun mountain, on the opposite side of which was Mulkah, the object of our expedition. It is patrolled by the Guide Corps, composed of cavalry and infantry.

The Guides are considered the flower of the Punjab Irregular force and have their fixed head quarters at Hoti Murdan, in the fort built by Hodson[2] who belonged to them

[1] Formerly the 1st European Bengal Fusiliers in the service of the Hon. East India Company, and later the 1st Bn The Royal Munster Fusiliers (disbanded 1922).

[2] Major William Stephen Raikes Hodson (1821–58), one of the best-known and most controversial figures of the Indian Mutiny. He served with the 2nd Bengal Grenadiers in the 1st Sikh War and later with the

and earned a distinguished name in the Mutiny. The fort is simply a walled enclosure of some acres, built of sun dried mud bricks, and as the country had recently been flooded, it presented a very fragile and dilapidated appearance. It afforded comfortable quarters for the officers and no doubt could be held against any attack by the border tribes if provisioned. It is surprising how many British comforts have been provided in this inhospitable distant plain – an excellent billiard table, swimming bath, and library are among these – but much is required to compensate the banishment from civilisation and isolated life led by British officers at Hoti Murdan.

On our arrival we found the Guides had already gone to Bamkeyl on the Indus, and were watching the fanatics. Lieut Colonel Wilde,[1] in command, directed us to join him: we did, and halted at Nowa Killa until the 15th of October, when a force of 5000 men had collected, and General Neville Chamberlain[2] assumed command. We were not many miles from the base of the mountain called Mahabun on which our enemy had located himself, and to march up the rugged jungle covered face over its crest, to Mulkah on

16th Bengal Grenadiers and 1st European Bengal Fusiliers. He commanded the Guides, 1852–4; raised and commanded Hodson's Horse, 1857; obtained the surrender of the King of Delhi, whose sons and grandson he shot with his own hands. Killed at Lucknow, 12 March 1858.

[1] Lieutenant-Colonel Alfred Thomas Wilde, C.B. (1819–78), late 19th Madras Native Infantry and Commandant, Corps of Guides. He served on the Frontier and in the Indian Mutiny. Died a Lieutenant-General.

[2] Brigadier-General Sir Neville Bowles Chamberlain (1820–1902), Bengal Infantry. He was at the assault of Ghuznee, 1839 and with Major-General Sir William Nott's force in Afghanistan, 1842; in Gwalior Campaign and present at Maharajpore. Present at Chillianwallah and Goojerat. Field Marshal, 1900. The force of which he now found himself in command (5545 officers and men), consisted of a Half Bty 19th Brigade, R. A. Peshawur Mountain Train Battery; Huzara Mountain Train Battery; 71st Highland Light Infantry; 101st R. Bengal Fusiliers; one Company Sappers and Miners; Guides Infantry; 1st, 3rd, 5th and 6th Punjab Infantry; 20th and 32nd Punjab Native Infantry; 5th Goorkha Regiment.

its northern slope would have been the shortest route, but every step would have been contested, and the fanatics would in all probability have retreated with little loss, into the more distant ranges. In place of this direct advance, a plan of attack was conceived which in theory had much to commend it, but when an attempt was made to carry it out, the consequences were little short of disastrous, and the loss of life to our troops was without doubt greater than would have resulted from a disputed ascent of the southern mountain slope in our front.

The plan is easily understood if we assume the mountain to have been roughly triangular, that on its south east sides lie our own provinces, Euzofzai and Huzara, and on its north west face a mountain locked valley called Chumla. A stealthy and rapid march was contemplated into this valley, by which we should place ourselves in rear of the fanatics, cut off their retreat into the distant ranges, and be within a short climb of Mulkah. The ascent of the mountain in rear presented less difficulty, the northern slope being less steep and rugged than the faces looking upon our encampment in the plains. For obvious reasons this plan was kept with the greatest secrecy from all save the few to whom its knowledge was necessary.

During the time occupied in assembling our force, the tribe of Gudoons made apologies which were accepted by the commissioner of the district, Colonel Reynell Taylor,[1] and there were few in camp that expected more than a march to Mulkah and back, with scarce an interchange of hostile shots. Fifteen days' provisions accompanied us, and according with stringent orders, we discarded most of our baggage save bedding, and of this we took little enough though the nights were cold and at 8,000 feet – the height of Mahabun – we anticipated frost. On its summit we could,

[1] Lieutenant-Colonel Reynell George Taylor (1822–86), late 2nd Bengal Light Cavalry. Served in Gwalior, 1843; Sutlej, 1845–6, present at Mudkee; Punjab, 1848–9. Commanded Corps of Guides, 1855. General, 1880.

by the aid of a glass, see numerous clumps of pine from our position in the plains; we could also see the pass by which Sir Sidney Cotton entered in 1858, and which we also believed was destined to be our route. The fanatics and those who had sided with them were of the same impression and had done all they could to render the pass impracticable. It led, I believe, to Mungultana.

Late on the night of the 20th,[1] field force orders detailed three columns of troops; the first, under Lt Colonel Wilde, would move at once, a second at midnight, under Major Keyes, and the third, under Captain Salt of the Artillery,[2] at 3 a.m. No mention of route or destination was made. A depot was ordered to remain in the plains, and Major Ross[3] with a wing of the regiment of Ferozepore was to move about Euzofzai. One hundred sabres of my regiment, with Colonel Probyn and Lieutenant Macaulay,[4] accompanied the first column; the remainder were left in the plains.

As the night was excessively dark and our encampment ploughed fields, the three columns going in different directions at different times caused the greatest confusion; regiments too were broken up, entailing much extra trouble on their officers, and everyone appeared in a state of bewilderment. Accustomed as I had been to camp life, my impression was that the beginning was bad. The roads were mere field tracks, everywhere blocked by baggage animals, and Captain Salt's column, with which I marched,[5] was

---

[1] 20 October 1863.

[2] Major Charles Patton Keyes (1823–1896), 30th Madras Native Infantry and Commandant 1st Punjab Regiment. Later a General. Captain Thomas Henry Salt, Royal (Bengal) Artillery. Served in Punjab, 1848, present at Chillianwallah and Goojerat; at capture of Delhi, 1857.

[3] Major Campbell Claye Grant Ross (1844–92), 14th Native Infantry (formerly Ferozepore Regiment). General, 1890.

[4] Lieutenant Charles Edward Macaulay (late 51st Bengal Native Infantry), Adjutant, Probyn's Horse, with which he served in China.

[5] Sylvester had wished to go with Probyn, but was prevented from doing so by the Deputy Inspector-General of Hospitals, Surgeon John Macintire (1816–67), who, he states in his *Diary*, bore him a grudge.

unable to proceed: he himself knew not his destination and the guide provided by the political agent led him upon a road impracticable for guns. We awaited daylight and then General Chamberlain's plan of attack was apparent to all, and to the enemy also, who could look down upon us from his high position. Major Keyes had feigned an attack on the Mungultana pass while General Chamberlain and the main body had arrived at the mouth of another which was to lead us to the Chumla valley in rear of Mulkah, the head quarters of the fanatics.

When it was light enough to see our position I found that we were among low ranges of hills near a village called Rustoom. This was the position selected for the depot and sick of the European corps, viz. the 71st Highlanders and 101st Bengal Fusiliers. General Chamberlain continued his march through the village of Soorkhawai into the pass now well known to us as that of Umbeylah.

It is a fact that nothing was known to us as to the actual length or practicability of Umbeylah pass for guns, but we did know that the steep sides of the Mahabun mountain formed its walls on the right, and that a high range on the left separated it from the territory of Boneyr and Swat, both of which valleys were full of warlike men as proud of their honour and jealous of their homes as Englishmen. We have to imagine their astonishment and anger when, tending their goats and sheep among the cliffs of the pass at daylight on the morning of the 20th, they saw a force as five thousand men, and five times as many baggage animals and followers, entering their pass at Soorkhawai. The measure was necessary to carry out General Chamberlain's plan of attack, and though it is easy to be wise after the event, yet it is inconceivable how men of Frontier experience could have hazarded the experiment.

It is true that the previous night Colonel Taylor, the Commissioner, sent a proclamation to Chumla and Bonair informing them of our intended march into their valley, and its real purpose, assuring the tribes we should in nowise molest them, but even their rude politics could not brook our highhanded treatment.

Success so far attended the attempt that at three in the afternoon, the end of the pass was reached, and the advance guard stood at the head of the Chumla valley. The route proved to be one of extreme difficulty and was for the most part a watercourse, in many parts impassable to more than one laden animal abreast. Huge stones and boulders encumbered the way and a luxuriant growth of trees and shrubs, though adding to the picturesque, increased the difficulty. It really bade fair to be the ten days' picnic we imagined except that, as the fighting men had consumed the greater part of the day in marching nine difficult miles, there was little prospect of baggage animals arriving until the pangs of hunger had exceeded picnic limits, and indeed, the whole of the impedimenta did not arrive for two days more.

It was warmer in the pass than in camp on the plain; the high mountain barriers, some thousands of feet on either side, densely covered with trees and brushwood, tended to increase the midday heat, and it was more than fortunate that water was plentiful, otherwise an advance or retreat would have been imperative. The transit of the artillery was a matter of great difficulty and delay, overcome only by the aid of elephants.

A move into the valley would have abandoned the crowded pass to the mercy of either the fanatics or hillmen, and in the event of an attack from the heights, native drivers of baggage and ammunition laden animals would have deserted and brought about disorganisation; consequently, General Chamberlain halted in inaction at the end of the pass until the 23rd. During this delay there was much discomfort to be endured, and as no one had contemplated separation from their baggage and commissariat, food was very scarce. A rupee was given for a single chupattie.

The scenery at the Chumla extremity of the pass, as it

debouched into the valley, was very imposing: on our right
the Mahabun mountain, by a series of steep spurs, towered
to the height of seven or eight thousand feet; on our left the
beetling crags of Mount Goroo, the highest point of the
chain separating us from Boneyr, rose to about five thousand
feet. A great deal of forest covered both mountains, sufficient indeed to conceal large masses of men. Here and there
woodless eminences cropped out from among the pines and
were ere long to be the scenes of bloody contests. Mulkah
was not visible, being many miles in advance on our right.

From the halting place of our force on the watershed,
sloping gradually away in front, for a distance of about three
miles, were the grassy plains of Chumla, the mountains
opening wider and wider on either side. The valley bent
to the right after the distance I have mentioned, so that we
could not see its full length, but the small village of
Umbeylah, and a brook threading the valley, were visible,
and beyond fir clad ranges of hills, while in the extreme
distance the Hindoo Koosh, clad in snow, crossed the
horizon.

During this unfortunate delay, the tocsin of war rang
through the wild lands of Swat and Boneyr, and in every
village, even the thirty miles which Mahabun measures
from east to west, tribes of widely differing tenets of
Islamism (and on that account at feud with each other)
joined against their common enemy, artfully represented
by the Hindoostanees as invading their homes and crushing
their religion. So much success attended these misrepre-
sentations that the High Priest or Akhoond of Swat joined
cause against us and rallied thousands around his standard,
with which he marched to oppose our passage into Chumla.

On arriving at the crest of the pass, Colonel Probyn, with
a hundred men of the Sikh Cavalry, some Guide Cavalry
and sappers, proceeded with Colonel Taylor of the Engineers
to reconnoitre as far as the village of Koria, near the eastern
extremity of the valley. Umbeylah was passed to the left,
and the mountain gorge leading into Swat was seen crowded

with Boneyrwall, but no hostilities were manifested until the return of the party, when a body of men moved across the valley and endeavoured to cut off its retreat. The men of my regiment were compelled to charge those who advanced into the open ground, while crowds under shelter jeered and shouted defiance. A sandy watercourse embarrassed the horses. Adjutant Macaulay's charger and another fell; they were caught and carried off by the enemy; some others were wounded by sabre cuts, and one of the native officers, Anoop Singh, received a tulwar blow on the scalp. Emboldened by the desire of our party to regain the pass, the Boneyrwall followed them with the greatest determination, and closed with the 20th and 32nd Regiments of Punjab Infantry which had advanced from the pass to cover the retreat of our hard pressed party.

A breastwork of stores and whatever material fell to hand was immediately thrown across the pass, and a battery drawn up, defended by densely packed infantry. Other infantry were dispatched up the slopes of Goroo on the one side and Mahabun on the other, and to a considerable height we held these barriers.

Darkness in no degree damped the ardour of the enemy who from this time besieged us. General Chamberlain was too astute to attempt any further advance in the face of the rapidly increasing and enraged tribes, and retreat would have been as ruinous to our prestige as difficult through the crowded pass. Thus no alternative offered but to stand on the defensive until reinforcements had arrived. Unfortunately, too, the object of this circuitous route of attack had in great part failed already for the Hindoostanees had arrived in our front, and could retreat if ultimately beaten and leave us but their empty lair on the Mahabun.

There was a faint moonlight on the night the valley was reconnoitred, and as this grew dim and almost dark from cloud, the enemy made a furious attack on our position and succeeded in gaining the front of the breastwork over which one, more desperate than the rest, leapt and cut down an Engineer officer. Others crept through the brush-wood on the slopes and assailed him they met first. Heavy small arm firing continued until 3 a.m. the following morning. This was of necessity made at random or guided merely by sounds or flashes from matchlock or rifle. Very little damage was effected on either side by the desultory warfare; we however unfortunately lost Lieutenant Gillies[1] of the Artillery, who was shot through the heart. The light of the portfire was surmised by some to have attracted the shot.

A slight exposure to sun, cold or wet suffices to place the European soldier of the present day on the sick list, and as it was impossible to keep sick and wounded in camp, General Chamberlain sent a number already unfit for duty under a guard to Rustoom. Fifty men of my regiment, with sick, wounded, and shoeless horses, accompanied them. There was little prospect of cavalry being of further service in the pass, and though the charge of so many sick and wounded was an important one, I was, much against my inclination, chosen to take charge of the field hospital at the Euzofzai end of the pass. Besides sick and wounded, the European dead were sent on camels into Hoti Murdan or Peshawur, for burial.

Telegraphic communication with India was not estab-lished until later in the campaign, the required rein-forcements would be many days in arriving, the fifteen days' days provisions were being consumed, and the position of the force was critical, but not so serious as it would have been had the original intention of marching into the valley, without a halt, been carried out. Nothing however was spared to strengthen its unfortunate position. Our flanks, extending far up the mountain sides, were strengthened by half bastions built of stones and rocks – by the natives called *sungas*. The highest of these, on the Mahabun, was called the Crag Picket, the highest on Mount Goroo, the Eagle's Nest. In both cases the names give an idea of the

[1] Lieutenant William Adam Beaver Gillies, Royal (Bengal) Artillery.

character of the positions. The ascent to either was very toilsome, but the panoramic view of our whole position, as well as that of the Chumla valley with its moving masses of the enemy about Umbeylah, was very beautiful. These two highest pickets were the most important points in our defences but, situated far below the top of the heights, they were commanded by others above them.

On the 25th of October the enemy descended from the higher spurs of the Mahabun and attacked our right line of pickets; they were however driven back for some distance into the fastnesses of the mountain. On the following day a much more determined attack was made by the Hindoostanees and combined tribes upon the opposite heights, the hardest struggle being at the Eagle's Nest. Fortunately, General Chamberlain had in anticipation assembled a large body of infantry, consisting of the 71st Highlanders, several regiments of Punjab Infantry, the mountain train, and other native troops.

The attack was made from the crest of Goroo, down the steep declivities of which the enemy came with banners flying and deafening war cries. They were received by a very hot fire from our rifles and mountain artillery, but it was insufficient to check their advance on the picket which they were bent on carrying. It was noon when the assault on the Eagle's Nest commenced with a charge of Boneyrwall across the open plateau in its front. They managed to plant a standard beneath the walls, but notwithstanding this gallant advance, the fire from the men of the 20th Punjab Infantry was so well reserved and steadily delivered that the enemy were sent reeling up the hill after strewing the plateau with dead. Failing in their charge, they afterwards ensconced themselves among the trees and rocks, galling the Punjabees with a very precise matchlock fire.

Major (now Sir Charles) Brownlow,[1] who was commanding the 20th, lost two of his Lieutenants, Richmond and

[1] Major Charles Henry Brownlow (late 4th Bengal European Regiment), Commandant 20th Native Infantry. Served on frontier and in China, 1860.

Clifford,[1] in addition to his senior native officer and many men. Lieutenants Drake, Hoste, and Barron,[2] and nine native officers, were wounded in other parts of our position on the left, and in all our casualties up to dark numbered about one hundred and fifty.

Firing continued throughout the night, and to give some idea of the amount of ammunition expended, a party of twelve sharpshooters under Lieutenant Fosbery[3] shot away two thousand Enfield bullets.

The day after this onslaught, the enemy received permission to carry off their dead, and without any previous warning, late in the evening after dark, I received a large convoy of sick and wounded. Few had eaten food since early morning; I had none to give; there was neither village nor bazaar where it could be purchased. Many of the Europeans arrived without even the scanty amount of bedding allowed in the pass, and excepting a very small supply of medicine and instruments, I, with one native assistant, was left empty handed to attend some hundreds of severely wounded and sick officers and soldiers. The whole of my small store of brandy wine, arrowroot, sponge, lint and such like actual necessaries were expended at once. I had but one water carrier and the nearest supply was one mile distant. There were none to cook, nor was there a single bedstead. Fortunately, I found tents in camp and got almost an acre of ground covered, for it often rained heavily and the nights were bitterly cold.

On the 30th, the Akhoond's troop's, estimated at fifteen hundred men, attacked the stockade in front, while the Hindoostanees assaulted our highest picket on the Mahabun

[1] Lieutenant George Mitchell Richmond (late 54th Bengal Native Infantry) with 20th Native Infantry. Lieutenant Robert Clifford, Adjutant of the 1st Punjab Cavalry, was a volunteer with the 3rd Punjab Infantry.

[2] Lieutenant Thomas Henry Tyrwhitt Drake, Captain William Dashwood Hoste (Commandant 6th Punjab Infantry) and Lieutenant William Barron, Royal (Bengal) Artillery.

[3] Lieutenant George Vincent Fosbery, V.C. (late 4th Bengal Europeans).

– The Crag. The Swatees were repulsed from the front by the 71st Highlanders and 101st Bengal Fusiliers, and afterwards charged by the gallent 5th Goorkha Regiment who followed the enemy some distance down the pass, ripping open and beheading their victims with their *cookries*.

The attack on the Crag was a surprise, commencing as it did before daybreak. The fanatics advanced with so much *élan* as fairly to drive our troops from the sunga. It had been held through the night by Major Keyes and his regiment, the 1st Punjab Infantry. There was nothing precipitate in its retreat, and after re-forming and awaiting daylight, Major Keyes retook it with great dash and killed fifty of the enemy. The hand to hand fighting was very severe; Major Keyes, Lieutenant Pitcher[1] and two native officers were wounded, one native officer and twelve men were killed, while thirty-six others were wounded.

Matters had now taken a very serious turn, and judging from the opinion then prevailing in the force, General Chamberlain's great reputation was failing. None however was more alive to the critical state of his force and the frontier generally, and brave to a fault himself, he was almost too exacting with those under his command. He informed the Government of the probable extension of the war, and advised all spare troops to be pushed rapidly to the frontier, so that the roads of northern India were soon lined with troops, stores and munitions of war.

The wounded were naturally discontented that no provision should have been made for them, and at the outset I sent urgently for supplies and help, to the chief medical officer of the division, but he was far away on the cool heights of Murree, and some days would elapse 'ere he could sanction my appeal, and many more before the longed for assistance and stores could arrive. Meanwhile, and as usual, late at night, the wounded of the 30th instant added to my

---

[1] Lieutenant Henry William Pitcher (formerly 13th Bengal Native Infantry), 1st Punjab Infantry. Served in the Indian Mutiny.

painful responsibility: hospital gangrene had broken out, and despite every precaution, it spread throughout the many wounded. Dysentery and inflammation of the lungs were the chiefest causes of sickness, and the want of proper food was an evil I could not combat. The frequent deaths depressed the suffering living, and the native troops, from our want of success in the pass and bad provision for their unfortunate condition, drew conclusions not flattering to our prestige.

Calculating the number of minutes of daylight in those short days, and the number of sick and wounded in my charge, I discovered that one minute each was the average time I could allow to each, while an amputation, if even so quickly done, occupied from twenty minutes to half an hour. I indented on all the adjacent villages for the common bedsteads in use, the worth of each perhaps less than six-pence, still, they sufficed to keep the worst cases off the damp ground and above the cold wind which came sweeping in over the plain, beneath the bottom of the tent. The little straw I could procure in the villages I took also, and wrote to General Chamberlain that in Napoleon's retreat from Moscow nothing more terrible had occurred. He at once responded by sending a surgeon from the pass to my help, and all that could be spared from their scanty supply of medical stores. His telegram to Government after a while brought me numbers of medical officers and every kind of stores and comforts from Peshawur, not however until hospital gangrene and want of proper nourishment had inflicted great suffering and loss.

By availing myself of the resources of the country, a complaint was lodged against me by a subordinate political officer, Lieutenant Sandeman.[1] By writing, in my emer-gency, to General Chamberlain, rather than waiting until other lives were sacrificed while help came tardily through the head of my department at Murree, I offended again,

[1] Lieutenant Robert Groves Sandeman (1835–92), Junior Political Officer (late 14th Bengal Native Infantry). Was with 1st Sikh Cavalry at Lucknow. K.C.S.I., 1879.

but letters from General Chamberlain and constant enquiries for the sick and wounded satisfied me on both delinquencies. He knew that I had done my utmost for their welfare and sent Captain Bernard[1] and some orderlies to render what aid they could.

From the very first occupation of the pass much labour had been expended in clearing away trees and brushwood, and as the road back to Euzofzai, down the watercourse, was so impracticable yet so indispensable, and difficult to hold if disputed, General Chamberlain directed a new road to be constructed in rear of our right flank, down the Mahabun slopes to the plains.

The crowded encampment in the pass had become insanitary and disagreeable, and the water supply foul and unwholesome. It was on this and other accounts advisable the camp should be shifted entirely to the situation now occupied by the right flank, namely on the slopes of the Mahabun, so that paths up the mountain sides were made also by working parties composed of two companies of native sappers aided by men of the 71st and 101st Regiments. The first mentioned road was a work of some magnitude and in parts not only distant from camp, but winding as it did amongst pine clad spurs, was out of sight and at some parts offered great facility to the enemy for surprising the workers. There can be little doubt that the enemy who watched our proceedings from the eyrie heights of Mahabun and Goroo concluded we were providing a new road for retreat.

Friday, being the Mussleman Sabbath, was a day on which the enemy usually fought and prayed, and this observance was kept up as long as we were besieged. It appeared that each man served a week with his standard and was then relieved by another of his tribe, bringing with him a week's supply of food, a sword, matchlock, powder horn, and bag of bullets, a stout pair of limbs and lion's heart. He was an enemy by no means despicable. In addition

---

[1] Captain Henry Lionel Charles Bernard (late 4th Bengal Europeans), 5th Goorkhas. Served in several frontier campaigns.

to a splendid physique, the loose blue blouse, girt at the waist by an ample cloth, the massive turban, bearded chin, and sandaled legs and feet, gave a most imposing appearance. Fortified by prayer and promises of paradise, their Friday advances with war drum beating and shrill pipe screeling, produced a very profound impression on the garrisons of our advanced posts, who, impassive and overworked, had to watch bands of these brave fellows troop down the mountain side, swords flashing, to the attack.

Friday the 6th of November, when the sappers were working some distance from other support than their covering parties, the enemy threatened in large numbers and compelled them, unarmed as they were, to withdraw, and for what purpose their defenders should have remained it is difficult to understand, but General Chamberlain, as commandant of the Punjab force, made virtually every appointment in it and was accustomed to exact a most rigorous attention to orders, perhaps so much so as to leave too little discretion to his officers, who consequently feared to incur the smallest responsibility. Two of them on this occasion, Major Harding and Captain Rogers,[1] appear to have awaited orders before leaving an indefensible position.

The party furthest from camp was composed of fifty of the 71st Highlanders, commanded by Ensign Murray and a volunteer from the 79th Highlanders, Lieutenant Dougal.[2] Dougal was a great sportsman and good shot with his rifle, and had scarcely reached camp from Peshawur when he was detailed for this duty. Nearer camp was a second party of Brownlow's Punjabees under command of Captain Rogers: yet nearer camp a third party commanded by Major Harding almost completed the chain, with the nearest point in our camp, viz. the picket held by the 1st Punjab Infantry, under Major Keyes, a mile distant. Although I have said a chain was complete to camp, yet

[1] Major George Whittall Harding, 2nd Sikh Regiment, and Captain Robert Gordon Rogers (late 5th Bengal Europeans).

[2] Ensign Charles Balfour Murray (71st) and Lieutenant Thomas Ballard Dougal (79th). Dougal had served at Lucknow.

these parties were not in sight of each other and the rocky, precipitous, fir clad nature of the ground rendered it impossible for the one to help the other speedily.

The wily enemy, under leaders well acquainted with every part of the ground, almost imperceptibly surrounded the advanced party and forced them to retire on the Punjabees, but many had been wounded and embarrassed this movement exceedingly. The 5th Goorkhas went to the rescue, and Major Harding, senior officer, assumed command.

By this time the enemy was pressing them closely and all sheltered themselves under a breastwork of rock, upon which the Boneyrwall advanced from the opposite side and kept up a very precise matchlock fire. Dougal was said to have killed four men with his rifle, but together with Murray, was shot dead. Lieutenant Oliphant of the Goorkhas[1] received a bullet wound through the shoulder blade and Battye of the Guides[2] was disabled also.

Harding, perceiving their perilous situation, wrote for help, and with his killed and wounded lying round him, awaited the messenger's return with an anxiety one can only imagine. At length the answer came; he was to retire unassisted. Night was coming on: there was no possibility of carrying off his dead nor badly wounded, but those who could walk he bade get to camp as best they were able with Captain Rogers' party, while he and the brave Goorkhas tarried awhile longer to keep back the enemy who, emboldened by success, followed closely. It was Harding's sad fate to be shot through the neck and afterwards hacked to pieces when being carried to camp by the Goorkhas. Major Keyes went to their assistance and helped them to his picket from which the enemy was kept away by the fire of the mountain guns, and the Goorkhas, as much at home on the mountain side as the Boneyrwall, under cover of darkness managed to reach camp.

[1] Lieutenant James Stuart Oliphant, 5th Goorkhas.
[2] Lieutenant Wigram Battye (late 6th Bengal Europeans), Guides.

There can be no doubt that few soldiers ever saw fighting so severe as that in which our troops were engaged. Oliphant, who afterwards suffered from traumatic delirium, often raved for the expected supports, and one unfortunate private of the 71st Highlanders escaped death by hiding in the brushwood throughout the night, while the enemy close to him stripped and mutilated the dead and hacked to pieces the wounded by the light of pinewood torches.

In this affair of the working parties, we lost in killed, one native, three European officers, and thirty-four men, while two British officers, two native officers, and thirty-seven men were wounded. It was no part of the enemy's system of warfare to make prisoners, and one, badly wounded, who was taken by us, refused any service I proffered him and died.

Intelligence had been received that the Akhoond had summoned other tribes, from the borders of Cabool, and accordingly, three thousand men from Bajour responded. The greatest praise must be accorded these demi savages for the manner they held us at bay, nor must we forget they were without artillery or commissariat, and in many instances, armed with a sword only.

Reinforcements in the shape of half a Punjab battery, the 4th Goorkha Regiment, and the 14th Native Infantry joined our force in the pass at this time, and if anything spoke well of the favour of our military service with the natives of northern India, it was the fact that numbers almost equal to our casualties offered themselves for enlistment before we left the pass.

A great deal of parading music and other signs of activity in the valley near Umbeylah generally foreshadowed an attack and led General Chamberlain to strengthen the threatened position, and these indications on the 12th of November induced him to reinforce the Crag. Nearly two hundred men were placed in it and a mountain battery under Captain Hughes[1] was placed on an available spot of

---

[1] Captain Thomas Elliott Hughes (1830–86), Royal (Bengal) Artillery. Major-General, 1885.

K

ground, two hundred and fifty yards below, in the right rear. Major Brownlow was again chosen to command the responsible post and could shout orders to the mountain battery beneath.

At 10 o'clock, in a very dim light, the valley beneath the Crag was full of the enemy, sounding the war drum and screeling pipe – not unlike the bagpipe in sound. Under cover of this noise, their advanced skirmishers, conversing in whispers, stole through the rocks and brushwood until they had arrived so near as to be visible to our soldiery, then, breaking forth into shouts, advanced *en masse* to the assault. Major Brownlow, who had reserved his fire, now ordered a volley, and Hughes' guns threw shells in their midst. Great slaughter occurred and drove them into the ravine and jungle below. Again they rallied and returned to the charge and again, by the same steady fire, were repulsed. These attacks, at intervals, were repeated through the night until almost daybreak.

In the morning, the picket was relieved and placed in charge of Lieutenant Davidson[1] of the 1st Punjab Infantry. The garrison was chiefly composed of the sepoys of the Ferozepore Regiment and fifteen of Fosbery's sharp-shooters, men of the Bengal Fusiliers. The enemy's sabbath had dawned, and with the undaunted zeal imparted by the Mahomedan creed, he rushed furiously upon the position and carried it. Here again was an instance affording a brilliant example of the discipline reigning in the Punjab Force: Davidson and a few brave fellows of his regiment refused to leave their post, and died there. After peace had been declared, one of the old chiefs of Boneyr spoke of Davidson's heroism, and would contrary to all custom, have spared his life could he have controlled his followers.

General Chamberlain could not brook a reverse for an instant, and directed H.M.'s 101st Foot, then under arms, to retake it forthwith, but as I have already related, it was a

[1] Captain John Paton Davidson, 1st Punjab Infantry. Served in the Indian Mutiny and several frontier campaigns.

work of considerable toil and time to mount the steep, which entirely overlooked and commanded our entire position; great therefore was the consternation in camp among servants and camp followers while the enemy held possession. The scene in camp closely approached a panic, which was appeased with great difficulty by Major Keyes, Ross, and other officers on the scene. Many of our followers had already been wounded while tending cattle on the outskirts, or by stray shots into camp, for sometimes, at dead of night, the darkness would sparkle with matchlock fire, and random shots disturbed the sleepers.

Responding to General Chamberlain's order, the 101st and Regiment of Ferozepore sped up the rugged steep and carried the work at the bayonet's point, without much opposition.

Our loss in this second battle of the Crag was severe; in killed, one British and one native officer, with forty-nine men; six wounded, one British[1] and three native officers, with one hundred and four men. These two last affairs were followed by very large convoys of sick and wounded, but I had now received help; stores, necessaries, clothing, rum, wine and other comforts, a liberal dispensation of which restored the large number in hospital to contentment. The European dead were in all cases sent to Peshawur for burial, while the native troops disposed of theirs after their own custom, in camp, and burnt the bodies of the enemy, which was deserved, by their brutal treatment of all our wounded who fell into their hands.

Fortunately, besiegers as well as besieged required time to bury their dead, and from the 13th to the 18th, little beyond desultory firing disturbed the camp, but the new road to the plains, which had cost us so dear, was complete, and there no longer existed need to hold the pass and opposite chain of pickets on Mount Goroo. All baggage and encumbrances were therefore carried up in rear of our right flank, to the new ground, and taking advantage of the

[1] This probably refers to Captain Davidson and Lieutenant Pitcher.

hours of darkness, our positions on the slopes of Goroo, and the fouled spot in the pass were evacuated, and troops, with the exception of a picket half way down the right on Mahabun, had all moved up on the right barrier of the pass. This single picket was commanded by Lieutenant Mosley[1] and a party of sepoys of the Regiment of Ferozepore.

Hitherto, and save one attack on the Eagle's Nest, the enemy's attention seems to have concentrated on the Crag as the key to our position on the Mahabun, but no sooner had daylight revealed our changed position than hordes of the enemy flocked to the abandoned ground on the crest of the pass. This time, under a mounted leader, they appeared greatly astonished. Some could be seen examining, with the curiosity of connoisseurs, empty soup and ham tins; others picked up bottles and scraps of anything strange in their eyes. It was, however, soon apparent that they had concluded we were commencing a retreat by the new route, and assailed Mosely's slender position behind a breastwork of stones, furiously. Mozely's ammunition was soon expended; his only chance was to leap over the breastwork and charge with the bayonet, which he did, and together with those who followed, fell, overpowered, and were hacked to pieces.

His Commanding Officer, Major Ross, with Lieutenant Inglis[2] and a body of the Ferozepore Regiment, two companies of Highlanders under Captain Smith,[3] some of the Bengal Fusiliers under their Adjutant, Chapman,[4] all rushed to the rescue, but such was [the] determination of these brave mountaineers that they too were hurled back up the steep. Captain Smith, Lieutenant Jones [a volunteer from the 79th Highlanders][5] and Lieutenant Chapman

---

[1] Lieutenant William Fielden Mosley, 14th Native Infantry (Ferozepore Regiment). Formerly in 35th Bengal Native Infantry. Present at several minor affairs in the Indian Mutiny.

[2] Lieutenant David Alexander Cator Inglis, 14th Native Infantry.

[3] Captain Charles Francis Smith, 71st. Served in the Crimea.

[4] Lieutenant Henry Howard Chapman, Adjutant, Bengal Fusiliers.

[5] Lieutenant Thomas Sheridan Gore Jones, 79th. Served in the Indian Mutiny.

were killed, the latter in the act of carrying Smith's body from the *mêlée*. Major Ross was slightly wounded, and Inglis received a bayonet wound in the chest, but not a serious one.

For two days our killed and wounded remained at the mercy of the enemy. On the 19th, a party went out to recover them but returned, unsuccessful. Lieutenant Aldridge of the 71st[1] and two of his men were killed, and Lieutenant Stockley of the 101st,[2] wounded in both arms.

These continued losses and acting on the defensive dispirited all, and cast a gloom over camp. Besides the loss of four officers in the change of position, forty men were killed and one hundred and seven were wounded. No sooner had I, by using every exertion and appliance, provided for one convoy of sick and wounded, and sent the carriage to the pass, than it again returned, each time bringing more, until I had accumulated an enormous camp, and what with reports, returns, indents, and tramping in thick mud and often rain the whole day long, in attending first on one line of tents and then another, I began fairly to tire, and wrote to General Chamberlain begging to be allowed a change of duty to the Mahabun, which he promised on the advance of the force.

On the 19th, Major Hugh James,[3] the Peshawur Commissioner arrived in the pass from England. He possessed much influence over the frontier tribes and was in no way surprised at the position into which our want of courtesy had brought us. His presence in camp was estimated highly by the natives of our force who could not understand our refusing to bring matters to an immediate issue by a determined advance which they maintained would be at once decisive and successful. Unquestionably they were tired of the continued struggle: many of them, and notably soldiers

---

[1] Captain Robert Barttelot Aldridge, 71st. Served in the Crimea.

[2] Lieutenant Charles More Stockley, 101st Bengal Fusiliers.

[3] Major Hugh Rees James, C.B. (late 44th Bengal Native Infantry), Peshawur Commissioner.

of the Guide corps were fighting against men of their own tribe, and one of this regiment declared he saw his old father in the enemy's breastwork and immediately took a shot at him.

XVII

The Umbeylah Campaign, 1863 (2)

GENERAL Chamberlain's command had now become a very anxious one, and the following telegram shewed he felt it to be so:

The troops have now been hard worked day and night for a month and having to meet fresh enemies with loss is telling. We much need reinforcements. I find it difficult to meet the enemy's attacks and provide convoys for supplies and wounded sent to the rear. If you can give some fresh corps to relieve those most reduced in numbers and dash the relieved corps can be sent to the plains and used in support. This is urgent.

This telegram created considerable alarm in the plains, and the Lieutenant Governor of the Punjab,[1] whose little war it was, became anxious to stay the conflagration, and it was reported, desired peace at any price.

So close were the enemy's breastworks to our advanced positions that taunts were often shouted to our native soldiery, and so indeed were threats of impending attacks, and in this manner we knew that a grand effort to drive the force off Mahabun would soon be made. The 20th[2] was a Friday, their day to pray and fight; accordingly the combined tribes appeared on the heights above the Crag picket. It was morning time and the garrison consisted of a hundred men of H.M.'s 101st Regiment, with three officers and an Assistant Surgeon: the officers were Major Delafosse, of Cawnpore celebrity, Captain Goad, Ensign Sanderson, and

---

[1] Sir Robert Montgomery (1809–87), Lieutenant-Governor of the Punjab, 1859–65. Appointed a member of the council of the Secretary of State for India, 1868.

[2] 20 November 1863.

Dr Pile.[1] In addition, Captain Rogers of the 20th Punjab Regiment was present with a hundred of his men.

The attack lasted greater part of the day, when about 3 o'clock in the afternoon, an officer of the 101st and a whole company of his men were seized with a remarkable desire to leave the fight, which mishap gave the enemy so much advantage that they gained the upper part of the picket, which was divided from the lower by huge rocks running across it. Delafosse, Sanderson, Pile and Rogers, with the remaining company of the 101st and Punjabees, fought desperately to retain the lower half, but Pile and Sanderson, together with two thirds of the men, were killed. The matter thus being utterly hopeless, the brave defenders yielded, and for the third time the enemy's standards flaunted in the Crag. The capture of a position was a great boon to the enemy in the shape of rifles and ammunition, besides bedding and uniforms. Retreats from this picket were almost frightful to witness from below, and anything more distressing than the scene at 3 o'clock could scarcely be imagined.

General Chamberlain ordered the Highlanders, 5th Punjab Infantry and 5th Goorkhas under arms without delay, and placing himself and Staff, with a few other officers, in front, led the way, all artillery shelling the position until they approached the base of the Crag, and here a deadly shower of rocks, stones, bullets and other missiles greeted them. The dust, noise, yells, smoke and enemy's war drums heightened the excitement which already ran high. Every shot fired by the enemy told on the dense mass of soldiery advancing; fortunately their small bullets did little more than temporarily disable the limb struck, unless they hit more vital parts. At the foot of the

[1] Major George Henry Delafosse (1835–1905), 101st (late of the 53rd Bengal Native Infantry). One of the survivors of the siege and massacre of Cawnpore. Was at Lucknow and capture of Cawnpore. In Sikkim campaign, 1860–1. Captain George Soden Goad, Ensign Algernon Robert Sanderson, and Assistant-Surgeon William Pile (all 101st).

Crag, Colonel Hope[1] re-formed his Highlanders and directed the Goorkhas to turn the flank of the enemy, but the sight of a hedge of bayonets steadily advancing was too much for the courage of even the brave mountaineers, for whom also some allowance must be made on account of a long and fruitless attempt to dislodge us, only occasionally encouraged by a temporary success.

A large list of wounded men and officers attended this re-capture; foremost among the latter was General Chamberlain himself, in whose forearm a matchlock ball entered, and traversing the muscles, caused him much subsequent suffering. Colonels Hope, Wylde, Vaughan, Tyler, Major Campbell and Lieutenant Anderson,[2] and one hundred and ten men were wounded also.

When the intelligence of this continued severe fighting reached the Lieutenant Governor, and Major James reported that a further reinforcement of six thousand men from Dher had joined the hostile tribes, he, fearing some disastrous reverse would shortly follow before our force could be recruited in numbers, councilled that General Chamberlain should withdraw into the plains. As I have before written, not only was the little war of the Lieutenant Governor's making, but its conduct now rested almost solely with him, for at this crisis, Lord Elgin[3] was on his deathbed. Fortunately, the Commander in Chief, Sir Hugh Rose, who never could understand the anomalous condition

[1] Lieutenant-Colonel William Hope (1819–98), 71st. Served in the Crimea. General, 1881.

[2] Colonel Wilde of the Guides.

Lieutenant-Colonel John Luther Vaughan, Commandant 5th Punjab Infantry. Formerly 21st Bengal Native Infantry. Served at Maharajpore; with Turkish contingent in the Crimea; Euzofzai, 1857, and in Indian Mutiny, including capture of Lucknow.

Major John Peter William Campbell, Commandant 5th Goorkhas.

Lieutenant Wardlaw Cortlandt Anderson, 3rd Punjab Cavalry, Orderly Officer to General Chamberlain who accompanied the storming column.

[3] James Bruce, 8th Earl of Elgin and Kincardine (1811–63). Signed Treaty of Tienstsin with China, and went out to obtain ratification in the Chinese War, 1860.

K2

of the Punjab force, and who deprecated the hurried manner and limited scale on which the expedition to Mulkah set out, declared against anything but a vigorous prosecution of the war, and was himself, despite much opposition, hurrying to the fray. A report of his advent reached camp and many of us believed the matter would not rest until, led by him, we should carry fire and sword through every hostile tribe to Cabool.

Sir Hugh Rose however was not permitted to proceed beyond Lahore. He was called upon to furnish regiment after regiment to battle in the pass and stay the conflagration around Peshawur valley and along the frontier, and it certainly appeared a singular arrangement that General Chamberlain, commanding the force in the pass, should be under other authority than his, and it certainly was fortunate that the Lieutenant Governor had selected an officer brave and resolute as General Chamberlain. His severe and painful wound, combined with much previous anxiety and hard work, completely prostrated him, but he commanded from his bed, and was entirely adverse to a retreat.

Any hurriedly written description or telegraphic news failed to convey a conception of our position in the pass to those outside, at a distance, and Sir Hugh Rose sent two of his staff – Colonel Adye and Captain Roberts[1] – to report on our position. Their presence in camp was the subject of much adverse comment, but I believe they were enabled to make a favorable report to their master. Major James, although deprecating the discourteous manner in which we had entered the valley, advocated that our adopted plan should be vigorously prosecuted, and though authorised to withdraw the force to the plains, would not entertain the idea. At this juncture, Sir William Denison[2] temporarily

[1] Colonel John Miller Adye, C.B., R.A. (1819–1900). Later General Sir John Adye. Deputy Adjutant General (R.A.), Bengal Army. Captain Frederick Sleigh Roberts, V.C. (1832–1914), Royal (Bengal) Artillery. Later Field Marshal Lord Roberts.

[2] Colonel Sir William Thomas Denison, R.E. (1804–71), Governor of Madras.

filled the place of Lord Elgin as Governor General and
added his testimony that, to withdraw from our position
would be deemed a measure of defeat by the natives.

The many and gallant attempts to drive us from their
valleys had not been made by the brave mountaineers
without grave losses, for though it is true besiegers have
advantages over besieged, and though they knew every foot
of the strange ground we occupied, yet we possessed the
insuperable advantages of artillery. Under all the circumstances, however, many of the tribes were losing heart, and
this fact, combined with the influence of Major James, induced them to retire from the contest; in short, the entire
affair was almost settled peaceably by the negotiations of the
Commissioner. Fortunately, however, for our reputation,
the Boneyr chiefs determined on fighting out the issue.

After the desperate attempt made to drive us from the
pass on the 20th of November, there followed a lull in which
desultory firing continued, but no engagement of note took
place until the 15th of November.[1] During this quiet
interval, the chiefs of the tribes were often in our camp,
negotiating with the Commissioner, and as General
Chamberlain was lying helpless, he had been succeeded by
Major General Garvock who was said to have seen some
active service at the Cape.

At the time of his arrival, all was in readiness to move
out from our position in the event of our terms meeting
with refusal from the enemy, and it was a piece of very
ill fortune to General Chamberlain, after all his anxious
command, that he was unable to remain with his force the
few days of hostilities remaining, for indeed the enemy
was at this time virtually beaten, and every arrangement
made to conclude the campaign.

In addition to the advantage of meeting a dispirited
enemy, General Garvock arrived with a large reinforcement
of fresh troops, eager to join in the fray, and as there was
quite a possibility of the Boneyrs acceding to our terms, no

[1] Should be 15 December.

time was lost in advancing after the arrival of messengers dallying with our terms.

It was a momentous time with the new General for as yet he had not received honours from his sovereign, and as the war had assumed large dimensions, honours would of necessity be commensurate, provided another pass of arms would give him the opportunity to write a dispatch. The opportunity occurred on the 15th of December when the force was divided into two Brigades of about three thousand men in each, and advanced from our entrenched positions, to guard which about three thousand were left in camp.

The 1st Brigade, under Colonel Turner,[1] comprised the Mountain Train, 71st Highlanders, 7th Royal Fusiliers, 5th Goorkhas, 1st, 3rd and 5th Punjab Infantry Regiments, 20th Bengal Native Infantry, and 32nd (Pioneers). In the 2nd Brigade, under Colonel Wilde, were H.M.'s 101st Foot, Guides, Heavy Guns, Huzara Mountain Train, 6th Regiment Punjab Infantry, 14th Regiment Punjab Infantry, and 23rd Regiment of Punjab Infantry.

It was with a feeling akin to deliverance that we left our entrenchment at daybreak, after two months' harrassing defence: one's eyes almost refused belief on seeing our scarlet coated soldiery trooping up the declivity which led to the crest of Mahabun, down which the brave Boneyrwall had so often streamed to assail the Crag. The distance from our camp to the nearest position held by the enemy was computed at two miles. Here and there on the way were rocks and small breastworks behind which a few outposts tarried for a moment, fired, and fell back upon their position which was a conical hill about five hundred yards higher than the mountain crest. It was therefore a most commanding spot and rendered difficult by a stone breastwork which ran across it and down the side towards the village of Lalloo behind.

Nothing could be more picturesque than our advance

[1] Lieutenant-Colonel William West Turner, 97th Foot. Served in China, 1842, Ceylon, 1848, the Crimea, and Indian Mutiny.

through the tall pines and lichen covered rocks along the crest of Mahabun, halting just without matchlock range of the Conical hill. The brigades reformed, to assault the position which appeared crowned by the enemy.

When all was ready, the mountain batteries opened, the advance sounded, and the two brigades sped across a few hundred yards of level ground in front of the hill, and commenced the steep ascent. The splendid order in which the 7th Royal Fusiliers crossed this space under the enemy's fire, and the cool audacity of their adjutant[1] was the admiration of all present. It was impossible to be otherwise than pleased with the rivalry amongst the regiments, native and European, and I need scarcely add that the enemy retreated precipitately, even as was foretold by our native soldiery who for weeks passed could not understand the reason for delay, declaring the tribes would at once fly before a determined advance.

The British colours were soon waving from the summit of the Conical hill, and Brigadier Turner endeavoured to turn the enemy's left by marching round Lalloo, but the flight was general. The mountaineers, hitherto so brave, fled down down each ravine and gorge, and in thousands crossed the narrow valley of Chumla, to Umbeylah and the passes beyond. It occurred to me there was little disposition shown to stay them, or why was it the cavalry were not sent into the valley until the day following? It is a matter for regret that this advance was almost bloodless, the more so as we were in a position to deal a blow which would have ensured a lasting peace on our north-west frontier.

During the capture of the Conical hill, and burning of Lalloo, a number of the enemy from Umbeylah made a feigned attack upon our entrenched camp and caused some little alarm to the diminished garrison. Major Keyes, who was left in command, proved equal to the occasion and drove off the assailants, but in point of fact, all serious fighting was at an end; the enemy, though reluctant to give in, had

[1] Lieutenant Henry Alexander Little. Served in the Crimea.

been thoroughly disconcerted and beaten since the third recapture of the Crag by General Chamberlain.

It was decided that the troops should bivouac for the night about Lalloo, and early on the morrow the brigades moved down the mountain slopes into Chumla. My regiment accompanied Colonel Wilde's brigade. We led our horses down for miles over boulders, through brushwood, fallen trees, and a score of other obstacles. It was strange ground indeed for cavalry, but we succeeded in reaching the valley though few of our horses brought their shoes with them and our saddlery and accoutrements suffered lamentably. The horses appeared delighted once again to gain the open ground after the necessary confinement they had endured while perched up among the rocks and pines on the heights of our late position.

Colonel Turner's brigade which had descended by a longer route, arrived at a point in the valley considerably above the village and some little time after ourselves, but troops arriving from two opposite directions served to heighten the alarm of the enemy, who, though showing themselves in considerable masses on a low ridge before Umbeylah village, speedily withdrew under shelter of the houses, trees, and low ravines between it and the pass into Boneyr and on the lower slopes of Mount Goroo.

So far as my regiment was concerned, we were grievously disappointed that we had not been sent into the valley on the first advance the previous day, for then, unquestionably we could have attacked the masses crossing. Throughout the day I acted as staff officer to Colonel Probyn, and accompanied by our orderlies and a few Guide Corps troopers, we rode into the village and found it deserted. The enemy watched us from the lower spurs of the adjacent hills. We found a heap of smouldering ashes and quickly succeeded in firing the thatch of one or two houses, from whence the flames spread rapidly until they enveloped the whole of Umbeylah.

The adjacent slopes and crest of the Boneyr pass literally

teemed with angry mountaineers who would beyond a
doubt have swept down upon a smaller force than ours, and
for some time it appeared they would molest us no further,
and Colonel Probyn and myself, with some half dozen
troopers, rode amongst the lower spurs of the hills, little
knowing a large body of desperate men were forming up in
an adjacent ravine in order to make one last assault while
their brethren in arms looked on, but as I have said, we did
not know of the proximity of any large number, but came
upon one or two armed men whom we captured, and
emerging from the ravines, met Captain Chamberlain[1] and
his regiment of Muzbee Sikhs. He asked us to move from
his front as he was dressing his line. We had scarcely
cleared from his way when a large body of Ghazees opened
a heavy fire, and shouting wildly, rushed upon the unfortunate Chamberlain and his corps, and sent them
flying. Lieutenant Alexander was killed, Chamberlain,
Wheeler, Marsh and Nott,[2] all officers of the Muzbees,
wounded. The fugitives, seeing two companies of the 7th
Fusiliers advancing rapidly to their support, rallied again,
faced the enemy, and drove him within his fastness.

This affair was seen by General Garvock and his staff who
occupied elevated ground at some distance. Although the
struggle was so brief, the loss to Captain Chamberlain's men
was very great indeed. Nearly two hundred casualties had
been added to our list during the advance from the pass.

We had left our entrenchment without tents or bedding,
and with no more baggage than could be carried in our
holsters, and now that our work was done and we were
considerably wearied, the prospect of a sojourn in the
valley we had captured was far from pleasant. The night

[1] Captain Charles Francis Falcon Chamberlain, Commanding Muzbee
Sikhs (23rd Native Infantry) and formerly of the 26th Bengal Native
Infantry.
[2] Lieutenant Charles David Peter Nott (late 4th Bengal Europeans),
Lieutenant George Alexander (23rd Punjab Native Infantry), Major
Trevor Wheler and Lieutenant Frank Hale Berwick Marsh (both 32nd
Punjab Native Infantry).

was bitterly cold and a hoar frost fell upon us. On our old ground on the heights we had never wanted for abundance of wood, and slept alongside burning pine logs, so that, although half frozen on one side, we were thoroughly warm through on the other.

As the excitement was now at an end, we were desirous to get out of these uncomfortable quarters and were glad to learn that the Commissioner's influence had arranged the closing act of the drama. This was not a difficult business, for most of the tribes had left for their homes, and the Boneyrwall, in whose territory we were, found themselves left alone in the dilemma, their village destroyed, their valleys overrun, provisions consumed, and ten thousand British troops still encamped on their soil. Thus it was that this gallant tribe agreed to the terms which had been proposed some weeks previously, and which even then they would have accepted but for the Akhoond's influence. These terms were that they should proceed to Mulka, the fanatic village, and destroy it, taking with them a few of our officers and some of the Guide Corps to witness the destruction.

It was a miserable morning, cold, with a thick drizzling rain, more like an English day than could be anticipated in these regions, when the mountain chiefs and a few followers, clad as agriculturalists with their rude weapons slung about them, assembled to start for the completion of the object of our campaign. I watched the little party start on their march, which proved to be about twenty-five miles. It gave me the impression of being a most inglorious termination of the war. In all our movements, haste to patch up a peace was apparent and the smoke of the burning village had scarcely vanished into thin air before our troops were hurried back into the plains.

Mulkah, the home of the fanatics, was burned, but its inhabitants once again escaped British vengeance: the destruction of a few pine built huts could hardly be a great punishment when a forest of these giant trees spread over the northern slopes of Mahabun for many a broad mile.

On Christmas Day, the entire force left the pass. My regiment had done so some days previously. The Commissariat experienced a great difficulty in supplying us with barley, on which our horses were fed; indeed, how the department managed to send it up the pass in the earliest days of our occupation is a marvel. We halted at Nowa Killa, where again I assumed charge of the Field Hospital, now replete with every necessary. General Chamberlain requested me to examine his arm: it was swollen to a very great size, so much so that it was difficult then to pronounce a very decided opinion as to the presence of the ball which had caused the wound. The pain was so acute that it prohibited all meddling, and from these circumstances I pronounced the ball yet to be in the limb. This was so, and six weeks afterwards, when the swelling had abated, it was extracted at Rawalpindee.

On Christmas Day we left Nowa Killa before daybreak and marched to Hoti Murdan. While breakfasting, we learnt that the tribe of Mohmunds had commenced hostilities at one of our old outposts, Shubkudhr, and being desirous to share in that affair also, we started at once and marched until 9 o'clock that evening, reaching Nowshera. We had been about eighteen hours in the saddle, the night was bitterly cold, a piercing wind blew across the plains from the Swat river, our baggage was miles behind us, we were hungry, cold, and miserable. Colonel Probyn advocated continuing our way to Peshawur, another thirty miles, but, a Government telegraph station existing some two miles distant, he rode there and dispatched a message to General O'Grady Haly[1] saying we would march on at [once?], did there exist any necessity for our services. We received an ungracious reply to the effect that we should be ordered on if required. Meanwhile that we awaited an answer, a Royal Artillery battery, encamped at no great distance, heard of our arrival and sent us an invitation to dine, and thus

[1] Major-General O'Grady Haly, C.B., commanding a Brigade in Peshawur District. Served in the Crimea.

a most unexpected Christmas dinner offered, and although the hour was very late, we gladly accepted. Next morning a lady of the 7th Hussars[1] sent us a turkey pasty which, having been discussed, we marched to Taroo, and on the following day, to Peshawur.

On arrival we discovered that the report of a rising among the Mohmunds was of old date. So long before as the 5th of December they had menaced Shubkudhr and had been attacked by Lieutenant Bishop[2] and a detachment of the 6th Bengal Cavalry. His men did not support him so well as they might have done and Bishop was killed.

The regiments of the force which had assembled in Umbeylah were differently distributed and it was our ill luck to be ordered to one of the worst stations in Bengal, to wit Mooltan, but as the Commander in Chief had arrived in Peshawur and was about to hold some great field days, we remained to take part, neither did we leave for Mooltan until the 5th of February. Our regiment so far as all the officers were concerned, save myself, was in high favor with Sir Hugh Rose, and though so unpopular as a commander, it was always a pleasure to us to serve near him. He was profuse in his praise of the regiment, which was undoubtedly first of its kind, and still maintains its high efficiency, to which Lord Napier of Magdala recently testified in a letter he wrote me.

Sir Hugh had not been many days in Peshawur before he visited the Khyber Pass with an escort of our troopers. I know not what his impressions may have been, but I for two years owned and resided in the last habitation of our Indian possessions; I have experienced the capabilities of the needy mountain tribes for rapine and plunder; I have slept in nightly dread of losing my horses from my stables; I have known regimental horses stolen from walled lines

---

[1] Mrs Trevelyan. (*Diary*.) Major Harrington Astley Trevelyan was an officer of the 7th Hussars.

[2] Lieutenant St George Meadows Bishop (1st Goorkha Regiment) serving with the 6th Bengal Cavalry.

under guard of loaded sentries, yet withal I could never look upon the dismal shadows of the Khyber and its rugged chain of walls without believing it to be the natural boundary of our long and splendid line of conquests in Asia.

It is true that Affghanistan alone divides us from Russian territory lately acquired, but it is far better her sentries should be planted in the inhospitable defiles of the Hindoo Khoosh, than that Britain should ever again cross the line of neutral territory bounding the valley of Peshawur. There, with a splendid force, and every appliance of war, she may calmly await Russia's advanced armies which would have to wage war hundreds of miles from their base and through tracts peopled with treacherous savages.

At the time Sir Hugh Rose was in Peshawur, the Banda and Kirkwee prize money had scarcely become a matter of dispute, much less of law. Sir Hugh confidently believed that the force which had served under him would share it, as indeed it well deserved to do, and one night, while dining with him, he told me that we were almost certain to share it. 'Some silly people' said he, 'have gone to law about it, but the Queen may give it to whom she likes and I will let you know the moment it is settled.' Though doubtless well acquainted with the law's delays, Sir Hugh little thought many years would elapse before a decision would be arrived at, and one, too, so obviously unfair. Otherwise, when Commander in Chief he was most scrupulous in the observance of any promise even casually made, and a really good officer had always something to hope for in his reign, for he scouted the old seniority system, and so far as he was able, gave appointments by merit only.

In the dispatches relative to the campaign in Umbeyla pass, General Garvock did me the honor of a casual mention, but Sir Neville Chamberlain, when lying wounded, wrote the following recognition of my services, a recognition which, added to my former services in the Field during the Mutiny and Pursuit of Tantia Topee, ought fairly to have brought its reward, and would moreover, in the case of

Dowb, have brought him great military distinction, but now as ever, interest is at the bottom of all military distinction, and he is unwise who enters the British Army unless he possesses it.

General Sir Neville Chamberlain's dispatch was as follows:

Camp Nowakilla
16th December, 1863

To

    The Adjutant General

Sir,

      Although no longer in command of the Euzofzai Field Force, I trust that His Excellency the Commander in Chief will allow me to bring to his notice the excellent service rendered by Assistant Surgeon Sylvester, 11th Bengal Cavalry, whilst in Medical charge of the sick and wounded of the native troops at Nowakilla; when Assistant Surgeon Sylvester was first appointed to the charge, the arrangements were not what they ought to have been, but by his systematic care, skill, and kind treatment, he infused perfect order and confidence amongst all ranks and everything was conducted in the most regular and satisfactory manner.

on 4th Decr.

sick	316
wounded	190
	——
	506
	——
officers	
wounded	
5	

      Dr Sylvester's means, considering the number of sick and wounded (noted in the margin) were very limited, there being only one other Assistant Surgeon with him, but by his unwearied diligence, and working the entire day, no man's wound remained undressed or his wants uncared for.

      All the various officers that from time to time I requested to visit the camp were unanimous in according to Dr Sylvester the merit of the order and contentment which prevailed throughout the depot.

      His Excellency will I know concur with me that the sick and wounded should at all times receive the very greatest consideration and I therefore beg to express the hope that he will cause to be conveyed to that officer his appreciation of his services whilst in medical charge of the Depot.

I have the honor to be,
Sir,
Your most obedient servant,
Neville Chamberlain
Brigadier General.

When this letter reached the supreme Government of India, Sir John, now Lord, Lawrence[1] was at its head. After a lapse of time I received a copy of the following letter which was addressed to the Government of Bombay, to which presidency I belonged:

No. 252

To
    The Secretary to Government,
Bombay.
Military Department.

Military Department
    Sir,
    I am directed to transmit to you for the information of the Government of Bombay, the accompanying Copy of a communication from the Adjutant General No. 1360 ED/27th ultimo, forwarding one from Brigadier General Sir Neville Chamberlain K.C.B., late Commanding the Euzufzai Field Force, bringing to notice the excellent services rendered by Assistant Surgeon Sylvester, 11th Bengal Cavalry, while in Medical charge of the sick and wounded at Nowakilla and intimating that His Excellency the Commander in Chief has thanked that officer for the service performed.

I have the honor to be,
Sir,
Your most obedient servant,
H. K. Burne, Major.
Secretary to the Government
of India.

Sir Hugh Rose's letter was as follows:

No. 204 A
Field operations
A. G. O. Head Quarters
Camp Hussun Abdool, 24th December, 1863.

Sir,
    By direction of the Commander in Chief I have the honor to transmit for your information, copy of a letter dated 16th instant from Brigadier General Sir Neville B. Chamberlain, K.C.S.I., late commanding the Field Force in which he brings to notice the excellent

---

[1] Lord Lawrence (Sir John Laird Mair Lawrence) (1811–79). One of the most distinguished of the British administrators of India.

services of Assistant Surgeon J. H. Sylvester, 11th Bengal Cavalry, whilst in Medical charge of the sick and wounded at Nowakilla and I am to request that you will convey to the Assistant Surgeon His Excellency's appreciation of the value of these services.

Sir Hugh Rose desires me to add that he will not fail to bring Dr Sylvester's services under the notice of his Departmental superiors and of Government.

I have the honor to be,
Sir,
Your most obedient servant,
D. M. Stewart, Colonel,
Adjutant General.

The force in the Peshawur valley during the early part of the year 1864 was a very large one, and during Sir Hugh Rose's brief stay, we had some very brilliant parades – parades in which there was great earnest. Both horses and men were killed by accident, which mostly happened among the artillery, from the treacherous nature of the ground.

After a very critical review of my regiment, of which he was much pleased, Sir Hugh Rose directed Colonel Probyn to call singly from the ranks any officer or soldier who had distinguished himself.[1]

[1] It is at this point that Sylvester's narrative ends, but it seems, from his *Diary*, that this may have been the occasion when 'the Chief . . . called me to the front of the regiment when it was inspected and told me he was proud to see me at the head of my Regiment and that he had not forgotten the distinguished services I had rendered in Central India &c. &c.'

Postscript

As has been seen, Sylvester's narrative ends abruptly, so abruptly in fact that it appears evident that it was his intention to continue with his reminiscences, but for some unknown reason he never did so. It may be that some other interest in life completely overshadowed his desire to write, or that, even more likely, he had, temporarily, tired of writing and as so often happens, had never raised the enthusiasm to take it up again. It is of course more than possible that, although at first intending to cover the whole period of his career in India, his existence after the Umbeylah campaign became so humdrum that he did not consider it worth recording. If this is so, then why the abrupt ending when just on the point of describing so flattering a recognition by Sir Hugh Rose? One thing only is certain; whatever the cause, we will never know.

There was one activity which he did not give up for several years; this was the writing of his *Diary* (in two volumes) in which not only did he enter events of each day (often so trivial), but in which he contrived to reveal so much of his own character. It is by means of this *Diary* that it is possible to record the happenings of a few more years of his life though without the ability otherwise to draw on his memory.

It is from the diary that we learn that, on about 5th February 1864, Sylvester and the regiment took a sorrowful farewell of Peshawur and left for the dreaded Mooltan which, on arrival, seemed not as bad as expected, but this early impression very soon wore off, and to make matters worse, to quote Sylvester's own words: 'Messing is sinfully extravagant, it vexes me much but I am powerless to help it. None of us can afford it but Probyn will think so for appearances even in this wretched place, but he is so good natured & ready to help one in all things I cannot bear to oppose him in anything.'

On 12 April Sylvester took charge of the public garden which he found to be a perfect jungle, and from that date his *Diary* reflects the horrible dullness of life in Mooltan, only slightly relieved by invitations to dinner which cannot in any way have lessened his continual sufferings from indigestion, from which he obtained relief only by drinking water and by total abstinence from alcohol. It also eased the strain on his pocket. He must have greatly envied his Commanding Officer of whom he wrote: 'Probyn amuses himself by driving a four in hand of the Brigadier's, he is a man of most happy disposition apparently most regardless of morrow and expense.'

A break from life 'as dull as dullest ditchwater' (when even attempts to get up private theatricals were unsuccessful owing to lack of energy on the part of the officers of the 89th)[1] came on 15 July, on which day he left once more on sixty days' leave to Cashmere where for part of the way he travelled with Captain Segrave[2] of the 71st Highlanders ('a jolly & amusing fellow is Segrave about 6 ft 6" high') and accompanied by his dog 'Digs'. The description in the *Diary* of this trip to Cashmere is very similar to that already given by him of his earlier tour and contains little of particular interest.

On his return to Mooltan on 17 September he received 'a box which I had packed 10 years ago on departure to Persia & left in Bombay. The full dress suit & cocked hat I brought out with me was in it, my diplomas . . . The full dress which was so useless to me cost me about £20 for now I have sent it to the Bazaar – where I imagine it will scarce

---

[1] Later 2nd Bn The Royal Irish Fusiliers. Early in February 1865 they were replaced by the 35th (now 1st Bn The Royal Sussex Regiment). (*Diary*.)

[2] Captain William Francis Segrave.

fetch so many rupees! My bill from Pulford & Co has arrived, fortunately I only ordered a stable jacket & that is charged about eighteen guineas, some of the other fellows are properly let in, Drummond & Dick for about £150. I fancy Probyn's bill must be £300, but I have done, I'll buy no more full dress, & take good care to spend little as possible in uniform. . . . On arrival I was appointed Staff Surgeon, it is little enough remuneration, it brings but 30 Rs a month, helps pay House Rent. I am now living with a jolly old Bengallee – Colonel Nuthall who commands the 3rd N. I.'[1]

Two entries in the *Diary*, on 23 September and 13 December, make an interesting change from continual complaints of indisposition, bad weather and expense. 'I observe Woodhall of the firm Chesson & Woodhall is dead, they have paid me nothing for my last Tale – *Red Lancers of Bundlekunde* so I have written to dun them. . . . Chesson & Woodhall paid up R390 when I placed the debt for the *Red Lancers* in the hands of Mr Leathe's solicitors.' In addition to his other accomplishments, Sylvester was a writer of fiction although it is not known how much of it appeared in print.

The advent of 1865 found Sylvester still in the much hated Mooltan, busily recording the weather, the state of his health, and his ever-growing interest in financial matters and the making of money, but on 22 February (his birthday) he wrote: 'I am 35, I believe it appears I am very old,' and on 15 March: 'Big parade again this morning, I did A.D.C. to General Maxwell[2] & lamed poor "Master George", sprained his fetlock, I hope he will soon be right for the C in Chief. Col Biddulph[3] comes in Colonel Nuthall's place to live with me today, the 3rd marched yesterday . . .

[1] Lieutenant-Colonel William Frost Nuthall, 3rd Bengal Native Infantry, which regiment, in pre-Mutiny days, was the 32nd.

[2] Brigadier-General Maxwell was the Colonel George Vaughan Maxwell who had co-operated with Sir Hugh Rose at Calpee.

[3] Lieutenant-Colonel Michael Anthony Shrapnel Biddulph, R.A. 1823–1904).

persuaded Probyn to do away with the Choga [a long-sleeved garment rather like a dressing-gown] and adopt the men's blue Garibaldi shirt.' A few days later: 'Sir Wm Mansfield[1] came in on Sunday to Shere Shah & by train on Monday morning, all the C.O.'s & a troop of our men mounted on greys received him. I called on him the following day with Col Biddulph, he was very civil & polite, but a hard featured cold mannered man such indeed as I have so often heard him described, he was writing for the English mail. This morning all the troops turned out to parade and marched past, I did A.D.C. to General Maxwell on Col Biddulph's young Arab but a more unbroken unwieldy young colt I never bestrode, he would not go near an Infantry column & bolted with me bang into one of the Barracks where I fortunately stopped him. I am to dine with the General and meet the Comr in Chief this evening, his A.D.C. Christie & Capt Flood[2] the Military secretary, both seem nice fellows.'

On 22 March Sylvester again dined with General Maxwell and the Hon. Colonel Chichester,[3] and the following night he dined with General van Cortlandt,[4] and as far as the entries in the *Diary* show, these appear to be the two most exciting events for many weeks during which he continued to buy and sell stocks and shares, as well as horses, in efforts to make money, but his selling of horses although in general highly successful financially, were not always crowned with success. On 15 April he tried to sell 'Adonis' to Mowbray R.A.[5] but 'Adonis' bolted with Mowbray and threw him on

[1] Lieutenant-General Sir William Rose Mansfield (1819–76). Entered the British Army as an Ensign of the 53rd Foot, 1835. Served in the 1st Sikh War; the Punjab, 1849, and acted as Chief of Staff to Sir Colin Campbell during the Indian Mutiny. Raised to the peerage as 1st Baron Sandhurst, 1871.

[2] Lieutenant Henry Toffrey Christie, Bombay Infantry (General List), and Major Frederick Richard Solly Flood, 82nd Foot.

[3] Lieutenant-Colonel the Hon. Augustus George Charles Chichester, 77th Foot.

[4] This is the General Van Cortlandt already referred to.

[5] Possibly Lieutenant Philip Henry Mowbray, Royal Artillery.

his head. On 13 May, however, Sylvester seemed to be happier having taken delivery of a new waler which he had ordered: it appeared very quiet and good tempered, but four days later he was to get an 'eye-opener'. 'Got on my new horse this morning & he buck-jumped worse than any horse I ever knew and threw me hurting my back on a peg on which I fell – bad beginning, I fear he is vicious & if so useless.'

An entry on 25 May sums up fairly what for some time he reiterated almost daily: 'Heat is a mild phrase for the terrible suffering we are now undergoing, I scarcely felt anything to equal it but strange I never get indigestion or pains now – simply because that I have turned teetotaller. Water agrees best with me though De Renzy[1] maintains it gives people scurvy which is very prevalent here. . . . My poor greyhound feels the heat very sadly.' On this day the new waler was not forgotten as it was recorded that he threw Jemadar Sadool Singh that morning, after having gone quietly for some time. Sylvester himself felt too weak and relaxed by the terrible heat to mount him.

On 1 June is the entry: 'Jemadar Sadool Singh has ridden the new waler twice during the dusk of morning to take the fire out of him he says. I don't believe in the dodge.' His horse 'Master George', described as 'growing old though very showy and handsome', was bought by Captain Miller,[2] 90th Light Infantry, two days later.

Much of Sylvester's spare time was spent in writing home, with a correspondingly heavy receipt of mail from his family and it is of interest to learn that on 3 June he heard from his brother, the Reverend Edward Henry Sylvester (who had obtained the curacy at Deene, and the appointment

[1] Assistant-Surgeon Annesley Charles Castriot De Renzy (1828–1914). Served with the Bengal Artillery in Burma, 1852–4. Present on the occasion of the mutiny of the 15th Bengal Native Infantry at Nusseerabad, and at the siege of Lucknow.

[2] Captain George Robert Miller, who had served in the Indian Mutiny with Sir James Outram and Lord Clyde. The 90th Perthshire Light Infantry later became 2nd Bn The Cameronians (Scottish Rifles).

as Domestic Chaplain to the famous Earl of Cardigan who led the Light Brigade at Balaclava) to the effect that, as he put it, 'Edward has had a little turn up with old Cardigan about his pupils which is provoking'.

It was not long before the new waler, which had most appropriately been named 'Gladiator', forced his way once more into the record. 9 June: ' "Gladiator" is breaking in most quietly;' 22 June: 'My waler was getting on quietly & well until lately & he has twice thrown Sadool Singh. I have a boil on my seat and cannot ride, otherwise am pretty well.'

At 6 a.m. on 15 July Sylvester was once again off to Cashmere, returning to Mooltan on 17 September, to find 'Gladiator' fat and well, but within a few days he 'buck-jumped me off the night before', and at the beginning of the following month 'he kicked Beadon's[1] greyhound yesterday & broke the poor things ribs for which I am very sorry'. Beadon's feelings are not recorded.

On 13th October Sylvester sold a pony and bought another waler but was again thrown by the terrible 'Gladiator', who, judging by the entries in the *Diary* at that time, was the sole cause of any excitement apart from the welcome news that the regiment was to move to Umballa. On 8 November 'Gladiator' again threw Sylvester when he was least expecting it although 'I rather took it out of him for it afterwards'. This lesson seems to have had little effect as, two days later, it was decided that he must be got rid of as he had become so dangerous. 'I'm very sorry for he is a rattling fine horse: but I fear his breaking my collar bone.' The decision was a wise one, but getting rid of 'Gladiator' was to prove no simple matter.

The beginning of December brought better weather but unwelcome visitors, for, on the 3rd of the month 'clouds cleared off and the weather is bright & in early morning

---

[1] Probably Captain Richard Beadon (late of the old 4th Bengal European Cavalry). Served with the 3rd Sikh Cavalry in the Indian Mutiny and in China, 1860. At the time of which Sylvester was writing, he may have been A.D.C. to the Lieutenant-Governor of Bengal, and an officer of the 5th Bengal Cavalry.

very cold but the sun makes itself very speedily felt. I
moved into a tent today to make room for the Lord Bishop
of Calcutta[1] and suite expected tomorrow; this is a terrific
annoyance having these people in the Mess.' The annoyance
was in a way lessened by a feeling of 'seediness' experienced
some days later 'due probably to a very cold night in tents;
laid awake with cold to which I am acutely sensitive, the
Bishop's wife, governess & child came yesterday, the old
party & his chaplain today, I haven't seen him yet.' Much
to Sylvester's relief, the 'old party' and his family took
themselves off on 13 December.

It is in an entry in the *Diary* for 3 December that (as
once before when depressed and disgruntled in Calcutta)
Sylvester shows us that that he was himself aware of his
peculiarly restless character and of his desire for recognition
but this had by this time become tinged with a certain
sadness which must strike a responsive cord in all those who
have started off in life full of ambition, only to realize that,
after years of striving, they have not risen to the hoped-for
heights. 'This I suppose is my last day as an Assistant
Surgeon. I feel thankful for promotion, though sad I don't
know why. I'm getting antique and like old customs, I am
not always craving for change of appointments as hcreto-
fore, but that was engendered by the roving life I led in
the Mutiny.[2] I am now content with mediocrity and steady
but slow acquisition of money, most thankful too my health
is spared me.'

Although it cannot be said that the entries in the *Diary*
now became immediately more cheerful, at least they
appear somewhat less despondent towards the end of
December when on the 20th Sylvester was able to write:
'Thank Goodness my promotion appeared in orders last
night in the Bombay Gazette and I received an intimation

[1] The Rt Rev. George Edward Lynch Cotton (1813–66).
[2] Sylvester seems to have forgotten his early attempts to join Burton
and Speke in their explorations, almost immediately after having set
foot in India.

to that effect from the Military Fund office,' and to make matters even better, he could report, on 12 January 1866, the glad news that, with the regiment, he had left the 'abominable place' and had made the move to Umballa where life at once appeared to be more interesting and where, soon after arrival, he bought himself a couple of houses, but ' "Gladiator" is still with me, I cannot sell him as everybody fears to ride him though he is far quieter than I knew him heretofore. He threw Shakespeare[1] the instant he got on his back.'

By this time Probyn had left India, the command of the regiment devolving on Lieutenant-Colonel Wright,[2] 'a sharp business-like fellow' but not, according to Sylvester, so impressive as Probyn, although it must be remembered that he too was somewhat of a disappointment when first seen, and in any case Probyn was an outstanding and colourful character whose shoes it would be hard for any average man to fill.

Whilst in Umballa, Sylvester very evidently took part in the social life and did not feel 'that miserable dullness and solitude I did in Mooltan'. He made many friends, particularly the family of Major Henry Nicoll,[3] described by him as 'the nicest people I ever met'. By May, however, all those who could manage to do so (including the Nicolls) had fled to the cooler weather of Simla and in its turn Umballa was stigmatized as 'very dull', but on 15 June, Sylvester also left for a short stay in Simla where he struck up a friendship with Major Lane[4] of the 21st Hussars and took a great deal

---

[1] Captain George Robert Shakespeare, Bengal Staff Corps, serving with the 11th Bengal Cavalry.

[2] Lieutenant-Colonel Thomas Wright (late of the old 46th Bengal Native Infantry). Served in the Punjab, 1848–9, when he was present at Ramnuggur, Chillianwallah and Goojerat.

[3] Major Henry Nicoll (1816–1907), Assistant Adjutant-General, Umballa Division. He was an officer of the Bengal Infantry who had served in Bundlekunde, 1842; the Gwalior Campaign, 1842–3; the Punjab, 1848–9, and was Brigade Major, Delhi Field Force, 1857. General, 1889.

[4] Brevet-Major Charles Powlett Lane (late 3rd Bengal European

of interest in life in general and rode in nearly every event in the races. By 6 July he was back in Umballa where he 'went to the Jervis Court Martial, twice heard Sir Wm Mansfield cross examined, his answers were particularly lucid'.[1]

So great an impression had Simla made on Sylvester that he once again reverted to his old habit of applying to be sent somewhere other than where he was, and this time he put in for the 'joint medical charge of Simla' though with no great hopes, which was just as well as he did not get the appointment. Nevertheless, his sixty days' leave again became due and this time there was no thought of Cashmere and its solitudes; it was to Simla that he contrived to 'slope off' on 20 July.

Shortly before his departure, Sylvester heard news, by telegram, of that matter of such great import and disappointment, the Kirwee prize money, which, it was stated, had been decided in favour of Whitlock's column. The following day his dashed hopes were raised for a short while by the arrival of an amendment which was so confused in its wording that he could not understand it.

The sixty days' leave in Simla were spent in ways far different to those of Cashmere. 'I then went in for the usual Simla life, calling, picnics, At Homes, balls, dinners, croquet, flirtations and the like. Alas! it was all vanity indeed: the Club was most comfortable but I missed Lane when he left soon after very much, but I made friends with Stockwell of the 95th[2] and Hawkins of the Civil Service,

---

Cavalry). Served in the Punjab, 1848, when he was present at Ramnuggur, Chillianwallah and Goojerat. Served in the Indian Mutiny.

[1] Captain Ernest Scott Jervis, 106th Bombay Light Infantry (formerly 2nd Bombay European Light Infantry), was A.D.C. to Sir William Mansfield. Although Jervis was dismissed the service on disciplinary grounds, the Court-Martial severely damaged Mansfield's reputation as, of a string of charges of peculation and falsifying of accounts which he brought against Jervis, none could be substantiated or justified.

[2] Captain John W. Inglis Stockwell, 95th Foot. Served in the Crimea and the Indian Mutiny.

the Club soon became quite full and I was placed on the House Committee and made myself useful to the institution which is certainly a great boon to Simla.'

On his return to Umballa he was kept busy, being placed in medical charge not only of his own regiment, but also of the 31st Native Infantry, four miles distant, and he was soon to receive a nasty blow when he heard, privately, that the Bombay Government had applied for his services. It caused him a terrible shock. 'I felt quite sick at heart, with all my connections severed, my houses, property, and Bank Shares . . . it troubled me exceedingly. Flood, Military Secretary, promised me an interview with the Chief on the morrow and accordingly I went and he was uncommonly civil and polite promising I should not go if he could stay me and unless I was ordered back by the Supreme Government – he then asked me a great deal about remounts for Cavalry saying he knew I took great interest in the subject. I talked some time with him, he then told me to go home & write all I knew on the subject which I did and sent it next day & he asked might he use my name as an authority!! Very flattering.'

Whatever his thoughts might have been on the Kirwee prize money, and on the proposal that he should return to Bombay, in one respect at least his drooping spirits were raised, for, on 13 October he wrote: 'If the brute is not returned to me I have sold "Gladiator" to Capt Manderson, Royal Artillery[1] for £100 so I have gained something by the brute at last and very thankful I feel to have got rid of him, fortunately he allowed Manderson to mount him twice and ride him without giving him a cropper. I only hope he will behave himself among the guns which I doubt, he pays me by cheque on Calcutta. I have bought Stockwell's big Arab for 1,400/. and a magnificent animal he is – the finest Arab in the Punjaub I should say.'

---

[1] Probably Captain George Rennie Manderson, Royal Bengal Artillery, who had served in Burma in 1852. There was also a Captain Wardlaw Manderson in the Royal Artillery.

On the same day he also recorded that Sir William Mansfield 'wrote a most flattering letter urging I should be retained in Bengal as I was an officer of great promise & had written a valuable treatise on Horse Breeding just sent up to Government and that I rendered ex-officio much valuable aid to my Commanding Officer. . . . I wonder whether they will offer me Medical charge of Simla, I strongly suspect not, indeed I suppose it is just on the cards I return to Bombay, if I do and as report says Sir Robt Montgomery[1] comes out as Governor, I shall fall on my legs again.'

The next three entries in the *Diary*, for 14, 15 and 23 October are chiefly of interest where they touch on the subject of horses. Sylvester was at that time looking after other people's mounts as well as his own and 'the brute "Gladiator" threw Manderson at once and I was obliged to take him back again as Manderson declared he would not mount him again for £100. I had paid away 500/. of the money which I was unable to return but M. said there was no hurry: this morning however I sold my Buggy Horse and Harness for 700/. clearing 150/. by the "Turn out". I am to be paid in a week and then I shall repay Manderson.' In the course of the next few weeks he sold five horses, always at a profit but was unfortunately unable to accept an offer for the redoubtable 'Gladiator' which had just been sent off to the sales at Agra. This may really have been a blessing as 'Gladiator' would doubtless have been returned to him yet once again by some alarmed purchaser.

The beginning of 1867 found Sylvester in cheerful spirits but on Sunday, 21 January, the blow fell. He received a letter informing him that the order had gone forth, and he was to leave his regiment and return to Bombay. He had thought that this contingency had blown

[1] Sir Robert Montgomery (1809–87) was Lieutenant-Governor of the Punjab during the Umbeylah Campaign. Member of the Council of India, 1868–87.

L

over, but the Governor-General[1] had given in to the head
of his department. The news completely spoilt his dinner
and he went wretchedly to bed.

All appeals to be allowed to remain in Bengal were in
vain and so overcome was he at the thought of leaving that
he spent sleepless nights and no longer enjoyed parties or
hunting. He dreaded the thought of beginning life anew
amidst strangers and in a bad climate and did not know how
he was to get rid of all his property in Umballa. He was to
discover that, on the last score, he had no cause for worry:
no sooner did he advertise than things sold thick and fast.
The horses he disposed of were 'Azeezee', 'Gymnast', two
strawberry roan carriage horses, a grey, and 'Ruby', a
chestnut Arab, and of his two houses, he sold one and let
the other. He made money on all he sold. His only failure
was his effort to sell his uniform to his successor, Assistant-
Surgeon N. J. Grant.[2] It would not fit Grant so he had to
take it away with him, with the firm resolve never to buy
any more and to live economically in Bombay. According to
Sylvester, Grant was a fine fellow and a plunger, but mean;
he would not buy anything of Sylvester's, not even his
regimental belts and saddlery. In this case at least, he seems
to have met his match!

On his last day in Umballa, all the native officers called
and admired his house with its papered walls – a rarity in
the India of those days.

The last two entries in the diary were made in Bombay.
On 11 April 1867, he wrote: 'Really most wondrous
metamorphoses I undergo, I am now Professor of Opthalmic
Surgery. I have had no time of late for entries in my diary –
it must be done in arrears. I certainly have been followed
by my usual luck – it is now 8.30 and the delicious coolness
& freshness of the evening now that dinner is over which

---

[1] Sir John Lawrence.

[2] Assistant-Surgeon Nathaniel James Grant (1831–1914). Served on
the Peshawur Frontier, 1854–5; with the Field Force in the annexation
of Oude, 1856, and in the Indian Mutiny.

prompts me to write it down. I am dressed in a woollen coat & waistcoat, the drops of the chandelier are ringing pleasantly in the sea breeze, the thermometer on the table stands at 80°, I should have thought it 70, so jolly cool does it feel. How sorrowing and sad I came to Bombay and went straight in for the only appointment which seemed made on purpose for me and the Governor in most flattering terms gave it me & said he was proud to serve so distinguished an officer: he is a thorough English gentleman is Sir Seymour.[1] Rogers who had written to ask me to stay with him I found living in Carey Coles' old bungalow, strange to say where I first landed in India. . . . Operated on 3 cataract cases was very anxious & nervous over the first, am getting confidence now: like my work. Dined with Hewlett & Payne Barras last night.'

The final entry, on 21 July 1867: 'No time for making notes – this book, my watch, chain, medals . . . and many other things including all my papers were stolen. I recovered all but the valuables: am still living with Rogers & getting a decent practice some 350/ a month. I have drawn 1050/ per month while Acting Oculist & now 1150/. I was appointed pukka Professor of Physiology and Acting 2nd Physician & yesterday made University Examiner in Botany & Materia Medica & Anatomy. . . . My practice is chiefly consultation; have been successful in my eye operations.'

On this confident and cheerful note the *Diary* ends, with Sylvester back in the old familiar surroundings of his first years in India, in the city of Bombay, where he was destined to spend a further six successful years.

[1] Sir William Robert Seymour Vesey Fitzgerald (1818–85). Succeeded Sir Bartle Frere as Governor of Bombay, 1867, and held the appointment until 1872.

Appendix A

AMONGST a considerable number of old letters both from and to Surgeon-General Sylvester, and now in Miss Hodder's possession, is the following, written by Jemadar Nezam Oodeen Khan of the 11th Bengal Cavalry shortly after Sylvester had left the regiment for Bombay. The phraseology is certainly quaint but the recipient was doubtless pleased to know that he had been so much appreciated by his Indian colleagues. The Jemadar appears (No. 18) in the group photograph of the officers, taken in Peshawur, in 1862.

Umballa
2nd April
1867

Sir,

after your departure – head of my desires was thus waving with excitement and imagination (as the flag shakes to all sides with every wind) for certain news of your good health –

        Sir

I am now glad too and thankful our officer who gave me news all about your honor – with these rare qualities that your majesty arrived all right; in that place at ten oclock where you were before and left last ten years ago – otherwise I was joyful by listening being your flattered on that situation –

        Sir

although by hearing news of your good health also praise I am mixed with joy – but your servant and well-wisher remembers our greif and your consolations which is marked on heart as the plan indelible –

Hakoomutra Duffadur and Kader Buksh native Doctor desire me to send his sullam to your honor –

believe me sir awaiting allways news at your good health – to be your obet. servant

Nezam oodeen Khan   5th troop
    11th Regiment

PRINCIPAL SOURCES CONSULTED DURING
COMPILATION OF THE FOOTNOTES

The Bombay Artillery, List of Officers, Compiled by Colonel F. W. M. Spring, 1902.

King George's Own Central India Horse, Major-General W. S. Watson, 1930.

History of the Hyderabad Contingent, Major Reginald George Burton, 1905.

Our Soldiers during the reign of Her Majesty Queen Victoria, William H. G. Kingston.

The History of the Indian Revolt, G.D.

British Battles on Land and Sea, edited by Field-Marshal Sir Evelyn Wood, V.C., C.M., G.C.B., G.C.M.G., D.C.L., 1915.

British Battles on Land and Sea, James Grant.

The Invasion of the Crimea, A. W. Kinglake, 6th edn, 1877.

List of Officers of the Bengal Army, 1758–1834, arranged and annotated by Major V. C. P. Hodson, 1927–47.

Recollections of the Campaign in Malwa and Central India, Assistant Surgeon John Henry Sylvester, F.G.S., 1860.

Roll of the Indian Medical Service, 1615–1930, D. G. Crawford, 1930.

The Scottish Highlands, Highland Clans and Highland Regiments, edited by John S. Keltie, .F.S.A.S.

From Midshipman to Field Marshal, Evelyn Wood, F.M., V.C., G.C.B., G.C.M.G., 1906.

Historical Records of the Services of the 33rd (Queen Victoria's Own) Light Cavalry, compiled by Major A. P. Currie, Major M. H. Anderson, and Captain E. S. J. Anderson, 1914.

The History of Probyn's Horse (5th King Edward's Own Lancers), Major C. A. Boyle, D.S.O., 1929.

A History of the XI King Edward's Own Lancers (Probyn's Horse), Captain E. L. Maxwell, 1914.

The History of the Prince of Wales's Leinster Regiment (Royal Canadians), Lieutenant-Colonel F. E. Whitton, C.M.G., 1924.

Historical Record of the 14th (King's) Hussars, 1715–1900, Colonel H. B. Hamilton, 1901.

A History of the Thirtieth Lancers, Gordon's Horse, Major E. A. W. Stotherd, 1912.

A History of the Indian Mutiny, T. Rice Holmes, 1904.

The Indian Mutiny of 1857, by Colonel G. B. Malleson, C.S.I., 1891.

Ubique: War Services of all the Officers of H.M.'s Bengal Army, compiled by Captain T. C. Anderson, 1863.

The Dictionary of National Biography.

Dictionary of Indian Biography, compiled by C. E. Buckland, 1906.
East India Registers.
The Indian Army and Civil Service Lists.
Hart's Army Lists.
The Journal of the Society for Army Historical Research.
'Clemency' Canning, Michael Maclagan, 1962.

Index of Persons and Places

Bold numerals indicate the page references for the footnote identifying persons mentioned in Sylvester's narrative and giving details of their rank and career.

Index of Regiments
and other Military Formations